Other Books and Seri

1901-1907 Native American Census Sen
Modoc, Ottawa, Peoria, Quapaw, and Wy
School, Indian Territory)

1932 Census of The Standing Rock Sioux Reservation with Births And Deaths 1924-1932

Census of The Blackfeet, Montana, 1897- 1901 Expanded Edition

Eastern Cherokee by Blood, 1906-1910, Volumes I thru XIII

Choctaw of Mississippi Indian Census 1929-1932 with Births and Deaths 1924-1931   Volume I

Choctaw of Mississippi Indian Census 1933, 1934 & 1937, Supplemental Rolls to 1934 & 1935 with Births and Deaths 1932-1938, and Marriages 1936-1938   Volume II

Eastern Cherokee Census Cherokee, North Carolina 1930-1939 Census 1930-1931 with Births And Deaths 1924-1931 Taken By Agent L. W. Page   Volume I

Eastern Cherokee Census Cherokee, North Carolina 1930-1939 Census 1932-1933 with Births And Deaths 1930-1932 Taken By Agent R. L. Spalsbury   Volume II

Eastern Cherokee Census Cherokee, North Carolina 1930-1939 Census 1934-1937 with Births and Deaths 1925-1938 and Marriages 1936 & 1938 Taken by Agents R. L. Spalsbury And Harold W. Foght Volume III

Seminole of Florida Indian Census, 1930-1940 with Birth and Death Records, 1930-1938

Texas Cherokees 1820-1839 A Document For Litigation 1921

Choctaw By Blood Enrollment Cards 1898-1914 Volumes I thru XIII

Visit our website at **www.nativestudy.com** to learn more about these and other books and series by Jeff Bowen

CHOCTAW BY BLOOD
ENROLLMENT CARDS
1898-1914
VOLUME XIV

TRANSCRIBED BY

JEFF BOWEN

NATIVE STUDY
Gallipolis, Ohio
USA

This series is dedicated to
Mike Marchi,
who keeps my spirits up.

CREEK CENSUS.

SECOND NOTICE.

Members of the Dawes Commission will be present at the following times and places for the purpose of enrolling Creek citizens, as required by Act of Congress of June 10, 1896:

At Muskogee, Nov. 8 to 30, 1897, inclusive.
At Wagoner, Nov. 8 to 13, " inclusive.
At Eufaula, Nov. 8 to 13, " inclusive.
At Sapulpa, Nov. 15 to 20, " inclusive.
At Wetumpka, Nov. 15 to 20, " inclusive.
At Okmulgee, Nov. 22 to 30, " inclusive.

All persons who have not heretofore enrolled before the Dawes Commission should appear and enroll. Parents and guardians can enroll their families and wards.

TAMS BIXBY,
FRANK C. ARMSTRONG,
A. S. McKENNON,
THOS. B. NEEDLES,
Commissioners.

The above illustration is similar in nature to what was found throughout Indian Territory for different tribes as far as postings on bulletin boards, public centers, or wherever they could be read so people would be notified of where and when they needed to be for enrollment with the Dawes Commission.

This is a picture of the Dawes Commission at Camp Jones in Stonewall, Indian Territory on September 8, 1898.

The images below are of two of the original cards given on the microfilm. The cards given in this book have been formatted to fit on one page and still give all the information found on the original cards.

Choctaw Nation — Choctaw Roll (Not Including Freedmen)

Card No. / Field No. 1

Residence County. Post Office: Kiamitia Ind. Ter.

Dawes Roll No.	NAME	Relationship to Person First Named	AGE	SEX	BLOOD	Tribal Enrollment Year	County	No.	Name of Father	Year	County	Name of Mother	Year	County
1	Bell, Rebecca		25	F	1/4	1895	Atoka	1825	John Donnelly	Dead	Choctaw roll	Henrietta LaFlo-Dead		Choc. roll
2	" Zola Alice	Dau.	3	F	1/8	1896	"	1826	King G. Bell		White man	No.1		
3	" Thetas Lee	Son	2	M	1/8	1827	"	1827	" " "		" "	No.1		
4	" King	Husb.	35	M	I.W.	1896	"	14,151	J.B.Bell	Dead	Non-Citz.	Margaret Bell	Dead	Non-Citz.

ENROLLMENT
APPROVED BY THE SECRETARY
OF INTERIOR Dec.12, 1902

No.3 on Choctaw roll as Lee Bell
No.4 on 1895 Choctaw census roll as K.G.Bell
No.4 transferred from Choctaw card #D.3.See decision of April 20,1903.
No.1 Died prior to September 25,1902;not entitled to land or money.
(See Indian Office letter of June 20,1910 D.S.# 836-1910)

Notation made Jan. 7,1916
Date of Enrollment Sept. 1895

ENROLLMENT
June 13, 1903

Date of Application for Enrollment

Choctaw Nation — Choctaw Roll (Not Including Freedmen)

Card No. / Field No. 268

Residence County. Post Office: Miller, Ind. Ter.

Dawes Roll No.	NAME	Relationship to Person First Named	AGE	SEX	BLOOD	Tribal Enrollment Year	County	No.	Name of Father	Year	County	Name of Mother	Year	County
568	Dillard, Hamilton		36	M	1/16	1896		3631	Wm Dillard	Dead	Non-Citizen	Elizabeth Dillard		
497	" Victoria	Wife	31	F	Full	1896		4947	T.M. Burdines		"	Emily Burdines	Dead	Non-citizen
569	" Lee Hamilton	Son	14	M	1/16	1896		3644	No.1			No.2		
570	" Joseph Bryant	Son	13	M	1/16	1896		3645	No.1			No.2		
571	" William Grey	Son	10	M	1/16	1896		3646	No.1			No.2		
572	" Fannie Victoria	Dau	8	F	1/16	1896		3647	No.1			No.2		
573	" Birdie Maurice	"	5	M	1/16	1896		3648	No.1			No.2		
574	" Guff Crockett	Son	3	M	1/16	1896		3649	No.1			No.2		
575	" Floyd	"	1	M	1/16				No.1			No.2		
576	" Nellie Dawson	"		F	1/16				No.1			No.2		
577	" Douglas	Son		M	1/16				No.1			No.2		
563	" Walter			M	1/16				No.3			Alpha Victoria Dillard intermarried		

ENROLLMENT
OF NOS. APPROVED BY THE SECRETARY
OF INTERIOR

Date of Application for Enrollment Sept. 03/98

Introduction

This series of Choctaw Enrollment Cards for the Five Civilized Tribes 1898-1914 has been transcribed from National Archive Film M-1186 Rolls 39-46.

The series contains more than 6100 Choctaw enrollment cards. All of the cards list age, sex and degree of blood, the parties' Dawes Roll Numbers, and date of enrollment by the Secretary of Interior for each person. The contents also give the enrollee's parents' names as well as miscellaneous notes pertaining to the enrollee's circumstances, when needed. Most entries indicate whether or not a spouse is an Intermarried White, with the initials I.W.

Enrollment wasn't as simple a process as most would think just by going through these pages. The relationships between the Five Tribes and the Dawes Commission were weak at best. There were political battles going on between the tribes and the U.S. Government as it was, but the struggles didn't stop there. Each tribe had its own political factions pulling it from every direction. On top of everything else, people from every corner of the United States were trying to figure how to get in on the spoils (Money and Land Allotment) by means of political favor. Kent Carter, author of *The Dawes Commission*, describes the continuous effort required to enroll the different tribes and the pressure the Commission incurred from people all over the country who tried to insinuate themselves into the equation:

"In May 1896 the Dawes Commission Returned To Indian Territory for its third visit, establishing its headquarters at Vinita in the Cherokee Nation. It now had to process applications for citizenship in addition to negotiating allotment agreements; these circumstances make the narrative of events more confusing because the commission attempted the two tasks concurrently. The commissioners resumed making their usual speeches to tribal officials and public gatherings to promote negotiations, but now they inevitably had to respond to questions about how the application process for citizenship would work. They also began receiving letters from people all over the United States asking how they could 'get on the rolls' so they could 'get Indian land'."[1]

For the actual process of Choctaw enrollment, "A commission was appointed in each county of the Choctaw Nation under an act of September 18 to make separate rolls of citizens by blood, by intermarriage, and freedmen; it was to deliver them to recently elected Chief Green McCurtain by October 20, but he rejected them even before they were completed because of charges that people were being left off for political reasons. On October 30, the National Council authorized establishment of a five-member

---

[1] *The Dawes Commission* by Kent Carter, page 15, para. 1

ix

commission to revise the rolls within ten days and then directed McCurtain to turn them over to the Dawes Commission on November 11, 1896. The Choctaws hired the law firm of Stuart, Gordon, and Hailey, of South McAlester to represent the tribe at all proceedings held by the Dawes Commission,"[2] another indication that throughout the Commission's efforts there was always controversy between the tribes and the negotiators.

When completed, this multi-volume series will contain thousands of names, all of them accounted for in the indexes carefully prepared by the author. Hopefully this work will help many researchers find their ancestors and satisfy the questions that so many have had about their Native American heritage.

Jeff Bowen
Gallipolis, Ohio
NativeStudy.com

---

[2] *The Dawes Commission* by Kent Carter, page 16, para. 5

Choctaw By Blood Enrollment Cards 1898-1914

RESIDENCE: Blue COUNTY.								
POST OFFICE: Caddo, I.T.	**Choctaw Nation**				**Choctaw Roll** (Not Including Freedmen)	CARD NO. FIELD NO. 3901		

Dawes' Roll No.	NAME	Relationship to Person First Named	AGE	SEX	BLOOD	TRIBAL ENROLLMENT		
						Year	County	No.
1	Smith, Mack D	Named	21	M	1/8			
2								
3								
4								
5								
6								
7								
8								
9								
10								
11								
12								
13								
14								
15								
16								
17								

TRIBAL ENROLLMENT OF PARENTS

	Name of Father	Year	County	Name of Mother	Year	County
1	W.H.P. Smith	Dead Non Citz		Mary A Loving		Choctaw
2						
3						
4						
5						
6						
7	No1 Denied in 96 Case #546					
8	Admitted by U.S Court, Central Dist.					
9	June 19/99, Case No 71. As to residence, see her[sic] testimony.					
10	Judgment of U.S. Court admitting No1 vacated and set aside by Decree of Choctaw Chickasaw Citizenship Court Dec 17/02					
11	No1 now in C.C.C.C. Case #807					
12						
13						
14						
15					Date of Application for Enrollment.	Aug 24/99
16						
17						

DENIED CITIZENSHIP BY THE CHOCTAW AND CHICKASAW CITIZENSHIP COURT

Case 16240 Oct 20/04

Choctaw By Blood Enrollment Cards 1898-1914

RESIDENCE: Blue   COUNTY. **Choctaw Nation**   **Choctaw Roll** *(Not Including Freedmen)*   CARD NO. FIELD NO. **3902**
POST OFFICE: Caddo, I.T.

Dawes' Roll No.	NAME		Relationship to Person First Named	AGE	SEX	BLOOD	TRIBAL ENROLLMENT Year	County	No.
10974	1 Paddock, James L	29	First Named	26	M	1/16	1896	Blue	10479
I.W. 145	2 " Venia	30	Wife	27	F	I.W.	1896	Blue	14976
10975	3 " William H	8	Son	5	M	1/32	1896	Blue	10480
10976	4 " Jesse	7	"	4	"	1/32	1896	"	10481
10977	5 " Rosa L	5	Dau	2	F	1/32			
10978	6 " Johnie R	2	Son	6mo	M	1/32			
10979	7 " Claude	1	Son	2mo	M	1/32			

ENROLLMENT OF NOS.1,3,4,5,6 and 7 HEREON APPROVED BY THE SECRETARY OF INTERIOR Feb 4 1903

ENROLLMENT OF NOS. 2 ~ HEREON APPROVED BY THE SECRETARY OF INTERIOR Jun 13 1903

17 For child of Nos 1&2 see NB (Apr 26-06) Card #496

TRIBAL ENROLLMENT OF PARENTS

Name of Father	Year	County	Name of Mother	Year	County
1 Reuben Paddock		Non Citz	Liza Paddock	Dead	Blue
2 Jno Templeton		" "	Lydia Templeton		Non Citz
3 No1			No2		
4 No1			No2		
5 No1			No2		
6 No.1			No.2		
7 No.1			No.2		

8 No.1 on 1896 roll as Jas L Paddock
9 No.3 on 1896 roll as Wm H Paddock   No.6 Enrolled June 11, 1900
10 No1 was admitted by Act of Choctaw Council No 46 approved November 5/88   7/23/02 See Choc D-20

13 No2 Evidence of marriage to be supplied:- On 1896 roll as Viney Pedock   #1 to 5 inc

Date of Application for Enrollment.   Aug 24/99

16 No2 evidence of marriage filed Dec 14/99   No.7 Born Dec. 4, 1901; enrolled Feby 24, 1902

2

Choctaw By Blood Enrollment Cards 1898-1914

RESIDENCE:	Blue	COUNTY.				
POST OFFICE:	Blue, I.T.		**Choctaw Nation**		Choctaw Roll *(Not Including Freedmen)*	FIELD NO. **3903**

Dawes' Roll No.	NAME		Relationship to Person First Named	AGE	SEX	BLOOD	TRIBAL ENROLLMENT		
							Year	County	No.
10980	₁ James, Walton	34	First Named	31	M	1/2	1896	Chick Dist	7388
~~DEAD.~~	₂ " ~~Lottie~~		~~Wife~~	~~24~~	~~F~~	~~I.W.~~			
10981	₃ " Julia	7	Dau	4	"	1/4			7389
10982	₄ " Vinnie M	5	"	2	"	1/4			
10983	₅ " Frank	4	Son	8mo	M	1/4			
I.W. 1420	₆ " Henrietta		Wife	21	F	I.W.			
	₇					ENROLLMENT			
	₈					OF NOS. ~~~ 6 ~~~ HEREON APPROVED BY THE SECRETARY			
	₉	ENROLLMENT				OF INTERIOR JUN 12 1905			
	₁₀	OF NOS. 1,3,4 and 5 HEREON							
	₁₁	~~APPROVED BY THE SECRETARY~~ OF INTERIOR MAR 10 1903							
	₁₂	~~No. 2 HEREON DISMISSED UNDER~~							
	₁₃	~~ORDER OF THE COMMISSION TO THE FIVE~~							
	₁₄	~~CIVILIZED TRIBES OF MARCH 31, 1905.~~							
	₁₅								
	₁₆								
	₁₇								

TRIBAL ENROLLMENT OF PARENTS

Name of Father	Year	County	Name of Mother	Year	County
₁ Jiman James	Dead	Blue	Mary James		Jackson
₂ ~~W.M. McCartey~~		~~Non-Citz~~	~~Mary McCartey~~		~~Non-Citz~~
₃ No1			No		
₄ No1			No2		
₅ No1			No2		
₆ Charley Shafer		non-citz	Emer Burlue		non-citz
₇					
₈	No3 on 1896 roll as Julian James				
₉	~~Nos4-5 Affidavits of birth to be~~				
₁₀	supplied:- Filed Nov 2/99				
₁₁	No.2 Died Jan 22,1900: Proof of death filed Dec 24 1902				
₁₂	~~Wife of No1 is Henrietta James: applicant today 12/24/02~~ ~~No6 originally listed for enrollment on Choctaw card #D-978~~				
₁₃	Dec. 24, 1902: transferred to this card May 15, 1905. See decision of Feb 7, 1905 #1			Date of App for Enrol	
₁₄				Aug 24	
₁₅					
₁₆	~~No6 Matoy I.T. 2/7/05~~				
₁₇	Antlers I.T. 12/24/02				

3

Choctaw By Blood Enrollment Cards 1898-1914

RESIDENCE: Blue   COUNTY. **Choctaw Nation**   **Choctaw Roll**   CARD No.
POST OFFICE: Caddo, I.T.   *(Not Including Freedmen)*   FIELD No. 3904

Dawes' Roll No.	NAME	Relationship to Person First Named	AGE	SEX	BLOOD	Year	County	No.
10984	1 Dillard, Tandy W ³³	First Named	30	M	1/8	1896	Blue	3540
I.W. 361	2 " Virginia ³¹	Wife	28	F	IW	1896	"	14475
10985	3 " Vera ¹²	Dau	9	"	1/16	1896	"	3541
10986	4 " Rice ¹⁰	Son	7	M	1/16	1896	"	3542
10987	5 " Jewel ⁸	Dau	5	F	1/16	1896	"	3543
10988	6 " Virgie M ⁴	"	5mo	"	1/16			
10989	7 " Tandy Russell ¹	Son	2wk	M	1/16			
	8							
	9							
	10							
	11	ENROLLMENT						
	12	OF NOS. 1,3,4,5,6 and 7 HEREON APPROVED BY THE SECRETARY						
	13	OF INTERIOR MAR 10 1903						
	14	ENROLLMENT						
	15	OF NOS. 2 HEREON APPROVED BY THE SECRETARY						
	16	OF INTERIOR SEP 12 1903						
	17							

TRIBAL ENROLLMENT OF PARENTS

	Name of Father	Year	County	Name of Mother	Year	County
1	Hamp Dillard	Dead	Non Citz	Eliz Dillard		Chick Dist
2	Arch Russell		" "	Clemie Russell		Non Citz
3	No1			No2		
4	No1			No2		
5	No1			No2		
6	No1			No2		
7	No1			No2		
8						
9	No1 on 1896 roll as T. W. Dillard					
10						
11	Evidence of marriage to be					
12	supplied:- Recd Oct 7/99					
13	No7 Enrolled October 9, 1901					
14	For child of Nos 1&2 see NB (Apr 26-06) Card #817				#106	
15	" " " " " " " (March 3-1905) " #781			Date of Application for Enrollment.	Aug 24/99	
16						
17						

4

Choctaw By Blood Enrollment Cards 1898-1914

RESIDENCE:	Blue	COUNTY.				
POST OFFICE:	Caddo, I.T.				CARD NO.	

Choctaw Nation **Choctaw Roll** *(Not Including Freedmen)* FIELD NO. 3905

Dawes' Roll No.	NAME	Relationship to Person First Named	AGE	SEX	BLOOD	TRIBAL ENROLLMENT		
						Year	County	No.
1	Cobb, George S	Named	52	M	1/8		D	
2	" Mary F A	Wife	48	F	IW		D	
3	Hogue, Edna	Dau	19	"	1/16		D	
4	Cobb, Ethel B	"	11	"	1/16		D	
5	Hogue, Charlie Herbert	Gran. dau	2mo	"	1/32			
6								
7								
8								
9								
10								
11								
12								
13	#5 DISMISSED							
14	JAN 21 1905							
15								
16	DENIED CITIZENSHIP BY THE CHOCTAW AND							
17	CHICKASAW CITIZENSHIP COURT							

No1 Denied by C.C.C.C. as Geo S Cobb
No2 " " " M F A Cobb
No3 " " " Ed A Cobb

TRIBAL ENROLLMENT OF PARENTS

	Name of Father	Year	County	Name of Mother	Year	County
1	Sam'l B. Cobb	Dead	Choctaw	Missie P Cobb	Dead	Non-Citz
2	W.T. Sanders	"	Non Citz	Nancy J Sanders	"	" "
3	No1			No2		
4	No1			No2		
5	C. H. Hogue	Dead	Non-citizen	No.3		
6						
7						
8	Nos 1 to 5 incl denied in 96 Case #734					
9	Admitted by U.S Court, Southern Dist					
10	Jany 18/98. As to residence, see testimony of No1			NOTICE OF DEPARTMENTAL ACTION APR 30 1907 MAILED PARTIES HEREIN		
11						
12	No3 admitted as Edna Cobb					
13	No5 Enrolled, June 23d, 1900					
14						
15				Date of Application for Enrollment	Aug 24/99	
16						
17						

Choctaw By Blood Enrollment Cards 1898-1914

RESIDENCE: Blue									

RESIDENCE: Blue
POST OFFICE: Caddo, I.T. COUNTY. **Choctaw Nation** Choctaw Roll *(Not Including Freedmen)* CARD NO. FIELD NO. 3906

Dawes' Roll No.	NAME	Relationship to Person First Named	AGE	SEX	BLOOD	TRIBAL ENROLLMENT Year	County	No.
1	Cobb, Simon S	Named	27	M	1/16		D	
2	" Claude	Son	4	"	1/32		D	
3	" Nina	Dau	3	F	1/32		D	
DP 4	" George D	Son	1	M	1/32			
DP 5	" Lena Kate	Dau	1 wk	F	1/32			
DP 6	" Martha Jewel	Dau	2	F	1/32			

No2 Enrolled by C.C.C.C. as Claude Cobb or Claud Cobb

No4 Evidence of marriage of parents to be supplied:-
Recd Oct 7/99

#4-5-6 DISMISSED JAN 21 1905

DENIED CITIZENSHIP BY THE CHOCTAW AND CHICKASAW CITIZENSHIP COURT

TRIBAL ENROLLMENT OF PARENTS

	Name of Father	Year	County	Name of Mother	Year	County
1	Geo S Cobb		Choctaw	Mary F A Cobb		Intermarried
2	No1			Florence Cobb		"
3	No1			" "		"
4	No1			Eula Cobb		Non Citz
5	No1			" "		" "
6	No 1			" "		" "

Nos1,2 &3 Denied in 96 Case #734
Nos1,2 &3 now in C.C.C.C. Case #33T
All but No4 were admitted by U.S. Court; Southern Dist, Jany 18/98 As to residence and birth of No4, which occurred July 17/98, see testimony of Geo S Cobb, Card No 3905

No1 is divorced from mother of Nos 2-3
No.5 born Jan 23, 1902; Enrolled Jan 29, 1902
No 6 Born July 22, 1900; enrolled Aug 6, 1902

Date of Application for Enrollment. Aug 24/99

6

Choctaw By Blood Enrollment Cards 1898-1914

RESIDENCE: Jackson   COUNTY.   **Choctaw Nation**   **Choctaw Roll** (Not Including Freedmen)   CARD No.

POST OFFICE: Jackson, I.T.   FIELD No. 3907

Dawes' Roll No.	NAME	Relationship to Person First Named	AGE	SEX	BLOOD	TRIBAL ENROLLMENT Year	County	No.
10900	1 Thompson, Jacob 24	First Named	21	M	1/4	1896	Blue	12426
DEAD.	2 " Nola	Wife	19	F	IW			
10901	3 " Minnie 2	Dau	8mo	F	1/8			
	4							
	5							
	6							
	7	ENROLLMENT						
	8	OF NOS. 1 and 3 HEREON APPROVED BY THE SECRETARY						
	9	OF INTERIOR MAR 10 1903						
	10	No. 2 HEREON DISMISSED UNDER						
	11	ORDER OF THE COMMISSION TO THE FIVE						
	12	CIVILIZED TRIBES OF MARCH 31, 1905.						
	13							
	14							
	15							
	16							
	17							

TRIBAL ENROLLMENT OF PARENTS

	Name of Father	Year	County	Name of Mother	Year	County
1	Green Thompson	Dead	Blue	Susan Thompson	Dead	Blue
2	Smith	"	Non Citz	Grace Orum		Non Citz
3	No.1			No.2		
4						
5						
6						
7			Evidence of marriage to be			
8		supplied:-	Recd Oct 7/99			
9		No.3 Enrolled April 12, 1901				
10		No2 died August 18, 1902; proof of death filed Nov 25, 1902				
11						
12						
13						
14					#1&2	
15				Date of Application for Enrollment	Aug 24/99	
16						
17	Academy I.T. 11/20/02					

7

Choctaw By Blood Enrollment Cards 1898-1914

RESIDENCE:	Blue	COUNTY.							
POST OFFICE:	Roberta, I.T.								

Choctaw Nation

Choctaw Roll *(Not Including Freedmen)*

CARD NO.

FIELD NO. 3908

Dawes' Roll No.	NAME	Relationship to Person First Named	AGE	SEX	BLOOD	TRIBAL ENROLLMENT		
						Year	County	No.
1	Alderson, Robert T	Named	40	M	IW			
2	" Ellen	Wife	37	F	1/8			
3	" Richard M	Son	16	M	1/16			
4	" Barley H	"	12	"	1/16			
5	" Jerry	"	2mo	M	1/16			
6								
7	No1 DISMISSED MAY -7 1904							
8								
9	No2,3 and 4 denied by C.C.C.C. March 28 04							
10	No 5 dismissed " " " " "							
11								
12								
13								
14	No5 DISMISSED							
15	MAY 25 1904							
16								
17	DENIED CITIZENSHIP BY THE CHOCTAW AND 2.3.4 CHICKASAW CITIZENSHIP COURT							

TRIBAL ENROLLMENT OF PARENTS

	Name of Father	Year	County	Name of Mother	Year	County
1	Richard Alderson	Dead	Non Citz	Mary Alderson	Dead	Non Citz
2	J. R. Marrs	"	" "	Jane Marrs		Choctaw
3	No1			No2		
4	No1			No2		
5	No.1			No.2		
6						
7	Nos 2,3&4 Denied in 96 Case #28					
8	Nos 2,3,4 and 5 now in C.C.C.C. Case #109					
9	Admitted by U.S. Court, Central Dist,					
10	Jany 10/98, Case No 88. As to re- sidence, see testimony of No1, also as to					
11	remarriage of No1, see testimony of himself.					
12	No.5 Born Jany 30, 1902 Enrolled April 7, 1902.					
13						
14						
15				Date of Application for Enrollment	Aug 24/99	
16						
17						

Choctaw By Blood Enrollment Cards 1898-1914

RESIDENCE: **Blue**   COUNTY. **Choctaw Nation**   **Choctaw Roll** *(Not Including Freedmen)*   CARD NO.

POST OFFICE: **Roberta, I.T.**   FIELD NO. **3909**

Dawes' Roll No.	NAME	Relationship to Person First Named	AGE	SEX	BLOOD	TRIBAL ENROLLMENT Year	County	No.
1	Hodge, Julia M	Named	13	F	1/16			
2	" Paul Eddison	Son	7mo	M	1/32			
3								
4								
5								
6								
7								
8								
9	2 MAY 27 1904 *DISMISSED*							
10								
11								
12								
13								
14								
15								
16								
17								

TRIBAL ENROLLMENT OF PARENTS

	Name of Father	Year	County	Name of Mother	Year	County
1	Robt. T. Alderson		Non Citz	Ellen Alderson		Choctawe
2	W.R. Hodge		non-citizen	No.1		
3						
4						
5						
6	No1 Denied in 96 Case #28					
7	Admitted by U.S. Court, Central Court, Jany 19/98, Case No 88. As to residence					
8	see testimony of Robert T. Alderson					
9	No.1 is the wife of W.R. Hodge, a noncitizen					
10	No.2 Enrolled May 24, 1901					
11						
12						
13						
14						
15				Date of Application for Enrollment	Aug 24/99	
16						
17						

DENIED CITIZENSHIP BY THE CHOCTAW AND CHICKASAW CITIZENSHIP COURT ... Mar 28 '04

Judgment of U.S.C. admitting No. vacated and set aside by Decree of Choctaw Chickasaw Citizenship Court Dec 17 02

No1 Denied by C.C.C.C. March 28 '04

No2 Dismissed

Choctaw By Blood Enrollment Cards 1898-1914

RESIDENCE: Jackson COUNTY. **Choctaw Nation** CARD NO.

POST OFFICE: Jackson, I.T. **Choctaw Roll** FIELD NO. 3910

(Not Including Freedmen)

Dawes' Roll No.	NAME	Relationship to Person First Named	AGE	SEX	BLOOD	TRIBAL ENROLLMENT		
						Year	County	No.
10992	1 Wilson, Louie ³⁷	First Named	34	M	Full	1896	Jackson	13801
	2							
	3							
	4							
	5	ENROLLMENT OF NOS. 1 HEREON						
	6	APPROVED BY THE SECRETARY						
	7	OF INTERIOR MAR 10 1903						
	8							
	9							
	10							
	11							
	12							
	13							
	14							
	15							
	16							
	17							

TRIBAL ENROLLMENT OF PARENTS

	Name of Father	Year	County	Name of Mother	Year	County
1	Wallace Wilson	Dead	Kiamitia	Melissa Wilson	Dead	Kiamitia
2						
3						
4						
5						
6			On 1896 roll as Louie Wilson			
7						
8						
9						
10						
11						
12						
13						
14				Date of Application for Enrollment.	Aug 25/99	
15						
16						
17	Caddo, I.T. 12/22/02					

Choctaw By Blood Enrollment Cards 1898-1914

RESIDENCE: Blue   COUNTY. **Choctaw Nation**   **Choctaw Roll**   CARD No.

POST OFFICE: Caddo, I.T.   *(Not Including Freedmen)*   FIELD No. **3911**

Dawes' Roll No.		NAME		Relationship to Person	AGE	SEX	BLOOD	TRIBAL ENROLLMENT		
								Year	County	No.
I.W. 1476	1	Lewis, Vicey	30	First Named	27	F	I.W.	1896	Blue	14778
15472	2	" Elmer L	9	Son	6	M	1/32	1896	"	8202
	3									
	4	No1 Dismissed								
	5	Sep 23 1904								
	6									
	7	ENROLLMENT								
	8	OF NOS. ~~ 2 ~~ HEREON								
	9	APPROVED BY THE SECRETARY OF INTERIOR May 9 1904								
	10									
	11	No1 – Granted								
	12	Jun 27 1905								
	13									
	14	ENROLLMENT								
	15	OF NOS. One HEREON								
	16	APPROVED BY THE SECRETARY OF INTERIOR Aug 22 1905								
	17									

TRIBAL ENROLLMENT OF PARENTS

	Name of Father	Year	County	Name of Mother	Year	County
1	W.W. Evans	Dead	Non Citz	Eliza Evans		Non Citz
2	C.S. Lewis		Blue	No1		
3						
4						
5						
6						

7	No.1 restored to roll by Departmental authority of January 19, 1909 (File 5-51)	
	Action of Commission to Five Civilized Tribes of September 23, 1904	
8	rescinded and under opinion of Assistant Attorney General for Dep't of Interior	
9	of March 24, 1905. No1 is enrolled. See decision of June 27, 1905	
10	No1 On 1896 roll as Eliza Vicey Lewis	
	Enrollment of No1 cancelled by order of Department March 4, 1907	
11	No1&2 Admitted by Dawes Com Case No 1239. No appeal as to No2	
12	as Vicey Lewis appealed to U.S. Court as to No1 decision sustained	
13	No appeal to C.C.C.C	Date of Application for Enrollment.
	No2 On 1896 roll as E. L. Lewis	
14	No1 Evidence of divorce from Charles S Lewis filed Dec 26, 1902	Aug 25/99
15	Judgment of U.S. Ct admitting No vacated and set aside by Decree of CCCC Decr 17 '02	
16	No1 formerly wife of Charles S. Lewis, final roll No 9950	Intermarried Status
17	P.O. address: Bokchito I.T.	September 25, 1902

11

Choctaw By Blood Enrollment Cards 1898-1914

RESIDENCE: Jackson   COUNTY. **Choctaw Nation**   **Choctaw Roll**   CARD NO.
POST OFFICE: Atoka, I.T.   *(Not Including Freedmen)*   FIELD NO. 3912

Dawes' Roll No.		NAME	Relationship to Person First Named	AGE	SEX	BLOOD	TRIBAL ENROLLMENT		
							Year	County	No.
10003	1	Carnes, Henry	DIED PRIOR TO SEPTEMBER 25, 1902	39	M	1/4	1896	Jackson	2829
	2								
	3								
	4								
	5	ENROLLMENT							
	6	OF NOS. 1 HEREON APPROVED BY THE SECRETARY							
	7	OF INTERIOR MAR 10 1903							
	8								
	9								
	10								
	11								
	12								
	13								
	14								
	15								
	16								
	17								

TRIBAL ENROLLMENT OF PARENTS

	Name of Father	Year	County	Name of Mother	Year	County
1	John Carnes	Dead	Bok Tuklo	Lizzie Carnes	Dead	Red River
2						
3						
4						
5						
6	No 1 died December -- 1900: Enrollment cancelled by Department May 1906					
7						
8						
9						
10						
11						
12						
13						
14						
15					Date of Application for Enrollment.	Aug 25/99
16						
17						

Choctaw By Blood Enrollment Cards 1898-1914

RESIDENCE: Blue COUNTY.
POST OFFICE: Bok Chito I.T.

Choctaw Nation

Choctaw Roll
(Not Including Freedmen)

CARD NO.
FIELD NO. **3913**

Dawes' Roll No.	NAME		Relationship to Person First Named	AGE	SEX	BLOOD	TRIBAL ENROLLMENT		
							Year	County	No.
10994	1 Boland, James	26	First Named	23	M	1/8	1893	Kiamitia	98
I.W. 362	2 " Kizzie	22	Wife	19	F	I.W.			
10995	3 " Arizona	4	Dau	9mo	"	1/16			
10996	4 " Sallie	1	Dau	3mo	F	1/16			
	5								
	6								
	7								
	8	ENROLLMENT							
	9	OF NOS. 1, 3 and 4 HEREON APPROVED BY THE SECRETARY							
	10	OF INTERIOR Mar 10 1903							
	11								
	12	ENROLLMENT OF NOS. 2 HEREON							
	13	APPROVED BY THE SECRETARY OF INTERIOR Sep 12 1903							
	14								
	15								
	16								
	17								

TRIBAL ENROLLMENT OF PARENTS

	Name of Father	Year	County	Name of Mother	Year	County
1	John Boland		Non Citz	Laura Kelly		Blue
2	W.C. Turner		" "	Sallie Turner	Dead	Non Citz
3	No1			No2		
4	No.1			No.2		
5						
6						
7	No1 on 1893 Pay Roll, Page 120, No 98,					
8	Kiamitia Co., as Jimmie Jackson					
9	No.4 Enrolled June 15, 1901					
10						
11	For child of Nos 1&2 see N.B. (Apr 26 '06) Card #259.					
12						
13						
14					Aug 25	
15				Date of Application for Enrollment.	25/99	
16						
17						

13

Choctaw By Blood Enrollment Cards 1898-1914

RESIDENCE:	Jackson	COUNTY.	**Choctaw Nation**			**Choctaw Roll**	CARD No.	
POST OFFICE:	Mayhew, I.T.					(Not Including Freedmen)	FIELD No. **3914**	

Dawes' Roll No.	NAME		Relationship to Person First Named	AGE	SEX	BLOOD	TRIBAL ENROLLMENT		
							Year	County	No.
10997	1 Lawrence, Canady	44	First Named	41	M	3/4	1896	Jackson	8134
10998	2 " Lucy	41	Wife	38	F	Full	1896	"	8135
10999	3 " William	16	Son	13	M	7/8	1896	"	8136
11000	4 " Osborne	12	"	9	"	7/8	1896	"	8137
11001	5 " Betsy	11	Dau	8	F	7/8	1896	"	8139
11002	6 " Annie	8	"	5	"	7/8	1896	"	8138
	7								
	8								
	9								
	10	ENROLLMENT							
	11	OF NOS. 1,2,3,4,5 and 6 HEREON APPROVED BY THE SECRETARY							
	12	OF INTERIOR Mar 10 1903							
	13								
	14								
	15								
	16								
	17								

TRIBAL ENROLLMENT OF PARENTS

	Name of Father	Year	County	Name of Mother	Year	County
1	Henry Lawrence	Dead	Jacks Fork	Becky Lawrence	Dead	Jacks Fork
2	I-me-tah	"	Nashoba	Wisey	"	Nashoba
3	No1			Liney Lawrence	"	Jacks Fork
4	No1			" "	"	" "
5	No1			" "	"	" "
6	No1			No2		
7						
8						
9	No4 on 1896 roll as Osbern Lawrence					
10	No3 On 1896 roll as Willie Lawrence					
11						
12						
13						
14						
15					Date of Application for Enrollment.	Aug 25/99
16						
17	No.4 P.O. Burse Okla 7/13/09					

14

Choctaw By Blood Enrollment Cards 1898-1914

RESIDENCE: **Blue**   COUNTY.
POST OFFICE: **Bok Chito I.T.**   **Choctaw Nation**
Choctaw Roll *(Not Including Freedmen)*
CARD No.
FIELD No. **3915**

Dawes' Roll No.	NAME		Relationship to Person First Named	AGE	SEX	BLOOD	TRIBAL ENROLLMENT		
							Year	County	No.
I.W. 363	₁ Labor, William	48	First Named	46	M	I.W.	1896	Blue	14779
11003	₂ " Phoebe	42	Wife	39	F	7/8	1896	"	8220
11004	₃ Parrish, Belhena	17	Dau	14	"	7/16	1896	"	8223
11005	₄ Labor Henry	12	Son	9	M	7/16	1896	"	8223
11006	₅ " Rena M	9	Dau	6	F	7/16	1896	"	8224
11007	₆ " Virgie	6	Son	3	M	7/16	1896	"	8225
11008	₇ " Alzona	5	Dau	2	F	7/16	ENROLLMENT		
11009	₈ " Namelia A	3	"	1mo	"	7/16	OF NOS. ~~ 9 ~~ HEREON APPROVED BY THE SECRETARY		
15843	₉ " Victoria		Dau	1	F	7/16	OF INTERIOR Jun 12 1905		
	₁₀								
	₁₁ ENROLLMENT								
	₁₂ OF NOS. 2,3,4,5,6,7 and 8 HEREON								
	₁₃ APPROVED BY THE SECRETARY OF INTERIOR Mar 10 1903								
	₁₄								
	₁₅ ENROLLMENT								
	₁₆ OF NOS. 1 HEREON APPROVED BY THE SECRETARY								
	₁₇ OF INTERIOR Sep 12 1903								

TRIBAL ENROLLMENT OF PARENTS

	Name of Father	Year	County	Name of Mother	Year	County
₁	William Labor	Dead	Non Citz	Precey Labor	Dead	Non Citz
₂	Wᵐ Watson	"	Nashoba	Betsey Watson		Nashoba
₃	No1			No2		
₄	No1			No2		
₅	No1			No2		
₆	No1			No2		
₇	No1			No2		
₈	No1			No2		
₉	No1			No2		
₁₀						

₁₁   No1 was admitted by Dawes Com Case | No9 born Jan 2, 1901
₁₂   No 851   His parents were Spaniards | application made and
₁₃   No8 is named Mela Ann Labor 11/17-02 | No9 placed hereon April
No2 on 1896 roll as Phebie Labor   3.1905
₁₄   No3 " 1896 " " Belle H "   For child of No 3 see NB (Mar 3-1905) #706
₁₅   No6 " 1896 " " Virgil "
Nº3 Is is[sic] now the wife of Ransom Parrish a non citizen
₁₆   Evidence of marriage filed October-25-1902   Date of Application for Enrollment.   Aug 25/99
₁₇   For child of No3 see NB (Apr 26-06) Card #206   ↘#1 to 8

15

Choctaw By Blood Enrollment Cards 1898-1914

RESIDENCE: **Blue** COUNTY. **Choctaw Nation** **Choctaw Roll** CARD No.

POST OFFICE: **Bok Chito, I.T.** *(Not Including Freedmen)* FIELD No. **3916**

Dawes' Roll No.	NAME	Relationship to Person First Named	AGE	SEX	BLOOD	TRIBAL ENROLLMENT		
						Year	County	No.
I.W.**364** ₁	Bugg, John H ⁴⁹	First Named	45	M	IW			
11010 ₂	" Narcissa ¹⁸	Wife	15	F	7/16	1896	Blue	8221
11011 ₃	" Benjamin T ³	Son	6wks	M	7/32			
₄								
₅								
₆								
₇	ENROLLMENT OF NOS. 2 and 3 HEREON							
₈	APPROVED BY THE SECRETARY OF INTERIOR MAR 10 1903							
₉								
₁₀	ENROLLMENT							
₁₁	OF NOS. 1 HEREON							
₁₂	APPROVED BY THE SECRETARY OF INTERIOR SEP 12 1903							
₁₃								
₁₄								
₁₅								
₁₆								
₁₇								

TRIBAL ENROLLMENT OF PARENTS

	Name of Father	Year	County	Name of Mother	Year	County
₁	William Bugg		Non Citz	Tina Bugg	Dead	Non Citz
₂	William Labor		Intermarried	Phoebe Labor		Blue
₃	No1			No2		
₄						
₅						
₆						
₇	No2 on 1896 roll as Narcissie Labor					
₈						
₉						
₁₀						
₁₁						
₁₂						
₁₃						
₁₄						
₁₅				Date of Application for Enrollment.	Aug 25/99	
₁₆				No3 enrolled Dec 16/99		
₁₇						

16

Choctaw By Blood Enrollment Cards 1898-1914

RESIDENCE: Blue   COUNTY. **Choctaw Nation**   **Choctaw Roll**   CARD NO.
POST OFFICE: Caddo, I.T.   *(Not Including Freedmen)*   FIELD NO. **3917**

Dawes' Roll No.	NAME	Relationship to Person First Named	AGE	SEX	BLOOD	TRIBAL ENROLLMENT Year	County	No.
15305	1 McLellan James A 49	First Named	46	M	1/4			
I.W. .80	2 " Mary E. A. 26	Wife	23	F	I.W.			
15307	3 " John F. 25	Son	22	M	1/8			
15308	4 " James C 20	"	17	"	1/8			
15309	5 " Robert D. 7	"	4	"	1/8			
15310	6 " Levi 5	"	2	"				
	7						ENROLLMENT	
	8					OF NOS. 2 HEREON APPROVED BY THE SECRETARY OF INTERIOR May 9 1904		
	9							
	10 No.6 born before Judgment							
	11 was rendered.							
	12 For child of No.1 see NB (Apr. 26 1906) 166.							
	13							
	14 No.6 was born April 30, 1896, subsequent to date						ENROLLMENT	
	15 of filing of original application in case of Jas. A					OF NOS. 1-3-4-5-6 HEREON APPROVED BY THE SECRETARY OF INTERIOR May 9, 1904		
	16 McLellan et al. vs Choctaw nation and is this date duly listed for enrollment and evidence of							
	17 birth is filed May 28, 1900.							

TRIBAL ENROLLMENT OF PARENTS

	Name of Father	Year	County	Name of Mother	Year	County
1	Frank McLellan	Dead	Non Citz	Dorethy[sic] McLellan	Dead	Choctaw
2	A.M. Murphey	" "		Mary Murphey	"	Non Citz
3	No 1			Polly A McLellan	"	" "
4	No 1			Melissa McLellan	"	" "
5	No 1			No 2		
6	No 1			No 2		
7						
8	Nos 1 to 5 incl admitted by C.C.C.C. March 21st 04					
9	Nos 1 to 5 incl denied in 96 Case #1331					
10	All but No6 were admitted by U.S. Court, Central Dist Aug 24/97, Case No 82 under					
11	name of McClellan. Judgement[sic] of U.S. Ct admitting No vacated and set aside by					
12	As to residence see testimony of No1 Decree of C.C.C.C. Dec 17 '02					
13						
14					Date of Application for Enrollment	
15					Aug 25/99	
16						
17						

17

Choctaw By Blood Enrollment Cards 1898-1914

RESIDENCE: **Blue**
POST OFFICE: **Caddo, I.T.**

COUNTY. **Choctaw Nation**

Choctaw Roll *(Not Including Freedmen)*

CARD NO.
FIELD NO. **3918**

Dawes' Roll No.	NAME		Relationship to Person First Named	AGE	SEX	BLOOD	TRIBAL ENROLLMENT		
							Year	County	No.
11012	1 Johnson, Sealy	38	First Named	35	F	Full	1893	Blue	208
11013	2 " Carrie	4	Dau	1	"	"			
11014	3 " Umpson	42	Husband	42	M	"	1893	"	682
	4								
	5								
	6								
	7	ENROLLMENT							
	8	OF NOS. 1,2 and 3 HEREON APPROVED BY THE SECRETARY							
	9	OF INTERIOR Mar 10 1903							
	10								
	11								
	12								
	13								
	14								
	15								
	16								
	17								

TRIBAL ENROLLMENT OF PARENTS

	Name of Father	Year	County	Name of Mother	Year	County
1	Thle-oh-tubbee	Dead	Towson		Dead	Towson
2	Umpson Johnson		Blue	No1		
3	Phillip Johnson	Dead	Choctaw	Nonah-hachale	dead	Choctaw
4						
5						
6	On 1893 Pay Roll, Page 19, No 208 Blue Co					
7	as Seely Bob					
8	No1 on 1896 Choctaw census roll page 120. No 4923 as Silly Gardner					
9	Husband of No1 and father of No2 on Choctaw card #5606, Nov. 14, 1902					
10	N°3 also on 1896 Choctaw census roll page 178 #7236 See testimony of No3 taken Nov. 17, 1902					
11						
12						
13					Date of Application for Enrollment.	
14						
15					Aug 25/99	
16						
17	No.3 P.O. Blue Okla 11/29/10					

18

Choctaw By Blood Enrollment Cards 1898-1914

RESIDENCE:	Blue	COUNTY.	**Choctaw Nation**	**Choctaw Roll**	CARD NO.	
POST OFFICE:	Caddo, I.T.			*(Not Including Freedmen)*	FIELD NO. **3919**	

Dawes' Roll No.	NAME	Relationship to Person First Named	AGE	SEX	BLOOD	TRIBAL ENROLLMENT		
						Year	County	No.
15311 ₁	McLellan Samuel J ㊼		44	M	1/8			
I.W. 802 ₂	" Sarah ⁴⁵	Wife	42	F	I.W.			
15312 ₃	" Edmund ²¹	Son	18	M	1/16			
15313 ₄	" Mary ¹⁹	Dau	16	F	1/16			
15314 ₅	" Samuel ¹⁷	Son	14	M	1/16			
15315 ₆	" Ollie ¹⁵	Dau	12	F	1/16			
15316 ₇	" George ¹⁰	Son	7	M	1/16			
15317 ₈	" Susan ⁸	Dau	5	F	1/16			
15318 ₉	" Orville D ³	Son	5mo	M	1/16	Born April 4 '99		
15319 ₁₀	Dickey Earnest G. ¹	G.Son	2mo	M	1/32	Born July 3 '01		
₁₁								
₁₂	For child of No4 see NB (Act Mar 3-05) Card #273							
₁₃	Nos 1 to 8 incl admitted by C.C.C.C. March 21, '04							
₁₄	For child of No6 see NB (Ap 26-06) Card #755							
₁₅	ENROLLMENT							
₁₆	OF NOS. 1,3,4,5,6,7,8,9,10 HEREON APPROVED BY THE SECRETARY							
₁₇	OF INTERIOR May 9 1904							

TRIBAL ENROLLMENT OF PARENTS

	Name of Father	Year	County	Name of Mother	Year	County
₁	Frank McLellan	Dead	Non Citz	Dorethy McLellan	Dead	Choctaw
₂	Caswell Burk	"	" "	Mary Burk		Non Citz
₃	No1			No2		
₄	No1			No2		
₅	No1			No2		
₆	No1		ENROLLMENT	No2		
₇	No1	OF NOS. 2 HEREON		No2		
₈	No1	APPROVED BY THE SECRETARY OF INTERIOR May 9 1904		No2		
₉	No1			No2		
₁₀	S.E. Dickey		non citizen	No4		
₁₁						
₁₂	Nos 1 to 8 incl now in C.C.C.C. Case #10					
₁₃	All but No9 were admitted by U.S. Court, Central Dist, Aug 24/97, Case No 82. As					
₁₄	to residence see testimony of No1 - Also as to					
₁₅	birth of child. Judgment by U.S. Ct admitting Nos 1 to 8 incl vacated and set aside by Decree of C.C.C.C. Decr 17 '02				Date of Application for Enrollment.	
₁₆	No.4 is now the wife of S.E. Dickey a non citizen. Evidence of marriage filed Sept 20, 1901. No10 Enrolled Sept 20, 1901.				Aug 25/99	
₁₇	No4 Boswell I.T. 6/2/04 Kait I.T. Wife of No3 on Card #6048					

3/20/05

19

Choctaw By Blood Enrollment Cards 1898-1914

RESIDENCE: Blue   **COUNTY.**   **Choctaw Nation**   **Choctaw Roll** *(Not Including Freedmen)*   **CARD NO.**
POST OFFICE: Caddo, I.T.   **FIELD NO.** 3920

Dawes' Roll No.		NAME	Relationship to Person First Named	AGE	SEX	BLOOD	TRIBAL ENROLLMENT		
							Year	County	No.
I.W. 803	1	McLellan, Susan E (31)	First Named	29	F	IW			
15320	2	" Franklin B 9	Son	6	M	1/16			
15321	3	" Abner D 7	"	4	M	1/16			
	4								
	5								
	6								
	7								
	8								
	9	ENROLLMENT OF NOS. ~~2-3~~ HEREON APPROVED BY THE SECRETARY OF INTERIOR MAY 9 1904							
	10								
	11								
	12								
	13	ENROLLMENT OF NOS. 1 HEREON APPROVED BY THE SECRETARY OF INTERIOR MAY 9 1904							
	14								
	15								
	16								
	17								

TRIBAL ENROLLMENT OF PARENTS

	Name of Father	Year	County	Name of Mother	Year	County
1	Samuel Black	Dead	Non Citz	Frances Black		Non Citz
2	Abner D McLellan	"	Choctaw	No 1		
3	" " "	"	"	No 1		
4						
5						
6						
7	Nos 1 to 3 incl Denied in 96 Case #1331 Admitted by U.S. Court, Central Dist					
8	Aug 24/97, Case No 82. As to residence see testimony of No1					
9	No 1 was admitted as Susie McLellan					
10	No 2 " " ' Franklin "					
11	Judgment of U.S. Ct admitting Nos 1,2 and 3 vacated and set aside by Decree of Choctaw Chickasaw Cit Court Dec 17 '02					
12	Nos 1,2 and 3 admitted by C.C.C.C. March 21 '04					
13						Date of Application for Enrollment.
14						
15						Aug 25/99
16						
17	P.O. Sugden[sic] AR. 3/20/08					

Choctaw By Blood Enrollment Cards 1898-1914

RESIDENCE: Blue	COUNTY.	**Choctaw Nation**	**Choctaw Roll**	CARD NO.
POST OFFICE: Folsom, I.T.			*(Not Including Freedmen)*	FIELD NO. 3921

Dawes Roll No.	NAME		Relationship to Person First Named	AGE	SEX	BLOOD	TRIBAL ENROLLMENT		
							Year	County	No.
15322	1 Hines, Oma	24		21	F	1/16			
	2								
	3								
	4								
	5								
	6								
	7	ENROLLMENT OF NOS. ~~~ 1 ~~~ HEREON							
	8	APPROVED BY THE SECRETARY OF INTERIOR MAY 9 1904							
	9								
	10								
	11								
	12								
	13								
	14								
	15								
	16								
	17								

TRIBAL ENROLLMENT OF PARENTS

	Name of Father	Year	County	Name of Mother	Year	County
1	Jeff McLellan		Choctaw	Sarah McLellan		Non Citz
2						
3						
4	No 1 Denied in 96 Case #1331					
5	Admitted by U.S. Court, Central Dist,					
6	Aug 24/97, Case No 82 as Oner McClellan					
7	As to residence, see her testimony					
8	No 1 now in C.C.C. Case #10					
9						
10	No 1 Admitted by C.C.C. March 21" 04					
11						
12	For child of No1 see NB (Apr. 26, 1906) Card No 209					
13	" " " " " " (March 3, 1905) " " 718					
14					Date of Application for Enrollment.	
15					Aug 25/99	
16						
17	P.O. Alma I.T. 3/27/05					

RESIDENCE: Blue COUNTY. **Choctaw Nation** Choctaw Roll CARD NO.
POST OFFICE: Folsom, I.T. *(Not Including Freedmen)* FIELD No. 3922

Dawes' Roll No.	NAME		Relationship to Person First Named	AGE	SEX	BLOOD	TRIBAL ENROLLMENT		
							Year	County	No.
15323	1	McLellan, Wade H (51)	First Named	48	M	1/8			
I.W. 800	2	" Kittie 44	Wife	41	F	IW			
15324	3	" Joseph M 22	Son	19	M	1/16			
15325	4	" John F 20	"	17	"	1/16			
15326	5	" Hattie 18	Dau	15	F	1/16			
15327	6	" Abner D 16	Son	13	M	1/16			
15328	7	" Adeline 12	Dau	9	F	1/16			
15329	8	" Dolly 9	"	6	"	1/16			
15330	9	" Wade 9	Son	6	M	1/16			
		" Monroe H 5	"	2	M	1/16			

ENROLLMENT
OF NOS. 1-3-4-5-6-7-8-9 HEREON
APPROVED BY THE SECRETARY
OF INTERIOR MAY 9 1904

12 Nos 1 to 9 incl admitted by C.C.C.C. March 21 04

ENROLLMENT
OF NOS. ~ 10 ~ HEREON
APPROVED BY THE SECRETARY
OF INTERIOR DEC 15 1904

TRIBAL ENROLLMENT OF PARENTS

	Name of Father	Year	County	Name of Mother	Year	County
1	Frank McLellan	Dead	Non Citz	Dorethy McLellan	Dead	Choctaw
2	J.C. Blocker		" "	Mary H Blocker		Non Citz
3	No 1			No 2		
4	No 1			No 2		
5	No 1			No 2		
6	No 1			No 2		
7	No 1			No 2		
8	No 1			No 2		
9	No 1			No 2		
10	Nº 1			Nº 2		
11	Nos 1 to 9 incl now in C.C.C.C Case #10			Nos 1 to 9 incl Denied in 96 Case #1331		

ENROLLMENT
OF NOS. 2 HEREON
APPROVED BY THE SECRETARY
OF INTERIOR MAY 9 1904

12 Admitted by U.S. Court, Central Dist Aug 24/97, Case No 82, under
13 name of McClellan
14 As to residence see testimony
15 of No1   No.3 is husband of Ada McLellan on 7-6036
15 Nº10 was enrolled on Choctaw card #R211. Transferred to this card upon presentation of proof of
16 birth subsequent to date of original application filed Aug. 25, 1902
17 Krebs I.T. 8/1/02   For children of No3 see NB (Act Mar 3-05) Card #294

Date of Application
for Enrollment.
Aug 25/99

PO Kiowa
PO Ashland I.T. 5/21/04

22

Choctaw By Blood Enrollment Cards 1898-1914

RESIDENCE: Blue   COUNTY.   **Choctaw Nation**   **Choctaw Roll** *(Not Including Freedmen)*

POST OFFICE: Caddo, I.T.   No. 3923

Dawes' Roll No.	NAME	Relationship to Person First Named	AGE	SEX	BLOOD	TRIBAL ENROLLMENT Year	County	No.
11015	1 Manning Matilda 62	First Named	59	F	1/2	1896	Blue	8771
DEAD.	2 " Charles A	Son	26	M	1/4	1896	"	8772
11016	3 " Thomas J 27	"	24	"	1/4	1896	"	8773
11017	4 " Arthur F 21	"	18	"	1/4	1896	"	8774
11018	5 Crutchfield, Gertrude 19	G.Dau	16	F	1/8	1896	"	12408
I.W. 749	6 " John W 28	HUSBAND OF NO 5	28	M	I.W.			
	7							
	8							
	9	ENROLLMENT						
	10	OF NOS. 1,3,4 and 5 HEREON APPROVED BY THE SECRETARY						
	11	OF INTERIOR MAR 19 1903						
	12							
	13	ENROLLMENT						
	14	OF NOS. ~~~~ 6 ~~~~ HEREON APPROVED BY THE SECRETARY						
	15	OF INTERIOR MAY -7 1904						
	16	Child of Nos 5&6 on NB (Apr 26-06) Card #294						
		" " No.4 " " (Mar 3-05) " #783						
	17	" " Nos 5&6 " " " " " #1262						

No. 2 HEREON DISMISSED UNDER ORDER OF THE COMMISSION TO THE FIVE CIVILIZED TRIBES OF MARCH 31, 1905.

TRIBAL ENROLLMENT OF PARENTS

	Name of Father	Year	County	Name of Mother	Year	County
1	Forbis LeFlore	Dead	Blue	Rebecca LeFlore	Dead	Blue
2	T.J. Manning	"	Non Citz	No1		
3	" "	"	" "	No1		
4	" "	"	" "	No1		
5	Fred Thompson	"	" "	Eliz. Thompson	Dead	Blue
6	John W Crutchfield		non-citizen	Evelyn L Crutchfield		non-citizen
7						
8						
9		No2 on 1896 roll as Chas A Manning				
10		No3 " 1896 " " Thos J "				
		No4 " 1896 " " Arthur "				
11	No.4 is now the husband of Nannie H Lawrence on Choctaw					
12	roll card #3678			Dec 24, 1901		
13	No.5 is now the wife of John W Crutchfield on Choctaw card #D.709: Mar. 13, 1902					
14				Date of Application for Enrollment.	Aug 25/99	
15	Nº2 Died Oct. 2, 1899, proof of death filed Dec 5 1902					
16	No.6 transferred from Choctaw card #D.709: see decision of Feby 27, 1904					
17						

Choctaw By Blood Enrollment Cards 1898-1914

RESIDENCE: **Blue** COUNTY. **Choctaw Nation** **Choctaw Roll** CARD NO.
POST OFFICE: **Caddo, I.T.** *(Not Including Freedmen)* FIELD NO. **3924**

Dawes' Roll No.	NAME		Relationship to Person	AGE	SEX	BLOOD	TRIBAL ENROLLMENT		
							Year	County	No.
I.W. **365**	₁ Harris, Jack L	32	First Named	28	M	IW			
11019	₂ " Amelia	25	Wife	22	F	1/4	1896	Blue	5865
11020	₃ " Thelma	6	Dau	3	"	1/8	1896	"	5866
11021	₄ " Fayne	5	Son	2	M	1/8			
11022	₅ " Kathleen	3	Dau	1mo	F	1/8			
DEAD.	₆ ~~" Amelia Clemmie~~	2	~~Dau~~	~~2w~~	~~F~~	~~1/8~~			
	₇								
	₈								
	₉	ENROLLMENT							
	₁₀	OF NOS. 2,3,4 and 5 HEREON APPROVED BY THE SECRETARY							
	₁₁	OF INTERIOR MAR 10 1903							
	₁₂	ENROLLMENT							
	₁₃	OF NOS. 1 HEREON APPROVED BY THE SECRETARY							
	₁₄	OF INTERIOR SEP 12 1903							
	₁₅	No. 6 HEREON DISMISSED UNDER							
	₁₆	ORDER OF THE COMMISSION TO THE FIVE CIVILIZED TRIBES OF MARCH 31, 1905							
	₁₇								

TRIBAL ENROLLMENT OF PARENTS

	Name of Father	Year	County	Name of Mother	Year	County
₁	J. C. Harris		Non Citz	Rebeca Harris		Non Citz
₂	J. Manning	Dead	" "	Matilda Manning		Blue
₃	No1			No2		
₄	No1			No2		
₅	No1			No2		
₆	No 1			No 2		
₇						
₈						
₉	No1 was admitted by Dawes Com					
₁₀	Case No 1357 as J.L. Harris. No3 was admitted in same case. No.6 Enrolled January 24, 1901					
₁₁						
₁₂						
₁₃	No.6 died Sept 23, 1901; proof of death filed Nov 28 1902 . Additional proof					
₁₄	of death filed Dec. 11, 1902				#1 to 4	
₁₅	For children of Nos 1&2 see NB (March 3 1905) #870			Date of Application for Enrollment.	Aug 25/99	
₁₆				No5 enrolled Nov 2/99		
₁₇						

24

Choctaw By Blood Enrollment Cards 1898-1914

RESIDENCE: Blue COUNTY.
POST OFFICE: Jackson, I.T.

Choctaw Nation

Choctaw Roll
(Not Including Freedmen)

CARD NO.
FIELD NO. 3925

Dawes' Roll No.	NAME		Relationship to Person First Named	AGE	SEX	BLOOD	TRIBAL ENROLLMENT		
							Year	County	No.
11023	1 Dobyns, Joanna	25	First Named	22	F	1/8	1896	Tobucksy	3319
11024	2 " Clifford	8	Son	5	M	1/16	1896	"	3320
11025	3 " Oscar Jr	6	"	3	"	1/16	1896	"	3321
I.W. 366	4 " Oscar	33	Husband	31	"	IW	1896	"	14464
11026	5 " Alice	2	Dau	8mo	F	1/16			
	6								
	7								
	8								
	9	ENROLLMENT							
	10	OF NOS. 1,2,3 and 5 HEREON APPROVED BY THE SECRETARY							
	11	OF INTERIOR MAR 10 1903							
	12	ENROLLMENT							
	13	OF NOS. 4 HEREON APPROVED BY THE SECRETARY							
	14	OF INTERIOR SEP 12 1903							
	15								
	16								
	17								

TRIBAL ENROLLMENT OF PARENTS

	Name of Father	Year	County	Name of Mother	Year	County
1	John Lacey	Dead	Non Citz	Sophie Lacey	Dead	Blue
2	Oscar Dobyns		" "	No1		
3	" "		" "	No1		
4	Kenaly Dobyns	dead	" "	Eliza Dobyns	dead	Non Citz
5	No.4			No1		
6						
7	Surnames on 1896 roll as Dobbins					
8						
9	No4 admitted by Dawes Commission					
10	Case 344					
11	No5 Enrolled Aug 29, 1907					
12	For children of Nos 1&4 see NB (March 3,1905) Card #585					
13					Date of Application for Enrollment.	
14					Aug 25/99	
15					No4 enrolled Dec 8/99	
16					no ticket issued	
17	Madill I.T. 1/22/00					

25

Choctaw By Blood Enrollment Cards 1898-1914

RESIDENCE:	Blue		COUNTY.	Choctaw Nation			Choctaw Roll	CARD No.	
POST OFFICE:	Caddo, I.T.						*(Not Including Freedmen)*	FIELD No. 3926	

Dawes' Roll No.	NAME	Relationship to Person First Named	AGE	SEX	BLOOD	TRIBAL ENROLLMENT		
						Year	County	No.
* 1	Riddle, Lemuel A	Named	46	M	1/8			
* 2	" Marvin	Son	12	"	1/16			
* 3	" Flora	Dau	8	F	1/16			
* 4	" Floy	"	8	"	1/16			
* 5	" Lemuel	Son	4	M	1/16			
6								
7								
8								
9								
10								
11								
12								
13								
14								
15								
16								
17								

TRIBAL ENROLLMENT OF PARENTS

	Name of Father	Year	County	Name of Mother	Year	County
1	Hampton Riddle	Dead	Choctaw	Nancy Riddle	Dead	Non Citz
2	No 1			Jennie Riddle		" "
3	No 1			" "		" "
4	No 1			" "		" "
5	No 1			" "		" "
6						
7						
8						
9	Nos 1 to 5 incl Denied in 96 Case #686					
10	Admitted by U.S. Court, Central Dist.,					
11	Aug 30/99, Case No 8. As to residence,					
	see testimony of No1					
12	Judgment of U.S. C. admitting Nos 1 to 5 incl vacated and set aside by Decree of Choctaw Chickasaw Citizenship Court Dec 17/02					
13	Nos 1 to 5 incl now in C.C.C.C. Case #108				Date of Application	
14	Nos 1 to 5 incl Denied by C.C.C.C. March 21/04				for Enrollment.	Aug 25/99
15						
16						
17						

26

Choctaw By Blood Enrollment Cards 1898-1914

RESIDENCE:		COUNTY.							CARD No.
POST OFFICE:			**Choctaw Nation**			**Choctaw Roll** *(Not Including Freedmen)*		FIELD No.	3927

Dawes' Roll No.	NAME	Relationship to Person First Named	AGE	SEX	BLOOD	TRIBAL ENROLLMENT		
						Year	County	No.
∗ 1	Johnson, Eva A	Named	18	F	1/16			
2	" Lottie E	Dau	7mo	"	1/32			
3	" James Cullen	Son	5w	M	1/32			
4								
5								
2,3 ~~DISMISSED~~ 6		MAY 27 1904						
7								
8								
9								
10								
11								
12								
13								
14								
15								
16								
17								

TRIBAL ENROLLMENT OF PARENTS

	Name of Father	Year	County	Name of Mother	Year	County
1	Lemuel Riddle		Choctaw	Jennie Riddle		Non Citz
2	Jas N Johnson		Intermarried	No 1		
3	"			No.1		
4	No 1 ~~DENIED CITIZENSHIP BY THE CHOCTAW AND~~					
5	~~CHICKASAW CITIZENSHIP COURT~~ Mar 28 '04					
6						
7	No1 Denied in 96 Case #686					
8	No1 admitted by U.S. Court, Central Dist, Aug 30/97, Case No8 as Eva					
9	Riddle. As to residence see testimony of					
10	Jas. N. Johnson, Card No D366					
11	Judgment of U.S.C. admitting No1 vacated and set aside by Decree of Choctaw Chickasaw Citizenship Court Dec 17'02					
12	No.3 Enrolled January 29, 1901					
13	No1 Denied by C.C.C.C. March 28 04					
14						
15					Date of Application for Enrollment	Aug 25/99
16						
17						

Choctaw By Blood Enrollment Cards 1898-1914

RESIDENCE: Chickasaw Nation COUNTY. **Choctaw Nation**   **Choctaw Roll** CARD NO.

POST OFFICE: Marlow I.T.   *(Not Including Freedmen)* FIELD NO. **3928**

Dawes' Roll No.	NAME	Relationship to Person First Named	AGE	SEX	BLOOD	TRIBAL ENROLLMENT Year	County	No.
11027	1 Dilliard, LeFlore ²⁴		21	M	1/8	1896	Chick Dist	3643
I.W. 978	2 " Cora ²⁶	Wife	23	F	I.W.			
14817	3 " John L ⁴	Son	8mo	M	1/16			
11028	4 " Willie May ²	Dau	2½mo	F	1/16			
	5							
	6							
	7							
	8	ENROLLMENT OF NOS. 1 and 4 HEREON APPROVED BY THE SECRETARY OF INTERIOR Mar 10 1903						
	9							
	10							
	11							
	12							
	13	ENROLLMENT OF NOS. 3 HEREON APPROVED BY THE SECRETARY OF INTERIOR May 20 1903						
	14					ENROLLMENT OF NOS. ~~2~~ HEREON APPROVED BY THE SECRETARY OF INTERIOR Sep 22 1904		
	15							
	16							
	17							

TRIBAL ENROLLMENT OF PARENTS

	Name of Father	Year	County	Name of Mother	Year	County
1	Ham Dilliard	Dead	Non Citz	Eliz Dillard[sic]		Chick Dist
2	William Floyd		" "	Sarah Floyd	Dead	
3	No1			No2		
4	No1			No2		
5						
6	No2 see decision of July 19 04					
7	No1 on 1896 roll as LeFlore Dillard					
8						
9	No3 Affidavit of birth to be					
10	supplied:- Filed Nov 2/99					
11	No4 Enrolled March 4, 1901					
12	For child of Nos 1 and 2 see NB (March 3, 1905) #1251					
13						#1 to 3 inc
14					Date of Application for Enrollment.	
15					Aug 25/99	
16						
17	Antlers I.T. 1/7/03					

Choctaw By Blood Enrollment Cards 1898-1914

RESIDENCE: Blue   COUNTY.
POST OFFICE: Caddo, I.T.

Choctaw Nation

Choctaw Roll *(Not Including Freedmen)*

CARD NO.
FIELD NO. **3929**

Dawes' Roll No.	NAME	Relationship to Person First Named	AGE	SEX	BLOOD	TRIBAL ENROLLMENT Year	County	No.
11029	1 Airington, William ⁵⁶	First Named	53	M	1/4	1896	Blue	389
11030	2 " Leroy ²⁶	Son	23	"	1/8	1893	"	36
5359	3 " Noah	"	21	"	1/8	1893	"	37
I.W. 1260	4 Airington Belle Haney ⁵⁵	Wife	55	F	I.W.			
I.W. 1630	5 " Amanda	Wife of No.2	16	"	I.W.			
	6							
	7	ENROLLMENT OF NOS. 1 and 2 HEREON APPROVED BY THE SECRETARY OF INTERIOR Mar 10 1903						
	8							
	9							
	10	No.5 placed hereon under order of the Commissioner to						
	11	the Five Civilized Tribes of Jan 7, 1907 holding						
	12	application was made for her enrollment within the time						
	13	provided by the Act of Congress Approved Apr 26-06						
	14	ENROLLMENT OF NOS. 2 and 4 HEREON APPROVED BY THE SECRETARY OF INTERIOR Dec 30 1904					ENROLLMENT OF NOS. 5 HEREON APPROVED BY THE SECRETARY OF INTERIOR Feb 19 1907		
	15							
	16							
	17	No.5 Granted Jan. 9, 1907						

TRIBAL ENROLLMENT OF PARENTS

	Name of Father	Year	County	Name of Mother	Year	County
1	Drew Airington	Dead	Non Citz	Nancy Airington	Dead	Red River
2	No 1			Belle Airington		Non Citz
3	No 1			" "		" "
4	William Labor	dead	non citizen	Preecy Labor	dead	non citizen
5	Newt Wall			Minnie Wall		
6						
7						
8						

9   Mother of Nos 2-3 is a Mexican. As to her
10 marriage to No 1 see testimony of Thomas
Ashford.
11   No2 on 1893 Pay Roll, Page 4, No 36, Blue Co. No2 enrolled December 11, 1900
12 as Leroy Arington.
13   No3 on 1893 Pay Roll, Page 4, No 36, Blue Co,
No4 originally listed for enrollment Nov. 21, 1902 on Choctaw card
14 #D-834: transferred to this card Dec 15, 1904. See decision of Nov 28, 1904
15   Wife of No1 appears on Choctaw card D#834
16 No3 transferred to Choctaw card #5359 December 11, 1900
17 Child of Nos 2 and 5 on N.B. #165 (Apr 26, 1906)

Date of Application for Enrollment.
Aug 25/99

29

Choctaw By Blood Enrollment Cards 1898-1914

RESIDENCE: **Blue**   COUNTY. **Choctaw Nation**   **Choctaw Roll** *(Not Including Freedmen)*   CARD NO.

POST OFFICE: **Caddo, I.T.**   FIELD NO. **3930**

Dawes' Roll No.	NAME		Relationship to Person First Named	AGE	SEX	BLOOD	TRIBAL ENROLLMENT		
							Year	County	No.
I.W. 367	1 Beard, Levi L	40	First Named	37	M	I.W.	1896	Blue	14323
11031	2 " Lucy A	27	Wife	24	F	1/4	1896	"	1710
11032	3 " Luther C	8	Son	5	M	1/8	1896	"	1711
11033	4 " Claudie	5	"	2	"	1/8			
11034	5 " Ruthie M	4	Dau	1	F	1/8			
11035	6 " Levi Lee	1	Son	2mo	M	1/8			
	7								
	8	ENROLLMENT OF NOS. 2,3,4,5 and 6 HEREON APPROVED BY THE SECRETARY OF INTERIOR Mar 10 1903							
	9								
	10								
	11	Nº6 Born May 12 1902; enrolled July 22, 1902							
	12								
	13	ENROLLMENT OF NOS. 1 HEREON APPROVED BY THE SECRETARY OF INTERIOR Sep 12 1903							
	14								
	15								
	16								
	17								

TRIBAL ENROLLMENT OF PARENTS

	Name of Father	Year	County	Name of Mother	Year	County
1	Calvin Beard	Dead	Non Citz	Sally Beard	Dead	Non Citz
2	Charley Beams	"	Blue	Nancy Beams	"	Cherokee
3	No1			No2		
4	No1			No2		
5	No1			No2		
6	Nº1			Nº2		
7						

No1 was admitted by Dawes Com Case No 926

No2 On 1896 roll as Lucy Ann Bieard

No3 " 1896 " " Luther C "

No2 Her mother, Nancy Beams, nee Hilderbrandt was a Cherokee. No2 was born and married in Choctaw Nation

See if on 1880 Roll. Also see her testimony No

Nos 4-5 Affidavits of birth to be supplied:- Recd Oct 7/99

No.3 admitted by Dawes Commission Case #926

#1 to 5 inc.

Date of Application for Enrollment.

Aug 25/99

Choctaw By Blood Enrollment Cards 1898-1914

RESIDENCE: Jackson   COUNTY. **Choctaw Nation**   Choctaw Roll   CARD NO.
POST OFFICE: Jackson, I.T.   *(Not Including Freedmen)*   FIELD NO. 3931

Dawes' Roll No.	NAME	Relationship to Person First Named	AGE	SEX	BLOOD	TRIBAL ENROLLMENT		
						Year	County	No.
11036	1 Ramsey, Mary N 43	First Named	40	F	Full	1896	Jackson	10875
11037	2 Barnes, Robert J 28	Son	25	M	"	1896	"	1477
11038	3 " Cornelius 24	"	21	"	"	1896	"	1478
11039	4 Ward, Joel 27	"	24	"	"	1896	"	13804
11040	5 Wilson, Tennessee 20	Dau	17	F	"	1896	"	13808
11041	6 " Elzara 19	"	16	"	"	1896	"	13809
11042	7 Lucas, Johnson 15	Son	12	M	"	1896	"	8140
11043	8 Barnes, Alice 6	Dau of No2	2	F	"			
	9							
	10							
	11							
	12							
	13							
	14							
	15							
	16							
	17							

ENROLLMENT
OF NOS. 1,2,3,4,5,6,7 and 8 HEREON
APPROVED BY THE SECRETARY
OF INTERIOR **MAR 10 1903**

No3 "Decl prior to Nov 25 1902, not entitled
to land or money." See copy of Indian
Office letter of Aug 4 1908 [Illegible]

TRIBAL ENROLLMENT OF PARENTS

	Name of Father	Year	County	Name of Mother	Year	County
1	Geo Ramsey	Dead	Jackson	Emiline Ramsey	Dead	Jackson
2	Jackson Barnes	"	Kiamitia	No1		
3	" "	"	"	No1		
4	Michael Ward	"	Jackson	No1		
5	William Wilson	"	"	No1		
6	" "	"	"	No1		
7	Johnson Lucas	"	Blue	No1		
8	Robert J Barnes		Jackson	Annie Battiest		Jackson
9						
10						
11						
12	No2 on 1896 roll as Robt. J. Barnes					
13	No3 " 1896 " " Cornelia "					
14	No6 " 1896 " " Lucy Wilson				#1 to 7	
15	No8- Affidavit of birth to be					Date of Application for Enrollment. Aug 25/99
16	supplied:- Received and filed Oct. 23d, 1900					
17	N°4 is now the husband of Emma Barnes on Choctaw card #3661. See copy of letter from him filed Sept 30 1902					No8 enrolled Aug 31/99

Choctaw By Blood Enrollment Cards 1898-1914

RESIDENCE: Jackson COUNTY.	POST OFFICE: Jackson, I.T.

Choctaw Nation — **Choctaw Roll** *(Not Including Freedmen)*

CARD NO. FIELD NO. **3932**

Dawes' Roll No.	NAME	Relationship to Person	AGE	SEX	BLOOD	TRIBAL ENROLLMENT Year	County	No.
11044	1 Jones, Sibby 27	First Named	24	F	Full	1896	Jackson	7115
11045	2 " Mary B 6	Dau	3	"	"	1896	"	7116
	3							
	4							
	5							
	6	ENROLLMENT						
	7	OF NOS. 1 and 2 HEREON APPROVED BY THE SECRETARY						
	8	OF INTERIOR Mar 10 1903						
	9							
	10							
	11							
	12							
	13							
	14							
	15							
	16							
	17							

TRIBAL ENROLLMENT OF PARENTS

Name of Father	Year	County	Name of Mother	Year	County
1 Dave Washington	Dead	Red River	Sukey Jones		Atoka
2 Robin Jones	"	Jackson	No1		
3					
4					
5					
6					
7 No2 on 1896 roll as Mary Belle Jones					
8					
9 No1 is wife of Solomon Ok chaya on Choctaw card #4480					
10 No2 "Died prior to Sept 25, 1902: not entitled to land or money." See copy of Indian Office letter of July 21-1908 (Land 45526-1908)					
11					
12					
13					
14					Date of Application for Enrollment.
15					Aug 25/99
16				No2 enrolled Aug 31/99	
17					

Choctaw By Blood Enrollment Cards 1898-1914

RESIDENCE: Blue   COUNTY.   **Choctaw Nation**   Choctaw Roll   CARD NO.

POST OFFICE: Albany, I.T.   *(Not Including Freedmen)*   FIELD NO. **3933**

Dawes' Roll No.	NAME		Relationship to Person First Named	AGE	SEX	BLOOD	TRIBAL ENROLLMENT		
							Year	County	No.
11046	1 Burks, Lucinda	28	First Named	25	F	1/2	1896	Blue	1730
11047	2 " Minnie M	7	Dau	4	"	1/4	1896	"	1731
11048	3 " Willie E	6	"	2	"	1/4			
11049	4 " Marvin F	3	Son	6mo	M	1/4			
11050	5 " Odra May	2	Dau	20mo	F	1/4			
	6								
	7								
	8								
	9	ENROLLMENT							
	10	OF NOS. 1,2,3,4 and 5 HEREON							
	11	APPROVED BY THE SECRETARY OF INTERIOR MAR 10 1903							
	12								
	13								
	14								
	15								
	16								
	17								

TRIBAL ENROLLMENT OF PARENTS

	Name of Father	Year	County	Name of Mother	Year	County
1	Ben Hampton		Blue	Charlotte Hampton	Dead	Blue
2	J. M. Burks		Non Citz	No 1		
3	" "		" "	No 1		
4	" "		" "	No 1		
5	" "		" "	Nº 1		
6						
7						
8	No2 on 1896 roll as Myrtle Burks					
9	Nº5 Born Feby 14, 1901, enrolled Oct 9, 1902					
10	For child of No1 see NB (Apr 26-06) Card #871					#1 to 4
11	" children " " 1 " " (Mar 3-1905) " #791					
12						
13						Date of Application for Enrollment
14						
15						Aug 25/99
16						
17	P.O. Tupelo IT 4/3/05					

Choctaw By Blood Enrollment Cards 1898-1914

RESIDENCE:	Blue	COUNTY.	**Choctaw Nation**		**Choctaw Roll**	CARD NO.	
POST OFFICE:	Caddo, I.T.				*(Not Including Freedmen)*	FIELD NO. **3934**	

Dawes' Roll No.	NAME		Relationship to Person	AGE	SEX	BLOOD	TRIBAL ENROLLMENT		
							Year	County	No.
11051	₁ Smith, Kittie	29	First Named	26	F	Full	1896	Blue	11608
11052	₂ Adams, Katie E	8	Dau	5	"	5/8	1896	"	401
I.W. 1127	₃ Smith, Ira L	29	Husband	29	M	I.W.			
	₄								
	₅								
	₆	ENROLLMENT							
	₇	OF NOS. 1 and 2 ~~APPROVED BY THE SECRETARY~~ HEREON							
	₈	OF INTERIOR Mar 10 1903							
	₉								
	10								
	11								
	12								
	13								
	14								
	15	ENROLLMENT OF NOS. 3 HEREON							
	16	APPROVED BY THE SECRETARY OF INTERIOR Nov 16 1904							
	17								

TRIBAL ENROLLMENT OF PARENTS							
Name of Father	Year	County		Name of Mother	Year	County	
₁	Dead	Blue		Louvina Nail	Dead	Atoka	
₂ Sam Adams		Blue		No1			
₃ J. L. Smith		non-citz		Mollie Smith	dead	non-citz	
₄							
₅							
₆							
₇	No. 3 restored to roll by Departmental authority of January 19, 1909 (File 5-51)						
₈	No2 on 1896 roll as Kitty Ertheral Adams						
₉	No.2 admitted by Dawes Commission in Choctaw case #1393						
10	~~No.3 transferred from Choctaw card #D-367, Oct. 31, 1904. See decision of Oct 15, 1904~~						
11	~~No.3 denied by U.S.Court Central Dist, I.T. July 13, 1896~~						
	As to remarriage see testimony of Kittie Smith						
12	~~Enrollment of No.3 cancelled by order of Department March 4, 1907~~						
13	~~No3 denied by Commission in 1896 Choctaw case No790 and also denied by U.S Court. No appeal to C.C.C.C.~~					#1&2	
14							
15						Aug 25/99	
16							
17							

34

Choctaw By Blood Enrollment Cards 1898-1914

RESIDENCE: Blue   COUNTY. **Choctaw Nation**   Choctaw Roll   CARD NO.

POST OFFICE: Caddo, I.T.   *(Not Including Freedmen)*   FIELD NO. **3935**

Dawes' Roll No.	NAME	Relationship to Person	AGE	SEX	BLOOD	TRIBAL ENROLLMENT		
						Year	County	No.
11053	1 Ward, William G 55	First Named	52	M	1/16	1896	Blue	13872
I.W. 485	2 " Eliza	Wife	53	F	I.W.	1896	"	15186
15054	3 " Timothy L	Son	34	M	1/32	1896	"	13878
15055	4 " Charles A	Son	27	M	1/32	1896	"	13874
15056	5 " Daisy	Dau	21	F	1/32	1896	"	13875
15057	6 Allen Cora E	Dau	19	F	1/32	1896	"	13876
15058	7 Ward, William H	Son	15	M	1/32	1896	"	13877
	8							
	9 ENROLLMENT OF NOS. 1 HEREON APPROVED BY THE SECRETARY OF INTERIOR Mar 10 1903							
	10							
	11							
	12 ENROLLMENT OF NOS. 2 HEREON APPROVED BY THE SECRETARY OF INTERIOR							
	13							
	14							
	15 ENROLLMENT OF NOS. 3-4-5-6-7- HEREON APPROVED BY THE SECRETARY OF INTERIOR Feb 16 1904							
	16							
	17							

TRIBAL ENROLLMENT OF PARENTS

	Name of Father	Year	County	Name of Mother	Year	County
1	Joseph Ward	Dead	Non-Citz	Elizabeth Ward	Dead	Atoka
2	C. M. Beck	"	"	Martha Beck		Cherokee
3	No 1			No 2		
4	No 1			No 2		
5	No 1			No 2		
6	No 1			No 2		
7	Wm G. Ward					
8			On 1896 roll as Wm G. Ward			
9						
10			Family on Card No D-368			
11	For child of No3 see NB (Apr 26-06) Card 692 For child of No6 see NB (March 3,1905) Card #917					
12	" " " " 6 " " " " 739					
13	No3 on 1896 roll as L. T. Ward					
14	No6 " " " " " Cora " No7 " " " " " W. H.					#1 to 7 incl
15	No6 is now the wife of Charley Allen on Choctaw card D.769 Aug 1,1902					Date of Application for Enrollment.
16	Nos 2 to 7 inclusive transferred from Choctaw card D368 August 5, 1903 See decision of July 30, 1903					Aug 25/99
17						

35

Choctaw By Blood Enrollment Cards 1898-1914

RESIDENCE:	Blue	COUNTY.	**Choctaw Nation**				Choctaw Roll	CARD NO.	
POST OFFICE:	Caddo, I.T.						*(Not Including Freedmen)*	FIELD NO. 3936	

Dawes' Roll No.	NAME	Relationship to Person First Named	AGE	SEX	BLOOD	TRIBAL ENROLLMENT		
						Year	County	No.
✓ 1	Smith, Charles P	Named	30	M	1/8		D	
DIV 2	" Ottoma	Dau	16mo	F	1/16		Dis	
✓ 3	" Olive	Dau	6mo	F	1/16		Dis	
✓ 4	" Charles Gordon	Son	7wks	M	1/16		Dis	
5								
No1 6	DENIED CITIZENSHIP BY THE CHOCTAW AND							
7	CHICKASAW CITIZENSHIP COURT							
8							Case #107 Oct 20 '04	
9	No.1 denied by C.C.C.C. as Charles							
10	P. Smith or Chas. P. Smith							
11								
#2-3-4- 12	DISMISSED							
13	NOV 12 1904							
14								
15								
16								
17								

TRIBAL ENROLLMENT OF PARENTS

	Name of Father	Year	County	Name of Mother	Year	County
1	W.H.P. Smith	Dead	Non Citz	Mary A Loving		Choctaw
2	No1			Ellie Smith		Non Citz
3	No.1			" "		" "
4	Nᴼ 1			" "		" "
5						
6						
7						
8	No1 Denied in 96 Case #546					
9	No1 Admitted by U.S. Court, Central					
10	Dist, Sept 11/97. As to residence and birth of No2, see his testimony					
11	Judgment of U.S. Court mitting not vacated and set aside by Decree of Choctaw Chickasaw Citizenship Court Dec 17 02					
12	Evidence of marriage of parents to be					
13	supplied:- Recd Oct 7/99					
14	No 1 to 4 incl not in C.C.C.C. Case #107					
	No.3 Enrolled June 7, 1900			Date of Application for Enrollment	Aug 25/99	
15	Nᴼ4 Born July 26, 1902; enrolled Sept. 11, 1902					
16	Nos 2,3 and 4 dismissed by C.C.C.C. for illegibility of Jurisdiction					
	Dec C 124					
17	P.O. Wade IT					

RESIDENCE:	Blue		COUNTY.	**Choctaw Nation**		**Choctaw Roll**	CARD NO.
POST OFFICE:	Durant, I.T.					*(Not Including Freedmen)*	FIELD NO. 3937

Dawes' Roll No.	NAME		Relationship to Person First Named	AGE	SEX	BLOOD	TRIBAL ENROLLMENT		
							Year	County	No.
11054	₁ Shannon, Rennie	24		21	F	1/8	1896	Blue	11603
11055	₂ " Anna	6	Dau	3	"	1/16	1896	"	11604
11056	₃ " Orrick L	4	Son	15mo	M	1/16			
11057	₄ " Edfred[sic] L	2	Son	1mo	M	1/16			
I.W. 750	₅ " Ober L	28	Husb	28	M	I.W.			
	6								
	7								
	8	ENROLLMENT							
	9	OF NOS. 1,2,3 and 4 HEREON APPROVED BY THE SECRETARY							
	10	OF INTERIOR MAR 10 1903							
	11								
	12	ENROLLMENT OF NOS ~~~~~5~~~~~ HEREON							
	13	APPROVED BY THE SECRETARY OF INTERIOR MAY -7 1904							
	14								
	15								
	16								
	17								

TRIBAL ENROLLMENT OF PARENTS

	Name of Father	Year	County	Name of Mother	Year	County
₁	Epps Taylor		Non Citz	Lou J. Taylor		Chick Dist
₂	Ober L. Shannon		white man	No1		
₃	" " "		" "	No1		
₄	" " "		" "	No.1		
₅	A.O. Shannon		non-citz	Eady Shannon	Dead	non-citz
6						
7						
8			No2 On 1896 roll as Aliya Shannon			
9						
10			Husband Ober L Shannon on			
11		Card No D373				
12			No.4 Enrolled Aug 22d, 1900			
13		N⁵ transferred from Choctaw card #D373. See decision of Feby 27, 1904				
14		For child of Nos 1&5 see NB (Apr 26-06) Card #425				
15		" " " " 1&5 " " Mar 3-05 " " 296		Date of Application for Enrollment	Aug 25/99	
16						
17						

37

Choctaw By Blood Enrollment Cards 1898-1914

RESIDENCE:	Blue	COUNTY.						

RESIDENCE: Blue   **COUNTY.**   **Choctaw Nation**   **Choctaw Roll** *(Not Including Freedmen)*   **CARD NO.**

POST OFFICE: Bok Chito, I.T.   **FIELD NO. 3938**

Dawes' Roll No.	NAME	Relationship to Person	AGE	SEX	BLOOD	TRIBAL ENROLLMENT		
						Year	County	No.
I.W. 368	1 Brackett, Thomas 35	First Named	29	M	I.W.			
11058	2 " Margaret 22	Wife	19	F	1/4	1896	Blue	1642
11059	3 " Fannie 7	Dau	4	"	1/8	1896	"	1643
11060	4 " Lennie ⊕ 6	Dau ~~Son~~	~~3~~	~~M~~ "F"	1/8	1896	"	1644
DEAD	5 ~~" William D~~ 4	Son	7mo	"	1/8			
11061	6 " Susan 2	Dau	1	F	1/8			
	7 ⊕ 3/26/1915 Sex of No4 changed from M to "F" per							
	8 Deptl authority of March 19, 1915 L-2264-1915							
	9 ENROLLMENT							
	10 OF NOS. 2,3,4 and 6 HEREON							
	APPROVED BY THE SECRETARY							
	11 OF INTERIOR Mar 10 1903							
	12							
	13 ENROLLMENT OF NOS. 1 HEREON							
	APPROVED BY THE SECRETARY							
	14 OF INTERIOR Sep 12 1903							
	15 No. 5 hereon dismissed under order of							
	16 the Commission to the Five Civilized							
	17 Tribes of March 31, 1905.							

TRIBAL ENROLLMENT OF PARENTS

	Name of Father	Year	County	Name of Mother	Year	County
1	Daniel Brackett		Non Citz	Sarah Brackett		Non Citz
2	Wm Labor		" "	Phoebe Labor		Blue
3	No1			No2		
4	No1			No2		
5	~~No1~~			~~No2~~		
6	No1			No2		
7						
8	No1 was admitted by Dawes Com					
9	Case No 914					
10	No2 on 1896 roll a Peggy Brackett					
11	~~No5 Affidavit of birth to be supplied:- Filed Nov. 2/99~~					
12	No.6 Enrolled Sept 4, 1901					
13						
14	~~No5 Died Dec 23, 1899; proof of death filed Nov 25 1902~~				Date of Application for Enrollment.	
15					Aug 25/99	
16						
17						

Choctaw By Blood Enrollment Cards 1898-1914

RESIDENCE: Blue   COUNTY. **Choctaw Nation**   Choctaw Roll   CARD NO.
POST OFFICE: Bok Chito, I.T.   *(Not Including Freedmen)*   FIELD NO. 3939

Dawes' Roll No.	NAME	Relationship to Person First Named	AGE	SEX	BLOOD	TRIBAL ENROLLMENT		
						Year	County	No.
11062	₁ Jackson Lena ²³		20	F	1/4	1896	Blue	4886
DEAD.	₂ " ~~Roy A~~ DEAD. ~~Son~~		~~2mo~~	"[sic]	~~1/8~~			
I.W. 1335	₃ Jackson, Jim Thompson ³⁹	Husband	39	M	I.W.			
	4							
	5							
	6	ENROLLMENT						
	7	OF NOS. 1 HEREON APPROVED BY THE SECRETARY						
	8	OF INTERIOR MAR 10 1903						
	9	~~ENROLLMENT~~						
	10	OF NOS. 3 HEREON APPROVED BY THE SECRETARY						
	11	OF INTERIOR MAR 14 1905						
	12	~~No. 2 HEREON DISMISSED UNDER~~						
	13	~~ORDER OF THE COMMISSION TO THE FIVE~~						
	14	~~CIVILIZED TRIBES OF MARCH 31, 1905.~~						
	15							
	16							
	17							

TRIBAL ENROLLMENT OF PARENTS

Name of Father	Year	County	Name of Mother	Year	County
₁ Emanuel Guess		Non Citz	Rhoda Guess		Blue
₂ ~~R.T. Madding~~		~~" "~~	~~No1~~		
₃ Carrel C Jackson		non citizen	Julia A Jackson		non citizen
4					

5 On Aug 31, 1902 No.3 was married to No.1 (formerly Madding, nee Guess)
6 For child of Nos 1 and 3 see NB (Mar 3,1905) #515
7 No.3 originally listed for enrollment on Choctaw card D-784 Sept 4,1902: transferred to this card Jan 28, 1905. See decision of Jan 12, 1905.
8 No1 On 1896 roll as Lena Guess
9 No1 is now the wife of Jim Thompson Jackson
10 on Choctaw D784. Evidence of marriage filed Sept 4, 1902
   ~~No1 was married to Jim Thompson Jackson under the name of Lenar Guess~~
11 Nº1 Evidence of divorce from R.L. Madding filed Sept 15, 1902 with
12 record in Choctaw #D784
13 No2 Died 1900: proof of death filed Nov 22 1902 filed Nov 22, 1902
   For child of Nos 1&3 see NB (Apr 26,1906) Card No. 63
14 Record as to enrollment of No.3 forwarded Department Mar 14, 1906
15 Record returned. See opinion of Assistant Attorney General of March 15,1906 in case of Omer R. Nicholson #1&2
16 | | Date of Application for Enrollment.
17 ~~No3 P.O. Caddo, I.T.~~ | | Aug 25/99

Choctaw By Blood Enrollment Cards 1898-1914

RESIDENCE: Blue	COUNTY. **Choctaw Nation**	**Choctaw Roll**	CARD NO.
POST OFFICE: Bok Chito, I.T.		*(Not Including Freedmen)*	FIELD NO. **3940**

Dawes' Roll No.	NAME	Relationship to Person	AGE	SEX	BLOOD	TRIBAL ENROLLMENT		
						Year	County	No.
11063	1 Guess, John 26	First Named	23	M	1/4	1896	Blue	4885
IW369	2 " Maud 26	Wife	23	F	I.W.			
DEAD	3 " ~~Ray~~ DEAD	~~Son~~	~~6mo~~	~~M~~	~~1/8~~			
11064	4 " Ruthie 2	Dau	3w	F	1/8			
	5							
	6							
	7 ENROLLMENT							
	8 OF NOS. 1 and 4 HEREON							
	9 APPROVED BY THE SECRETARY OF INTERIOR Mar 10 1903							
	10 ENROLLMENT							
	11 OF NOS. 2 HEREON							
	12 APPROVED BY THE SECRETARY OF INTERIOR Sep 12 1903							
	13							
	14 No. 3 hereon dismissed under order of							
	15 the Commission to the Five Civilized							
	16 Tribes of March 31, 1905.							
	17							

TRIBAL ENROLLMENT OF PARENTS

Name of Father	Year	County	Name of Mother	Year	County
1 Emanuel Guess		Non Citz	Rhoda Guess		Blue
2 Dan'l Brackett		" "	Sarah A Brackett		Non Citz
3 ~~No1~~			~~No2~~		
4 No1			No2		
5					
6					
7					
8 No3 – Affidavit of birth to be					
9 supplied – Rec'd Oct 4/99					
10					
11 No.4 Enrolled January 19 1901					
12 For child of Nos 1&2 see NB (Apr 26-06) Card #72					
13 ~~No.3 died October 16, 1899, proof of death filed Nov 29 1902~~					
14 ~~See affidavit of N°2 as to residence of No1 at the time of their marriage filed May 6, 1903~~					
15 For child of Nos 1&2 see NB (March 3 1905) #809			Date of Application for Enrollment.	Aug 25/99	
16					
17 P.O. Massey I.T. 4/18/05					

40

RESIDENCE: Atoka	COUNTY.							CARD NO.	

RESIDENCE: Atoka　　COUNTY.　**Choctaw Nation**　Choctaw Roll　CARD NO.
POST OFFICE: Coalgate, I.T.　　　*(Not Including Freedmen)*　FIELD NO. 3941

Dawes' Roll No.	NAME		Relationship to Person	AGE	SEX	BLOOD	TRIBAL ENROLLMENT		
							Year	County	No.
11065	1 Terry, Alice	28	First Named	25	F	1/4	1896	Blue	12415
11066	2 " Letha M	8	Dau	5	"	1/8	1896	"	12416
11067	3 " Ethel L	5	Dau	3	"	1/8	1896	"	12417
DEAD.	4 " ~~Lillian~~		"	3mo	"	1/8			
DEAD.	5 " ~~Vivian~~		"	3mo	"	1/8			
I.W. 751	6 " Noah M ③⑤	35	Husb	35	M	I.W.			
	7								
	8			No. 4 and 5 HEREON DISMISSED UNDER ORDER OF THE COMMISSION TO THE FIVE CIVILIZED TRIBES OF MARCH 31, 1905.					
	9	ENROLLMENT							
	10	OF NOS. 1,2 and 3 HEREON APPROVED BY THE SECRETARY							
	11	OF INTERIOR MAR 10 1903							
	12								
	13	ENROLLMENT							
	14	OF NOS. ~~~ 6 ~~~ HEREON APPROVED BY THE SECRETARY							
	15	OF INTERIOR MAY -7 1904							
	16								
	17								

TRIBAL ENROLLMENT OF PARENTS

	Name of Father	Year	County	Name of Mother	Year	County
1	Joe Kincade	Dead	Non Citz	Rhoda Guess		Blue
2	Noah M Terry		white man	No1		
3	" " "		" "	No1		
4	" " "		" "	~~No1~~		
5	" " "		" "	~~No1~~		
6	Brazil Terry		non-citz	Amanda Terry	Dead	non citz
7						
8	No3 – On 1896 roll as Ethel Terry					
9						
10	Nos 4-5 Affidavits of birth to be					
11	supplied:- Recd Oct 7/99					
12	Nºs 4 and 5 died in March 1902, proof of death filed Oct. 21, 1902					
13	See Choctaw D #374					
14	Nº6 transferred from Choctaw card #D374. See decision of Feby 27, 1904				#1 to 5 inc	
15						Date of Application for Enrollment
16	For child of Nos 1&6 see NB (Apr 26 '06) Card #196					Aug 25/99
17	" " " " " " " " (Mar 3-05) " #297					

41

Choctaw By Blood Enrollment Cards 1898-1914

RESIDENCE: **Blue**

POST OFFICE: **Caddo, I.T.**

COUNTY. **Choctaw Nation**

Choctaw Roll (Not Including Freedmen)

CARD NO.

FIELD NO. **3942**

Dawes' Roll No.	NAME	Relationship to Person First Named	AGE	SEX	BLOOD	TRIBAL ENROLLMENT		
						Year	County	No.
1	Smith, William R	Named	33	M	1/8		D	
2	" Arthur R	Son	5mo	"	1/16		Dis	
3	" Ella Eunice	Dau	2mo	F	1/16		Dis	
4								
5								
6	No1 denied by C.C.C.C. as W. R.							
7	Smith or Wm R Smith.							
8								
9	#2-3- DISMISSED							
10	NOV 12 1904							
11								
12								
13								
14								
15								
16								
17								

TRIBAL ENROLLMENT OF PARENTS

	Name of Father	Year	County	Name of Mother	Year	County
1	W.H.P. Smith	Dead	Non Citz	Mary A Loving		Choctaw
2	No1			Mary E Smith		Non Citz
3	Nᴼ 1			" "		" "
4						
5	No1					
6						
7	No1 Denied in 96 Case #546					
8	No1 – Admitted by U.S. Court, Central					
9	Dist, Sept 11/97, Case No 71. As to					
10	residence and birth of child which					
11	occurred, April 3/99, see testimony of No1					
12	Nᴼ3 Born July 15, 1902: enrolled Sept 15, 1902					
13						
14						
15						
16						
17	P.O. Roberta IT					

See C 134

Date of Application for Enrollment.   Aug 25/99

Choctaw By Blood Enrollment Cards 1898-1914

RESIDENCE: Jackson COUNTY.
POST OFFICE: Mayhew, I.T.

Choctaw Nation

Choctaw Roll
(Not Including Freedmen)

CARD NO.
FIELD NO. **3943**

Dawes' Roll No.	NAME	Relationship to Person First Named	AGE	SEX	BLOOD	TRIBAL ENROLLMENT		
						Year	County	No.
11068	1 Olson, Sarah 39	First Named	36	F	1/2	1896	Jackson	9995
11069	2 " Thomas 13	Son	10	M	1/4	1896	"	9996
11070	3 " Loftess 11	"	8	"	1/4	1896	"	9997
11071	4 " Rebecca 6	Dau	3	F	"1/4	1896	"	9998
I.W. 979	5 " Benjamin 54	Hus	54	M	I.W.	1896	"	14918
	6							
	7							
	8	ENROLLMENT OF NOS. 1,2,3 and 4 HEREON APPROVED BY THE SECRETARY OF INTERIOR Mar 10 1903						
	9							
	10							
	11							
	12							
	13	ENROLLMENT OF NOS. ~~~5~~~ HEREON APPROVED BY THE SECRETARY OF INTERIOR Sep 22 1904						
	14							
	15							
	16							
	17							

TRIBAL ENROLLMENT OF PARENTS

	Name of Father	Year	County	Name of Mother	Year	County
1	Wm Smallwood		Kiamitia	Mary Smallwood	Dead	Kiamitia
2	Ben Olson		Non Citz	No1		
3	" "		" "	No1		
4	" "		" "	No1		
5	Ola Olson		" "	Christina Olson		non citizen
6						
7						
8	No3 – On 1896 roll as Loftiest Olson					
9	Ben Olson, Husband of No1 on Choctaw Card D.409					
10						
11	No5 transferred from Choctaw card D#409, August 4, 1904					
12	See decision of July 19, 1904					
13						
14				Date of Application for Enrollment.		
15				Aug 25/99		
16						
17						

(Oberlin)

Choctaw Nation

COUNTY

Choctaw Roll
(Not Including Freedmen)

CARD NO.
FIELD NO. 3944

Roll No.	NAME		Relationship to Person First Named	AGE	SEX	BLOOD	TRIBAL ENROLLMENT		
							Year	County	No.
11072	1 Adams, Willie	25		22	F	1/4	1896	Kiamitia	10863
11073	2 Smallwood, Minnie	7	Dau	4	"	3/8	1896	"	10864
11074	3 Reed, Jack	5	Son	1	M	1/8			
11075	4 Adams, Anna	1	Dau	2mo	F	1/8			
	5								
	6								
	7								
	8	ENROLLMENT OF NOS. 1,2,3 and 4 HEREON APPROVED BY THE SECRETARY OF INTERIOR MAR 10 1903							
	9								
	10								
	11								
	12								
	13								
	14								
	15								
	16								
	17								

TRIBAL ENROLLMENT OF PARENTS

	Name of Father	Year	County	Name of Mother	Year	County
1	Ben Olson		Non Citz	Missie Harris		Kiamitia
2	Dan Smallwood		Blue	No1		
3	Jim Reed		Non Citz	No1		
4	J. L. Adams		non-citizen	No.1		
5						
6						
7						
8						

No1 – On 1896 roll as William Reed
No2 – " 1896 " " Minnie "
No3 – Affidavit of birth to be
supplied:- Reed Oct 7/99
No1 was married to J.L. Adams, a noncitizen, June 24, 1898. Evidence
of marriage filed June 6, 1901
No.4 Enrolled June 6, 1901
For child of No1 see NB (Apr 26 '06) Card #1235
" " " " " " (Mar 3-05) " " 298

#1 to 3

Date of Application
for Enrollment.

Aug 25/99

P.O. Boswell I.T. 4/12/25

Choctaw By Blood Enrollment Cards 1898-1914

RESIDENCE:	Blue	COUNTY.						CARD NO.	
POST OFFICE:	Caddo, I.T.							FIELD NO.	3945

Choctaw Nation

Choctaw Roll (Not Including Freedmen)

Dawes' Roll No.	NAME	Relationship to Person First Named	AGE	SEX	BLOOD	TRIBAL ENROLLMENT		
						Year	County	No.
✓ 1	Loving, Mary A		60	F	1/4		D	
2								
3								
4								
5								
6								
7								
8								
9								
10								
11								
12								
13								
14								
15								
16								
17								

TRIBAL ENROLLMENT OF PARENTS

	Name of Father	Year	County	Name of Mother	Year	County
1	J. D. Phillips	Dead, Non Citz		Eliz. Phillips	Dead	Choctaw
2						
3						
4						
5						
6						
7	No1 denied in 96 Case #546					
8	Admitted by U.S. Court, Central					
9	Dist, Sept 11/97, Case No 71. As to residence see her testimony.					
10	Judgment of U.S. Ct admitting No vacated and set aside by Decree of Choctaw Chickasaw Citizenship Court Dec 17'02					
11	No1 now in C.C.C.C Case #107					
12						
13			See C-134			
14						
15				Date of Application for Enrollment	Aug 25/99	
16						
17						

Choctaw By Blood Enrollment Cards 1898-1914

RESIDENCE: Atoka   COUNTY. **Choctaw Nation**   **Choctaw Roll**   CARD NO.
POST OFFICE: Coalgate, I.T.   *(Not Including Freedmen)*   FIELD NO. **3946**

Dawes' Roll No.	NAME	Relationship to Person First Named	AGE	SEX	BLOOD	TRIBAL ENROLLMENT		
						Year	County	No.
1	Ekberg, Henry O	Named	47	M	I.W.			
2								
3	Dismissed Sep 23 1904							
4	Dismissed Jan 17 1907							
5	Copy of decision forwarded applicant Jan 17 1907							
6								
7	Copy of decision forwarded							
8	attorney for applicant Jan 17 1907							
9	Copy of decision forwarded							
10	attorneys for Choctaw and							
11	Chickasaw Nations Jan 17 1907							
12								
13	Record forwarded							
14	Department Jan 17 1907							
15								
16	Decision prepared Nov 23/03							
17								

TRIBAL ENROLLMENT OF PARENTS

	Name of Father	Year	County	Name of Mother	Year	County
1	Peter Ekberg	Dead	Non Citz	Mary Ekberg	Dead	Non Citz
2						
3				Action approved by Secretary of Interior Feb 28 1907		
4						
5						
6				Notice of Departmental action		
7	No 1 Admitted in 96 Case #1096			forwarded attorneys for Choctaw and Chickasaw Nations Apr 16 1907		
8	Admitted by U.S. Court Central Dist, Aug 25/97 as an intermarried			Notice of Departmental action		
9	Choctaw, Case No 220, under name of			forwarded attorney for applicant Apr 16 1907		
10	Henry O Eckberg, Case No 220 As to					
11	residence see his testimony					
12	Decision Prepared					
	Judgment of U.S. Ct admitting No 1 vacated and set aside by Decree of Choctaw Chickasaw Citizenship Court Dec 17'02					
13	No appeal to C.C.C.C.			Notice of Departmental Action mailed applicant Apr 16 1907		
14						Date of Application for Enrollment
15	Notify Apple & Franklin of decision					Aug 25/99
16				11/14/03 Intermarried Status		
17						September 25, 1902

46

Choctaw By Blood Enrollment Cards 1898-1914

RESIDENCE: Blue   COUNTY.   **Choctaw Nation**   Choctaw Roll   CARD No.

POST OFFICE: Caddo, I.T.   *(Not Including Freedmen)*   FIELD No. **3947**

Dawes' Roll No.	NAME	Relationship to Person First Named	AGE	SEX	BLOOD	TRIBAL ENROLLMENT Year	County	No.
DEAD.	1 Freeny, James F		58	M	1/8	1896	Gaines	3996
11076	2 " Jasper D 24	Son	21	"	3/8	1896	"	3998
11077	3 " Robert L 14	"	11	"	3/8	1896	"	3999
I.W. 672	4 " Grace 19	Wife of No2	19	F	I.W.			
	5							
	6							
	7	ENROLLMENT						
	8	OF NOS. 2 and 3 HEREON APPROVED BY THE SECRETARY						
	9	OF INTERIOR MAR 10 1903						
	10	ENROLLMENT						
	11	OF NOS. 4 HEREON APPROVED BY THE SECRETARY						
	12	OF INTERIOR MAR 26 1904						
	13	No. 1 HEREON DISMISSED UNDER						
	14	ORDER OF THE COMMISSION TO THE FIVE						
	15	CIVILIZED TRIBES OF MARCH 31, 1905.						
	16							
	17							

TRIBAL ENROLLMENT OF PARENTS

	Name of Father	Year	County	Name of Mother	Year	County
1	Robert Freeny	Dead	Non Citz	Sally Freeny	Dead	Blue
2	No1			Mary Freeny	"	"
3	No1			" "	"	"
4	W. L. Cooper		noncitizen	Henrietta Cooper		noncitizen
5						
6						
7	No4 transferred from Choctaw card D673 January 21, 1904					
8	See decision of January 21, 1904					
9						
10	No1 on 1896 roll as J. Franklin Freeney					
11	No2 " 1896 " " Jasper					
	No3 " 1896 " " Robt L					
12	No2 Tribal enrollment number should be 3997					
13	No.2 is now the husband of Grace Freeny on Choctaw Card #D673 Nov 7, 1901					
14	Look out for child of No2 home since Sept 25, 1902				Date of Application for Enrollment	
15	For children of Nos 2&4 see NB (Mar 3 '05) Card #299				Aug 25/99	
16	No1 died Aug 21, 1902; proof of death filed Nov 25 1902					
17						

Choctaw By Blood Enrollment Cards 1898-1914

RESIDENCE: Blue COUNTY. **Choctaw Nation** **Choctaw Roll** CARD NO.
POST OFFICE: Caddo, I.T. *(Not Including Freedmen)* FIELD NO. 3948

Dawes' Roll No.	NAME	Relationship to Person First Named	AGE	SEX	BLOOD	TRIBAL ENROLLMENT		
						Year	County	No.
11078	1 Grubbs, William 22	First Named	19	M	1/8	1893	Blue	512
	2							
	3							
	4							
	5	ENROLLMENT						
	6	OF NOS. 1 HEREON APPROVED BY THE SECRETARY						
	7	OF INTERIOR MAR 10 1903						
	8							
	9							
	10							
	11							
	12							
	13							
	14							
	15							
	16							
	17							

TRIBAL ENROLLMENT OF PARENTS

	Name of Father	Year	County	Name of Mother	Year	County
1	Forbis Grubbs		Tobucksy	Tennessee Beard		Non Citz
2						
3						
4						
5						
6			Admitted by Act of Choctaw Council			
7			Approved Nov 1/84 Certified Copy of			
8			said Act herewith filed			
9			No1 On 1893 Pay roll, Page No 48, Blue Co as William Grubbs			
10						
11						
12						
13						
14				Date of Application for Enrollment. Aug 25/99		
15						
16						
17						

Choctaw By Blood Enrollment Cards 1898-1914

RESIDENCE:　　　　　　　　　COUNTY.　**Choctaw Nation**　　**Choctaw Roll**　CARD NO.
POST OFFICE:　　　　　　　　　　　　　　　　　　　　　　　*(Not Including Freedmen)*　FIELD NO. 3949

Dawes' Roll No.	NAME		Relationship to Person First Named	AGE	SEX	BLOOD	TRIBAL ENROLLMENT		
							Year	County	No.
DEAD.	1 Jones, Wilson N	75	Named	72	M	1/2	1896	Jackson	7159
I.W. 833	2 " Eliza B	70	Wife	68	F	IW	1896	"	14700
	3								
	4 No. 1 HEREON DISMISSED UNDER								
	5 ORDER OF THE COMMISSION TO THE FIVE								
	6 CIVILIZED TRIBES OF MARCH 31, 1905								
	7 ENROLLMENT								
	8 OF NOS. 2 HEREON APPROVED BY THE SECRETARY								
	9 OF INTERIOR MAY 21 1904								
	10								
	11								
	12								
	13								
	14								
	15								
	16								
	17								

TRIBAL ENROLLMENT OF PARENTS

	Name of Father	Year	County	Name of Mother	Year	County
1	Nat Jones	Dead	Bok Tuklo	Janie Jones	Dead	in Mississippi
2	Henry Hastings	"	Non Citz	Mary Hastings	"	Non Citz
3						
4						
5						
6						
7						
8			No1 on 1896 roll as W. N. Jones			
9			No2 " 1896 " " Isabelle "			
10			No1 died June 11, 1901; proof of death filed Dec 8 1902			
11						
12			I am reliably informed that these people have lived in			
13			Texas for several years last past. Tams Bixby		Aug 25/99	
14					Date of Application for Enrollment.	
15						
16						
17	Sherman					

49

Choctaw By Blood Enrollment Cards 1898-1914

RESIDENCE:	Jackson	COUNTY.								CARD No.	
POST OFFICE:	Caddo, I.T.		**Choctaw Nation**				**Choctaw Roll** *(Not Including Freedmen)*			FIELD No. 3950	

Dawes' Roll No.	NAME		Relationship to Person	AGE	SEX	BLOOD	TRIBAL ENROLLMENT			
							Year	County		No.
11079	1 LeFlore, Jincy	71	First Named	68	F	1/2	1896	Jackson		8147
	2									
	3									
	4									
	5	ENROLLMENT								
	6	OF NOS. 1 HEREON APPROVED BY THE SECRETARY								
	7	OF INTERIOR MAR 10 1903								
	8									
	9									
	10									
	11									
	12									
	13									
	14									
	15									
	16									
	17									

TRIBAL ENROLLMENT OF PARENTS

	Name of Father	Year	County	Name of Mother	Year	County
1	Nat Jones	Dead	Bok Tuklo	Janie Jones	Dead	in Misissippi
2						
3						
4						
5						
6						
7						
8						
9						
10						
11						
12						
13						
14					Date of Application for Enrollment.	
15					Aug 25/99	
16						
17						

Choctaw By Blood Enrollment Cards 1898-1914

RESIDENCE: Atoka COUNTY. **Choctaw Nation** Choctaw Roll CARD No.
POST OFFICE: Lehigh, I.T. (Not Including Freedmen) FIELD No. 3951

Dawes' Roll No.	NAME	Relationship to Person First Named	AGE	SEX	BLOOD	TRIBAL ENROLLMENT		
						Year	County	No.
11080	1 Thompson, Allen W ⁴²	First Named	39	M	1/2	1896	Atoka	12467
	2							
	3							
	4							
	5	ENROLLMENT						
	6	OF NOS. 1 HEREON APPROVED BY THE SECRETARY						
	7	OF INTERIOR MAR 10 1903						
	8							
	9							
	10							
	11							
	12							
	13							
	14							
	15							
	16							
	17							

TRIBAL ENROLLMENT OF PARENTS

	Name of Father	Year	County	Name of Mother	Year	County
1	G W Thompson	Dead	Blue	Mary Thompson	Dead	Jackson
2						
3						
4						
5						
6						
7						
8	No.1 on 1896 Choctaw roll as Allen Thompson					
9						
10						
11						
12						
13						
14					Date of Application for Enrollment	
15					Aug 25/99	
16						
17						

Choctaw By Blood Enrollment Cards 1898-1914

RESIDENCE: **Blue**
POST OFFICE: **Ego, I.T.**
COUNTY. **Choctaw Nation**
Choctaw Roll *(Not Including Freedmen)*
CARD NO.
FIELD NO. **3952**

Dawes' Roll No.	NAME		Relationship to Person First Named	AGE	SEX	BLOOD	TRIBAL ENROLLMENT		
							Year	County	No.
11081	1 Jones, Mary J	41	First Named	38	F	1/32	1896	Blue	7182
11082	2 " William C	18	Son	15	M	1/32	1896	"	7184
11083	3 " Luella	16	Dau	13	F	1/32	1896	"	7185
11084	4 " Pearly	14	"	11	"	1/32	1896	"	7186
11085	5 " Joseph L	12	Son	9	M	1/32	1896	"	7189
11086	6 " Lena L	10	Dau	7	F	1/32	1896	"	7188
11087	7 " Eula A	8	"	5	"	1/32	1896	"	7187
11088	8 " Allie C	3	"	1mo	"	1/32			
	9								
	10								
	11								
	12	ENROLLMENT OF NOS. 1,2,3,4,5,6,7 and 8 HEREON							
	13	APPROVED BY THE SECRETARY							
	14	OF INTERIOR Mar 10 1903							
	15								
	16								
	17								

TRIBAL ENROLLMENT OF PARENTS

	Name of Father	Year	County	Name of Mother	Year	County
1	G. H. Izard	Dead	Non Citz	Sarah E. Izard		Blue
2	Wᵐ T Jones		Choctaw	No1		
3	" " "		"	No1		
4	" " "		"	No1		
5	" " "		"	No1		
6	" " "		"	No1		
7	" " "		"	No1		
8	" " "		"	No1		
9						
10						
11	No1 = Was admitted by Choctaw Council					
12	with her mother Sarah A. Izard, in 1878 or					
13	1879					#1 to 7 inc
14	No2 on 1896 roll as Wᵐ Charles Jones					Date of Application for Enrollment.
15	No5 " 1896 " " Joseph Lee "					Aug 25/99
16	No6 " 1896 " " Liner L "					
	No7 " 1896 " " Uler A "					No8 enrolled Nov 2/99
17	Husband Wᵐ T Jones on					
	Card No D376					

52

Choctaw By Blood Enrollment Cards 1898-1914

RESIDENCE: Chickasaw Nation ~~COUNTY.~~
POST OFFICE: Hickory, I.T.

Choctaw Nation

Choctaw Roll
(Not Including Freedmen)

CARD NO.
FIELD NO. 3953

Dawes' Roll No.	NAME	Relationship to Person First Named	AGE	SEX	BLOOD	TRIBAL ENROLLMENT		
						Year	County	No.
11089	1 Putnam, Susan 18	First Named	15	F	1/4	1896	Kiamitia	5730
	2							
	3							
	4							
	5							
	6							
	7	ENROLLMENT OF NOS. 1 HEREON APPROVED BY THE SECRETARY OF INTERIOR MAR 10 1903						
	8							
	9							
	10							
	11							
	12							
	13							
	14							
	15							
	16							
	17							

TRIBAL ENROLLMENT OF PARENTS

	Name of Father	Year	County	Name of Mother	Year	County
1	Eastman Hart		Kiamitia	Mattie Hart		Non Cit
2						
3						
4						
5						
6						
7	On 1896 roll as Susan Hart					
8						
9	Evidence of marriage of parents to					
10	be supplied. Received and filed with Choctaw card #1512					
11	See Card 1512 for father's enrollment.					
12						
13	Mother on Choctaw card #D.587					
14	No1 is wife of S. G. Putnam; evidence of marriage filed Dec. 6, 1902					
15	For child of No.1 see NB (March 3, 1905) #1233			Date of Application for Enrollment	Aug 25/99	
16						
17	PO Midland IT 4/21/25					

53

Choctaw By Blood Enrollment Cards 1898-1914

| RESIDENCE: Blue | COUNTY. | Choctaw Nation | Choctaw Roll | CARD NO. |
| POST OFFICE: Academy, I.T. | | | (Not Including Freedmen) | FIELD NO. 3954 |

Dawes' Roll No.	NAME	Relationship to Person First Named	AGE	SEX	BLOOD	TRIBAL ENROLLMENT		
						Year	County	No.
1	Gardner, Rosetta		20	F	1/8			
2								
3								
4								
5								
6								
7								
8								
9								
10								
11								
12								
13								
14								
15								
16								
17								

TRIBAL ENROLLMENT OF PARENTS

	Name of Father	Year	County	Name of Mother	Year	County
1	Saml Riddle		Choctaw	Martha J Riddle		Non Citz
2						
3						
4						
5						
6						
7			Admitted by U.S. Court, Central Dist			
8			Aug 30/97, Court Case No 8, as Rosetta Riddle			
9			As to residence see her testimony			
10			also see enrollment of Samuel B Riddle, her			
11			father			
12						
13			Transferred to Choctaw card			
14			3809 with her husband,			Date of Application for Enrollment
15			Edward N Gardner. [Illegible Signature]			Aug 25/99
16						
17						

CANCELLED

54

Choctaw By Blood Enrollment Cards 1898-1914

RESIDENCE: Blue COUNTY. **Choctaw Nation** Choctaw Roll CARD NO.
POST OFFICE: Caddo, I.T. *(Not Including Freedmen)* FIELD NO. **3955**

Dawes' Roll No.	NAME	Relationship to Person First Named	AGE	SEX	BLOOD	TRIBAL ENROLLMENT		
						Year	County	No.
✻	1 Killian, Josie		29	F	1/8			
✓	2 " Ruth M	Dau	6mo	F	1/16			
	3							
	4							
	2 May 27 1904 Dismissed		No.1 Denied Citizenship by the Choctaw and					
	6		Chickasaw Citizenship Court Mar. 21 '04					
	7							
	8							
	9							
	10							
	11							
	12							
	13							
	14							
	15							
	16							
	17							

TRIBAL ENROLLMENT OF PARENTS

Name of Father	Year	County	Name of Mother	Year	County
1 Saml B Riddle		Choctaw	Martha Riddle		Non Citz
2 Henry Killian		non citizen	No1		
3					
4		No1 Denied in 96 Case #686			
5		Admitted by U.S. Court, Central Dist.			
6		Aug 30/97, as Josie Riddle Case No 8			
7		As to residence, see her testimony – also			
8		enrollment of father Samuel B Riddle			
		No2 born May 30 1902: enrolled Nov 28 1902			
9		Judgment of U.S. Ct admitting No1 vacated and set aside by Decree of Choctaw Chickasaw Citizenship Court Dec' 17'02			
10		No1 in C.C.C.C. Case #108			
11		No1 Denied by C.C.C.C. March 21 '04			
12					
13					
14					
15				Date of Application for Enrollment.	Aug 25/99
16					
17					

Choctaw By Blood Enrollment Cards 1898-1914

RESIDENCE: Blue	COUNTY.								CARD NO.	
POST OFFICE: Durant, I.T.	**Choctaw Nation**					**Choctaw Roll** *(Not Including Freedmen)*			FIELD NO. 3956	

Dawes' Roll No.	NAME	Relationship to Person First Named	AGE	SEX	BLOOD	TRIBAL ENROLLMENT		
						Year	County	No.
✓	1 Cooper, Noah W		63	M	1/4			
	2							
	3							
	4							
	5							
	6							
	7							
	8							
	9							
	10							
	11							
	12							
	13							
	14							
	15							
	16							
	17							

TRIBAL ENROLLMENT OF PARENTS

	Name of Father	Year	County	Name of Mother	Year	County
1	Caswell Cooper	Dead	Choctaw	Christiana Cooper	Dead	Non Citz
2						
3						
4						
5						
6	Admitted by U.S. Court, Central District,					
7	Ind. Ter, So McAlester , I.T. Jany 19, 1898					
8	in Court case #53					
9	~~Judgment of U.S. Court vacated and annulled by Decree of the U.S. Choctaw - Chickasaw Citizenship Court Dec 17/02~~					
	~~See Choctaw card D. 576 for child Jessie May Cooper~~					
10	~~No 1 now in C.C.C.C. Case #88~~					
11						
12	See Choctaw cards #D.576; #R.391 and #R.690 for children.					
13						
14						
15				Date of Application for Enrollment.		Aug 25/99
16						
17						

Choctaw By Blood Enrollment Cards 1898-1914

RESIDENCE: **Blue**   COUNTY.   **Choctaw Nation**   **Choctaw Roll**   CARD NO.

POST OFFICE: **Durant, I.T.**   *(Not Including Freedmen)*   FIELD NO. **3957**

Dawes' Roll No.	NAME	Relationship to Person First Named	AGE	SEX	BLOOD	TRIBAL ENROLLMENT Year	County	No.
1	Cooper, John E	Named	48	M	1/4			
2	" Robert E	Son	8	"	1/8			
3								
4								
5								
6								
7								
8								
9								
10								
11								
12								
13								
14								
15	See children on Choctaw card R. #612							
16								
17								

DISMISSED

SEP 22 1904

TRIBAL ENROLLMENT OF PARENTS

	Name of Father	Year	County	Name of Mother	Year	County
1	Caswell Cooper	Dead	Choctaw	Christiana Cooper	Dead	Non Citz
2	No 1					
3						
4						
5						
6						
7	Nos 1 and 2 denied by Court in 1896: case #729 Admitted by U.S. Court, Central District, Ind. Ter.					
8	So. McAlester, I.T. Jany 19, 1898 in court case #53					
9	No Appeal to C.C.C.C.					
10	Judgement of U.S. C't admitting Nos 1 & 2 vacated and set aside by Decree of Choctaw Chickasaw Citizenship Court Dec' 17'02					
11						
12						
13						
14						
15				Date of Application for Enrollment.	Aug 25/99	
16						
17						

Choctaw By Blood Enrollment Cards 1898-1914

RESIDENCE: Blue	COUNTY.								CARD NO.	
POST OFFICE: Caddo, I.T.	**Choctaw Nation**					Choctaw Roll (Not Including Freedmen)			FIELD NO. 3958	

Dawes' Roll No.	NAME	Relationship to Person	AGE	SEX	BLOOD	TRIBAL ENROLLMENT		
						Year	County	No.
11090	1 Lewis, Sophia ¹⁸	First Named	15	F	Full	1896	Blue	8186
	2							
	3							
	4							
	5	ENROLLMENT						
	6	OF NOS. 1 HEREON APPROVED BY THE SECRETARY						
	7	OF INTERIOR MAR 10 1903						
	8							
	9							
	10							
	11							
	12							
	13							
	14							
	15							
	16							
	17							

TRIBAL ENROLLMENT OF PARENTS

Name of Father	Year	County	Name of Mother	Year	County
1 Absalom Lewis	Dead	Blue	Nancy Lewis	Dead	Blue
2					
3					
4					
5					
6 On 1896 roll as Sophy Lewis					
7					
8					
9					
10					
11					
12					
13					
14					
15				Date of Application for Enrollment.	Aug 25/99	
16					
17					

58

Choctaw By Blood Enrollment Cards 1898-1914

RESIDENCE: Blue COUNTY. **Choctaw Nation** Choctaw Roll CARD No.
POST OFFICE: Caddo, I.T. *(Not Including Freedmen)* FIELD No. 3959

Dawes' Roll No.	NAME	Relationship to Person First Named	AGE	SEX	BLOOD	TRIBAL ENROLLMENT		
						Year	County	No.
11091	1 Folsom, John H ²⁴	First Named	21	M	1/4	1896	Blue	4382
	2							
	3							
	4							
	5 ENROLLMENT							
	6 OF NOS. 1 HEREON APPROVED BY THE SECRETARY							
	7 OF INTERIOR mAr 10 1903							
	8							
	9							
	10							
	11							
	12							
	13							
	14							
	15							
	16							
	17							

TRIBAL ENROLLMENT OF PARENTS

	Name of Father	Year	County	Name of Mother	Year	County
1	Dixon	Dead	Non Citz	Emma F Nail	Dead	Blue
2						
3						
4						
5						
6	On 1896 roll as Jno Henry Folsom					
7						
8						
9						
10						
11						
12						
13						
14						
15				Date of Application for Enrollment.	Aug 25/99	
16						
17						

Choctaw By Blood Enrollment Cards 1898-1914

RESIDENCE: Atoka   COUNTY. **Choctaw Nation**   **Choctaw Roll**   CARD NO.
POST OFFICE: Legal, I.T.   *(Not Including Freedmen)*   FIELD NO. 3960

Dawes' Roll No.		NAME		Relationship to Person First Named	AGE	SEX	BLOOD	TRIBAL ENROLLMENT		
								Year	County	No.
I.W. 370	1	Ninas, William	40	First Named	35	M	IW			
11092	2	" Tennessee	28	Wife	25	F	Full	1896	Atoka	9845
11093	3	" Alice	7	Dau	4	"	1/2	1896	"	9846
11094	4	" Flora B	5	"	2	"	1/2			
DEAD.	5	~~" Simeon~~		~~Son~~	~~1mo~~	~~M~~	~~1/2~~			
11095	6	" Josephine	1	Dau	4mo	F	1/2			
	7									
	8									
	9	ENROLLMENT OF NOS. 2,3,4 and 6 HEREON								
	10	APPROVED BY THE SECRETARY OF INTERIOR MAR 10 1903								
	11									
	12	ENROLLMENT OF NOS. 1 HEREON								
	13	APPROVED BY THE SECRETARY								
	14	OF INTERIOR SEP 12 1903								
	15	No. 5 HEREON DISMISSED UNDER								
	16	ORDER OF THE COMMISSION TO THE FIVE								
	17	CIVILIZED TRIBES OF MARCH 31, 1905.								

TRIBAL ENROLLMENT OF PARENTS

	Name of Father	Year	County	Name of Mother	Year	County
1	H. C. Ninas		Non Citz	Mary Ninas	Dead	Non Citz
2	Simeon Yamonubbee	Dead	Atoka	Serena Yamonubbee	"	Jackson
3	No1			No2		
4	No1			No2		
5	No1			No2		
6	No1			No2		
7						
8	For child of Nos 1&2 see NB (Apr 26-06) Card #580					
9	No4 Affidavit of birth to be					
10	supplied:- Filed Dec 14/99					
11	No6 Born Feb 15th 1902: Enrolled June 29" 1902					
12	No5 died Nov 25, 1900; proof of death filed Nov 26, 1902					
13	See affidavit of N°1 as to residence at the time of his marriage to N°2 filed May 6, 1903.					
14						#1 to 4 inc
15					Date of Application for Enrollment.	Aug 25/99
16					No5 enrolled Nov 2/99	
17						

Choctaw By Blood Enrollment Cards 1898-1914

RESIDENCE:	Atoka	COUNTY.							

POST OFFICE: Owl, I.T. — **Choctaw Nation** — **Choctaw Roll** *(Not Including Freedmen)* — **CARD NO.** — **FIELD NO.** 3961

Dawes' Roll No.	NAME	Relationship to Person	AGE	SEX	BLOOD	TRIBAL ENROLLMENT Year	County	No.
11096	1 Lawrence, Silas ⁶¹	First Named	58	M	1/4	1896	Atoka	8264
DEAD.	2 " Nellie	Wife	38	F	Full	1896	"	8265
11097	3 " Rosa A ¹⁵	Dau	12	"	5/8	1896	"	8267
	4							
	5							
	6							
	7	ENROLLMENT OF NOS. 1 and 3 HEREON						
	8	APPROVED BY THE SECRETARY						
	9	OF INTERIOR Mar 10 1903						
	10							
	11	No. 2 HEREON DISMISSED UNDER ORDER OF THE COMMISSION TO THE FIVE						
	12	CIVILIZED TRIBES OF MARCH 31, 1905.						
	13							
	14							
	15							
	16							
	17							

TRIBAL ENROLLMENT OF PARENTS

	Name of Father	Year	County	Name of Mother	Year	County
1	David Lawrence	Dead	Non Citz	Mary Lawrence	Dead	Jacks Fork
2	Fa-la-ta	"	Blue	Siney Falata	"	Atoka
3	No1			No2		
4						
5						
6						
7	No3 on 1896 roll as Rozella Lawrence					
8	N°2 Died May 18, 1902, proof of death filed Nov 22, 1902					
9	No3 now the wife of Sam A. Ott					
	For child of No.3 see NB (March 3 1905) #800					
10						
11						
12						
13						
14					Date of Application for Enrollment.	
15					Aug 28/99	
16						
17						

61

Choctaw By Blood Enrollment Cards 1898-1914

| RESIDENCE: | Atoka | COUNTY. | Choctaw Nation | | Choctaw Roll | CARD NO. | |
| POST OFFICE: | Owl, I.T. | | | | *(Not Including Freedmen)* | FIELD NO. 3962 | |

Dawes' Roll No.	NAME	Relationship to Person First Named	AGE	SEX	BLOOD	TRIBAL ENROLLMENT		
						Year	County	No.
11008	1 Alexander, Isham DIED PRIOR TO SEPTEMBER 25 1902		21	M	Full	1893	Atoka	895
	2							
	3							
	4							
	5	ENROLLMENT OF NOS. 1 HEREON APPROVED BY THE SECRETARY OF INTERIOR MAR 10 1903						
	6							
	7							
	8							
	9							
	10							
	11							
	12							
	13							
	14							
	15							
	16							
	17							

TRIBAL ENROLLMENT OF PARENTS

	Name of Father	Year	County	Name of Mother	Year	County
1	Aaron Alexander	Dead	Atoka	E-mul-icy	Dead	Atoka
2						
3						
4						
5						
6	No. 1 died November - 1902. Enrollment cancelled by Department May 7, 1906					
7	On 1893 Pay Roll, Page 90, No 896, Atoka					
8	County, as Isom Alexander. Also on 1896 roll as Alex Isom Page 155. No					
9	6323, Atoka Co					
10						
11						
12						
13						
14				Date of Application for Enrollment.	Aug 28/99	
15						
16						
17						

Choctaw By Blood Enrollment Cards 1898-1914

RESIDENCE: **Atoka** COUNTY. **Choctaw Nation** **Choctaw Roll** CARD NO.
POST OFFICE: **Atoka, I.T.** *(Not Including Freedmen)* FIELD NO. **3963**

Dawes' Roll No.	NAME	Relationship to Person	AGE	SEX	BLOOD	TRIBAL ENROLLMENT		
						Year	County	No.
11099	Folsom, Julius C	First Named	69	M	1/2	1896	Atoka	4428
I.W. 146	" Hattie I	Wife	31	F	IW	1896	"	14540
11100	" Tephi	Dau	3	"	1/4	1896	"	4430
11101	" Orilla	"	6mo	"	1/4			
11102	" Julius T.	Son	9mo	M	1/4			
6	CITIZENSHIP CERTIFICATE							
7	ISSUED FOR NO. 1&5 APR 24, 1903							
8								
9	ENROLLMENT							
10	OF NOS. 1,3,4 and 5 HEREON							
11	APPROVED BY THE SECRETARY OF INTERIOR MAR 10 1903							
12								
13	ENROLLMENT OF NOS. 2							
14	APPROVED BY THE SECRETARY HEREON							
15	OF INTERIOR JUN 13 1903							
16								
17								

TRIBAL ENROLLMENT OF PARENTS

	Name of Father	Year	County	Name of Mother	Year	County
1	Israel Folsom	Dead	Blue	Louvicey Folsom	Dead	Blue
2	Thos. Caughlin	"	Non-Citz	Louvenia Caughlin		Non-Citz
3	No.1			No.2		
4	No.1			No.2		
5	No.1			No.2		
6						
7						
8						
9	No1 On 1896 Roll as J.C. Folsom					
10	No2 " 1896 " " Hattie Fulsom					
11	No3 " 1896 " " Teplin "					
12						
13						
14						
15						
16						
17						Aug 28/99

Choctaw By Blood Enrollment Cards 1898-1914

RESIDENCE: COUNTY. **Choctaw Nation**   **Choctaw Roll**   CARD NO.
POST OFFICE: *(Not Including Freedmen)*   FIELD NO. 3964

Dawes' Roll No.	NAME	Relationship to Person First Named	AGE	SEX	BLOOD	TRIBAL ENROLLMENT Year	County	No.
DEAD	1 Riddle, Mary L DEAD		25	F	1/16	1896	Aipia	3600
11103	2 Daugherty, Myrtle 9	Dau	6	"	1/32	1/32	"	3601
DEAD.	3 Riddle, Johny D DEAD	Son	3mo	M	1/32	1/32		
	4							
	5							
	6							
	7							
	8							
	9							
	10							
	11							
	12							
	13							
	14							
	15							
	16							
	17							

ENROLLMENT OF NOS. 2 HEREON APPROVED BY THE SECRETARY OF INTERIOR MAR 10 1903

No. 1 HEREON DISMISSED UNDER ORDER OF THE COMMISSION TO THE FIVE CIVILIZED TRIBES OF MARCH 31, 1905.

No. 3 HEREON DISMISSED UNDER ORDER OF THE COMMISSIONER TO THE FIVE CIVILIZED TRIBES OF JULY 18, 1905.

TRIBAL ENROLLMENT OF PARENTS

Name of Father	Year	County	Name of Mother	Year	County
1 Joe Moore	Dead	Chick Dist	Mary Moore	Dead	Non Citz
2 Jas Daugherty	"	Non Citz	No1		
3 Jno. H. Riddle	" "		No1		

No1 on 1896 roll as Mary Louisa Dougherty
No2 " 1896 " " Martha "
No1 As to marriage of parents, see testimony of Julius C. Folsom
No3 enrolled Dec 18/99 Affidavit irregular and returned for correction
Recd & filed Jany 17, 1900
No3 died Sept 23d 1900. Evidence filed Ozzct 20, 1900
No.1 died November 6th, 1900
No2 is now living with Rebacca[sic] W Daugherty
Proof of death #3 acquired 8/15/05

Date of Application for Enrollment. Aug 28/99

64

Choctaw By Blood Enrollment Cards 1898-1914

RESIDENCE: Atoka   COUNTY. **Choctaw** Roll

POST OFFICE: Legal. I.T.   *(Not including Freedmen)*   FIELD NO. 5989

Dawes' Roll No.	NAME		Relationship to Person First Named	AGE	SEX	BLOOD	TRIBAL ENROLLMENT		
							Year	County	No.
11104	1 King, Mitchell	28	First Named	25	M	1/2	1896	Atoka	7651
11105	2 " Emma	25	Wife	23	F	1/2	1906	"	7652
11106	3 " Silas A.	6	Son	3	M	1/2	1906	"	7653
	4								
	5								
	6								
	7	ENROLLMENT							
	8	OF NOS. 1,2 and 3 HEREON APPROVED BY THE SECRETARY							
	9	OF INTERIOR MAR 10 1903							
	10								
	11								
	12								
	13								
	14								
	15								
	16								
	17								

TRIBAL ENROLLMENT OF PARENTS

	Name of Father	Year	County	Name of Mother	Year	County
1	Anderson King		Atoka	Sophie King	Dead	Atoka
2	Silas Lawrence		"	Nellie Lawrence		"
3	No 1			NP		
4						
5						
6	For child of Nos 1&2 see (Mar 2 '05) Card No 300					
7						
8						
9						
10						
11						
12						
13						
14					Date of Application for Enrollment.	
15					Aug 28/99	
16						
17						

Choctaw By Blood Enrollment Cards 1898-1914

RESIDENCE:	Blue	COUNTY.						

RESIDENCE: **Blue** COUNTY. **Choctaw Nation** **Choctaw Roll** CARD NO.
POST OFFICE: **Oconee, I.T.** *(Not Including Freedmen)* FIELD NO. **3966**

Dawes' Roll No.	NAME	Relationship to Person First Named	AGE	SEX	BLOOD	TRIBAL ENROLLMENT		
						Year	County	No.
1	Perkins, Albert		25	M	Full	1893	Atoka	8535
2								
3								
4								
5								
6								
7								
8								
9								
10								
11								
12								
13								
14								
15								
16								
17								

CANCELLED Sept. 3, 1902
Duplicate of Choctaw card #69

TRIBAL ENROLLMENT OF PARENTS

	Name of Father	Year	County	Name of Mother	Year	County
1	Sim Perkins	Dead	Blue	Sealey Perkins	Dead	Blue
2						
3						
4						
5						
6		On 1893 Pay Roll, Page 86, No 853, Atoka Co.				
7						
8						
9						
10						
11						
12						
13						
14					Date of Application for Enrollment.	
15					Aug 28/99	
16						
17						

Choctaw By Blood Enrollment Cards 1898-1914

RESIDENCE: Atoka   COUNTY. **Choctaw Nation**   Choctaw Roll   CARD NO.

POST OFFICE: Owl, I.T.   *(Not Including Freedmen)*   FIELD NO. **3967**

Dawes' Roll No.	NAME	Relationship to Person First Named	AGE	SEX	BLOOD	TRIBAL ENROLLMENT Year	County	No.
1	Goins, Robert G.	Named	77	M	1/4		D	
2	" Elizabeth	Wife	67	F	I.W.		D	
3								
4	Denied Citizenship by the Choctaw and Chickasaw							
5	Citizenship Court Case #39T, June 29,04							
6								
7								
8								
9								
10								
11								
12								
13								
14								
15								
16								
17								

TRIBAL ENROLLMENT OF PARENTS

	Name of Father	Year	County	Name of Mother	Year	County
1	Jeremiah Goins	Dead	Choctaw	Saraphine Goins	Dead	Non Citz
2	Brooks Williams	"	Non Citz	Sarah Williams	"	" "
3						
4						
5						
6						
7	No 1&2 Denied in 96 Case #55 Admitted by U.S Court, Southern					
8	Dist., Dec. 21/97, Case No 127 As to residence, see his testimony.					
9	Judgement[sic] of U.S. Ct admitting No vacated and set aside by Decree of Choctaw Chickasaw Citizenship Court Decr 17'02					
10	Nos 1&2 Now in C.C.C.C. Case #31T.					
11						
12						
13					Date of Application for Enrollment.	
14					Aug 28/99	
15						
16						
17						

Choctaw By Blood Enrollment Cards 1898-1914

RESIDENCE: Atoka   COUNTY. **Choctaw Nation**   Choctaw Roll   CARD NO.
POST OFFICE: Coalgate, I.T.   (Not Including Freedmen)   FIELD NO. 3966

Dawes' Roll No.		NAME	Relationship to Person	AGE	SEX	BLOOD	TRIBAL ENROLLMENT		
							Year	County	No.
I.W. 4631	1	Whitlock, William P 51	First Named	48	M	IW			
11107	2	" Isabelle 50	Wife	47	F	Full	1896	Blue	12411
11108	3	Hayes, Greenwood 13	S. Son	10	M	"	1896	"	5887
	4								
	5								
	6								
	7								
	8								
	9								
	10								
	11								
	12								
	13								
	14								
	15								
	16								
	17								

ENROLLMENT
OF NOS. 2 and 3 HEREON
APPROVED BY THE SECRETARY
OF INTERIOR   MAR 10 1903

ENROLLMENT
OF NOS. ~~~ 1 ~~~ HEREON
APPROVED BY THE SECRETARY
OF INTERIOR   FEB 19 1907

TRIBAL ENROLLMENT OF PARENTS

	Name of Father	Year	County	Name of Mother	Year	County
1	T. J. Whitlock	Dead	Non Citz	Lucy Whitlock	Dead	Non Citz
-	David Perkins	"	Blue	Alcie Perkins	"	Blue
3	Sidney Hayes	"	"	No2		
4						
5						
6						
7						
8						
9	No2 on 1896 roll as Isabelle Tehomba					
10	No3 " 1896 " " Green Hayes					
11	No2 " 1896 " " Elizabeth Perkins					
12	Page 270 No 1057A, Atoka County.					
13						
14	Notify Thos Norman Ardmore IT of decision as to No1					Date of Application for Enrollment.
15	5/05/06					Aug 28/99
16	No1					
17	PO 3/1 Tupelo I.T.	GRANTED	OCT 17 1906			

Choctaw By Blood Enrollment Cards 1898-1914

RESIDENCE: Atoka COUNTY. **Choctaw Nation** Choctaw Roll CARD NO.
POST OFFICE: Owl, I.T. *(Not Including Freedmen)* FIELD NO. 3969

Dawes' Roll No.	NAME	Relationship to Person First Named	AGE	SEX	BLOOD	TRIBAL ENROLLMENT Year	County	No.
11109	₁ Lawrence, Louis ²⁷	First Named	24	M	1/2	1896	Blue	8266
11110	₂ " Edna ³¹	Wife	28	F	Full	1896	"	7617
11111	₃ Sunny, Amy ²⁰	Ward	17	"	"	1896	Atoka	11657
	₄							
	₅							
	₆	ENROLLMENT						
	₇	OF NOS. 1 2 and 3 HEREON APPROVED BY THE SECRETARY						
	₈	OF INTERIOR MAR 10 1903						
	₉							
	₁₀							
	₁₁							
	₁₂							
	₁₃							
	₁₄							
	₁₅							
	₁₆							
	₁₇							

TRIBAL ENROLLMENT OF PARENTS

	Name of Father	Year	County	Name of Mother	Year	County
₁	Silas Lawrence		Atoka	Nellie Lawrence		Atoka
₂	Allen Battiest	Dead	"	Lena Battiest	Dead	"
₃	Turnway Sunny	"	"	Millie A Sunny	"	"
₄						
₅						
₆						
₇						
₈						
₉						
₁₀	No1 on 1896 roll as Lewis Lawrence					
₁₁	No2 " 1896 " " Edna King					
₁₂	No.2 also on 1896 Choctaw roll ad Edwin King: page 190: #7657					
₁₃						
₁₄					Date of Application for Enrollment	
₁₅					Aug 28/99	
₁₆					INTERMARRIED STATUS.	
₁₇					SEPTEMBER 25, 1902	

69

Choctaw By Blood Enrollment Cards 1898-1914

RESIDENCE: Jackson COUNTY.			Choctaw Nation				Choctaw Roll (Not Including Freedmen)		CARD NO. FIELD NO. 3970	

Dawes' Roll No.	NAME	Relationship to Person	AGE	SEX	BLOOD	TRIBAL ENROLLMENT		
						Year	County	No.
11112	1 Carnes, Ellen ⁷⁰	First Named	67	F	Full	1896	Jackson	2833
11113	2 " Eliza ¹¹	G.D.	11	"	"	1896	"	2934
	3							
	4							
	5							
	6							
	7	ENROLLMENT OF NOS. 1 and 2 HEREON						
	8	APPROVED BY THE SECRETARY OF INTERIOR Mar 10 1903						
	9							
	10							
	11							
	12							
	13							
	14							
	15							
	16							
	17							

TRIBAL ENROLLMENT OF PARENTS

	Name of Father	Year	County	Name of Mother	Year	County
1		Dead	Red River		Dead	Red River
2	Ben Carnes	"	Jackson	Sarah Anderson		Jackson
3						
4						
5						
6						
7						
8						
9						
10						
11						
12						
13					Date of Application for Enrollment.	
14					Aug 28/99	
15						
16						
17						

RESIDENCE:	Jackson	COUNTY.							
POST OFFICE:	Mayhew, I.T.		**Choctaw Nation**				Choctaw Roll *(Not Including Freedmen)*	CARD NO. FIELD NO. **3971**	

Dawes' Roll No.	NAME		Relationship to Person First Named	AGE	SEX	BLOOD	TRIBAL ENROLLMENT		
							Year	County	No.
DEAD	1 McClure, Joseph D		Named	48	M	Full	1896	Jackson	9411
11114	2 " Nicey	48	Wife	45	F	"	1896	"	9412
11115	3 " Douglas C	22	Ward	19	M	"	1896	"	9413
11116	4 " Lorena B	18	Dau	15	F	"	1896	"	9414
11117	5 " Benjamin	11	Son	8	M	"	1896	"	9415
11118	6 Hayes, Mary	12	Ward	9	F	"	1896	"	5833
	7								
	8								
	9								
	10	ENROLLMENT OF NOS. 2,3,4,5 and 6 HEREON APPROVED BY THE SECRETARY OF INTERIOR Mar 10 1903							
	11								
	12								
	13	No.1 hereon dismissed under order of the Commission to the Five Civilized Tribes of March 31, 1905.							
	14								
	15								
	16								
	17								

TRIBAL ENROLLMENT OF PARENTS

	Name of Father	Year	County	Name of Mother	Year	County
1	Wm McClure	Dead	Red River	Lucind[sic] McClure	Dead	Blue
2	Washington Carnes	"	Jackson	Ellen Carnes		Jackson
3	Cornelius Jones	"	Blue	Harriet S. Jones	Dead	Blue
4	No1			No2		
5	No1			No2		
6	Pickens Hayes		Jackson	Winey Hayes	Dead	Jackson
7						
8						
9						
10	No1 on 1896 roll as J.D. McClure					
11	No3 " 1896 " " Douglas O "					
12	No4 " 1896 " " Laurena B "					
	No2 " 1896 " " Nicey C "					
13	No1 died Aug 22, 1900: proof of death filed Nov 25, 1902				Date of Application for Enrollment.	
14	For child of No4 see NB (Apr 26-06) Card #681				Aug 28/99	
15	" " " " " (Mar 3 '05) " " 288					
16						
17						

Choctaw By Blood Enrollment Cards 1898-1914

Dawes' Roll No.	NAME		Relationship to Person First Named	AGE	SEX	BLOOD	TRIBAL ENROLLMENT		
							Year	County	No.
11119	1 Thomas, Mollie M	29	First Named	26	F	1/32	1896	Atoka	12463
11120	2 " Mary L	10	Dau	7	"	1/64	1896	"	12465
11121	3 " Minnie A	9	"	6	"	1/64	1896	"	12466
11122	4 " William	7	Son	4	M	1/64	1896	"	12464
11123	5 " Ethel	5	Dau	2	F	1/64			
11124	6 " John A	3	Son	5mo	M	1/64			
11125	7 " Burtie	1	Son	1mo	M	1/64			
	8								
	9								
	10								
	11	ENROLLMENT OF NOS. 1,2,3,4,5,6 and 7 HEREON							
	12	APPROVED BY THE SECRETARY							
	13	OF INTERIOR MAR 10 1903							
	14								
	15								
	16								
	17								

TRIBAL ENROLLMENT OF PARENTS

	Name of Father	Year	County	Name of Mother	Year	County
1	William Spain	Dead	Blue	Louisa Spain		Non Citz
2	Anderson Thomas		Non Citz	No1		
3	" "		" "	No1		
4	" "		" "	No1		
5	" "		" "	No1		
6	" "		" "	No1		
7	" "		" "	No1		
8						
9	Nos 1-7 inclusive descendants of Mary M Spain, who was admitted by Act of					
10	No1 As to marriage of parents, see			Council of Oct 31,1877		
11	enrollment of mother, Louisa Spain					
12	No1 On 1896 roll as Martha Thomas					
13	No2 " 1896 " " Louisa "					
14	No3 " 1896 " " Alice "					
15	Nos 5-6 Affidavits of birth to be supplied:- Recd Oct 7/99			Date of ... for E...		
16	No7 Enrolled May 23, 1901			Aug ...		
17	For children of No1 see NB (Act Mar. 3 '05) Card #289					
	PO Owl IT 3/29/05					

72

Choctaw By Blood Enrollment Cards 1898-1914

| RESIDENCE: | Atoka | COUNTY. | **Choctaw Nation** | | Choctaw Roll | CARD NO. | |
| POST OFFICE: | Coalgate, I.T. | | | | (Not Including Freedmen) | FIELD NO. 3973 | |

Dawes' Roll No.	NAME		Relationship to Person First Named	AGE	SEX	BLOOD	TRIBAL ENROLLMENT		
							Year	County	No.
I.W. 371	1 Spain, Louisa	57	First Named	54	F	IW			
	2								
	3								
	4								
	5								
	6								
	7								
	8 ENROLLMENT								
	9 OF NOS. 1 HEREON								
	APPROVED BY THE SECRETARY								
	10 OF INTERIOR SEP 12 1903								
	11								
	12								
	13								
	14								
	15								
	16								
	17								

TRIBAL ENROLLMENT OF PARENTS

	Name of Father	Year	County	Name of Mother	Year	County
1	William Huntress	Dead	Non Citz	Hannah Huntress	Dead	Non Citz
2						
3						
4						
5						
6						
7	No1 was wife of William Spain, deceased, who was son of Mary M Spain,					
8	admitted by Act of Choctaw Council of Oct. 31, 1877					
9	As to marriage, see her testimony and					
10	that of Rebecca W Daugherty					
11	Certified copy of record of marriage to be supplied:-					
12	Marriage certificate received 9/12/1899					
13	No.1 admitted by Dawes Commission in 1896 as an intermarried citizen: Choctaw case #798: no appeal.					
14						
15				Date of Application for Enrollment.	Aug 28/99	
16						
17						

Choctaw By Blood Enrollment Cards 1898-1914

RESIDENCE:	Atoka	COUNTY.	**Choctaw Nation**	**Choctaw Roll** *(Not Including Freedmen)*	CARD NO.
POST OFFICE:	Globe, I.T.				FIELD NO. 3974

Dawes' Roll No.		NAME		Relationship to Person First Named	AGE	SEX	BLOOD	TRIBAL ENROLLMENT		
								Year	County	No.
11126	1	Cabe, Rebecca W	34	First Named	31	F	1/16	1896	Atoka	3598
11127	2	Daugherty Elvin H	9	Son	6	M	1/32	1896	"	3599
	3									
	4									
	5									
	6	ENROLLMENT								
	7	OF NOS. 1 and 2 HEREON APPROVED BY THE SECRETARY								
	8	OF INTERIOR MAR 10 1903								
	9									
	10									
	11									
	12									
	13									
	14									
	15									
	16									
	17									

TRIBAL ENROLLMENT OF PARENTS

	Name of Father	Year	County	Name of Mother	Year	County
1	Joseph G. Moore	Dead	Chick. Dist	Mary E Moore	Dead	Non Citz
2	C. H. Daugherty		Non Citz	No1		
3						
4						
5						
6						
7	No1 on 1896 roll as Rebecca W Dougherty					
8	No2 " 1896 " " E. Harrison "					
9						
10	No1- As to marriage of parents, see					
11	enrollment of sister, Mary L Riddle					
12	Nº1 is now the wife of J. M. Cabe- non-citizen. Evidence of marriage received and filed Nov. 19, 1902					
13					Date of Application for Enrollment.	
14						
15					Aug 28/99	
16						
17	Coalgate I.T. 11/17/02					

Choctaw By Blood Enrollment Cards 1898-1914

	RESIDENCE: Atoka COUNTY.							

RESIDENCE: Atoka **COUNTY.** **Choctaw Nation** **Choctaw Roll** (Not Including Freedmen) **CARD NO.** **FIELD NO. 3975**
POST OFFICE: Coalgate, I.T.

Dawes' Roll No.	NAME		Relationship to Person First Named	AGE	SEX	BLOOD	TRIBAL ENROLLMENT		
							Year	County	No.
11128	1 Ott, John	26	First Named	23	M	Full	1896	Atoka	10020
11129	2 " Fannie	29	Wife	26	F	"	1896	"	10021
11130	3 " Gillam	4	Son	1	M	"			
11131	4 Billy, Lita	12	S.Dau	9	F	"	1896		1871
11132	5 Ott, Dora	1	Dau	1mo	F	"			
	6		ENROLLMENT						
	7		OF NOS. 1,2,3,4 and 5 HEREON						
	8		APPROVED BY THE SECRETARY OF INTERIOR Mar 10 1903						
	9								
	10								
	11								
	12								
	13								
	14								
	15								
	16								
	17								

TRIBAL ENROLLMENT OF PARENTS

	Name of Father	Year	County	Name of Mother	Year	County
1	Johnson Ott		Atoka	Bicey Ott		Atoka
2	Lyman Homma	Dead	"		Dead	Tobucksy
3	No1			No2		
4	Simon Billy			No2		
5	No.1			No2		
6						
7						
8						
9						
10						
11			No4 On 1896 roll as Littie Billy			
12			No3 Affidavit of birth to be			
13			supplied:- Filed Nov 2/99			#1 to 4 inc
14			No5 Enrolled Sept 16, 1901			Date of Application for Enrollment.
15			For child of Nos 1&2 see NB (Apr 26 '06) Card #1208			Aug 28/99
16			" " " " " " " (Mar 3,1905) " #645			
17						

75

Choctaw By Blood Enrollment Cards 1898-1914

RESIDENCE: Atoka   COUNTY. **Choctaw Nation**   **Choctaw Roll**   CARD N
POST OFFICE: Oconee, I.T.   *(Not Including Freedmen)*   FIELD NO. **3976**

Dawes' Roll No.	NAME		Relationship to Person	AGE	SEX	BLOOD	TRIBAL ENROLLMENT		
							Year	County	No.
I.W. 372	1 Mayo, John B	45	First Named	42	M	I.W.	1896	Atoka	14839
11133	2 " Tabitha A	31	Wife	28	F	1/32	1896	"	8820
11134	3 " Leonard	14	Son	11	M	1/64	1896	"	8821
11135	4 " Edna	12	Dau	9	F	1/64	1896	"	8823
11136	5 " Albert	9	Son	6	M	1/64	1896	"	8822
11137	6 " Lula	4	Dau	1	F	1/64			
11138	7 " John	2	Son	3w	M	1/64			
	8								
	9								
	10								
	11	ENROLLMENT OF NOS. 2,3,4,5,6 and 7 HEREON APPROVED BY THE SECRETARY OF INTERIOR Mar 19 1903							
	12								
	13								
	14	ENROLLMENT OF NOS. 1 HEREON APPROVED BY THE SECRETARY OF INTERIOR Sep 12 1903							
	15								
	16								
	17								

TRIBAL ENROLLMENT OF PARENTS

	Name of Father	Year	County	Name of Mother	Year	County
1	John A Mayo	Dead	Non Citz	Phoebe E Mayo		Non Citz
2	Geo H Izard	"	" " "	Sarah E Izard		Blue
3	No1			No2		
4	No1			No2		
5	No1			No2		
6	No1			No2		
7	No.1			No.2		
8						
9						
10						
11	No2 On 1896 roll as Tobiathy[sic] A Mayo					
12	No3 " 1896 " " Leonora	"				
13	No1 Admitted by Dawes Com Case No 1286. On 1896 roll as Jno. B. Maise					
14	No6 Affidavit of birth to be				#1 to 6	
15	supplied:- Recd Oct 7/99 No.7 Enrolled January 10th, 1901			Date of Application for Enrollment.	Aug 28/99	
16	For children of Nos 1&2 see NB (Mar 3rd 1905) Card #490					
17	Olney I.T. 11/19/02					

76

RESIDENCE: Chickasaw Nation ~~COUNTY~~.

POST OFFICE: Emet, I.T.

Choctaw Nation

Choctaw Roll *(Not Including Freedmen)*

CARD NO.

FIELD NO. 3977

Dawes' Roll No.	NAME		Relationship to Person First Named	AGE	SEX	BLOOD	TRIBAL ENROLLMENT		
							Year	County	No.
11139	1 Hamilton, Marnie	22	First Named	19	F	1/16	1893	Blue	1099
11140	2 " Alonzo F	5	Son	2	M	1/32			
11141	3 " Lorena H		Dau	3mo	F	1/32			
11142	4 " Lora Williams		Son	1mo	M	1/32			
	5								
	6								
	7								
	8								
	9								
	10								
	11								
	12								
	13								
	14								
	15								
	16								
	17								

ENROLLMENT
OF NOS. 1,2,3 and 4 HEREON
APPROVED BY THE SECRETARY
OF INTERIOR MAR 10 1903

TRIBAL ENROLLMENT OF PARENTS

	Name of Father	Year	County	Name of Mother	Year	County
1	E. Taylor		Non Citz	Lou Taylor		Chick. Dist
2	Wm H. Hamilton		" "	No1		
3	" " "		" "	No1		
4	" " "		" "	Nº1		
5						
6						
7						
8						
9						
10			No1 On 1893 Pay Roll, Page 106, No 1099,			
11			Blue Co, as ~~Minnie Taylor~~.			
12						
13			Wife of Wm H. Hamilton, Card			
14			No D383		Date of Application for Enrollment.	
15			Nº4 Born Aug. 25, 1902; enrolled Sept. 24, 1902		FOR Nos	
			For child of No1 see NB (Act Mar 3-05) Card #290		1 to 3 inc Aug 28/99	
16						
17	P.O. Bee I.T. 3/18/05					

77

Choctaw By Blood Enrollment Cards 1898-1914

RESIDENCE:	Atoka		COUNTY.	**Choctaw Nation**			Choctaw Roll	CARD No.	
POST OFFICE:	Atoka, I.T.						*(Not Including Freedmen)*	FIELD No. **3978**	

Dawes' Roll No.	NAME		Relationship to Person First Named	AGE	SEX	BLOOD	TRIBAL ENROLLMENT		
							Year	County	No.
I.W. 373	₁ Robb, David N	60	First Named	57	M	IW	1896	Atoka	14994
11143	₂ " Czarena	69	Wife	66	F	1/2	1896	"	10965
11144	₃ Walker, Rhoda	26	Ward	23	"	Full	1896	Red River	13699
11145	₄ Brown, Celia	23	"	20	"	"	1896	Atoka	1824
11146	₅ Williams, Sallie	22	"	19	"	"	1896	"	13978
11147	₆ Sexton, Martin	14	"	11	M	1/2	1896	"	11619
	₇								
	₈								
	₉								
	₁₀	ENROLLMENT OF NOS. 2,3,4,5 and 6 HEREON APPROVED BY THE SECRETARY OF INTERIOR Mar 10 1903							
	₁₁								
	₁₂								
	₁₃	ENROLLMENT OF NOS. 1 HEREON APPROVED BY THE SECRETARY OF INTERIOR Sep 12 1903							
	₁₄								
	₁₅								
	₁₆								
	₁₇								

TRIBAL ENROLLMENT OF PARENTS

Name of Father	Year	County	Name of Mother	Year	County
₁ William Robb	Dead	Non Citz	Margaret Robb	Dead	Non Citz
₂ Israel Folsom	"	Blue	Louvicey Folsom	"	Blue
₃ Sin-te-nosh	"	"	Litey	"	"
₄ Louis Brown	"	Gaines		"	Gaines
₅ Williams	"	"		"	"
₆		Non Citz	Eliza Sexton		Tobucksy
₇					
₈ No1 on 1896 roll as D. N. Robb					
₉					
₁₀ No2 admitted as an intermarried citizen by Dawes Commission Choctaw Case #1189: No appeal					
₁₁ For child of No.4 see NB (March 3, 1905) #817					
₁₂					
₁₃					
₁₄					
₁₅			Date of Application for Enrollment.	Aug 28/99	
₁₆					
₁₇					

Choctaw By Blood Enrollment Cards 1898-1914

RESIDENCE: Atoka   COUNTY. **Choctaw Nation**   **Choctaw Roll**   CARD No.
POST OFFICE: Oconee, I.T.   *(Not Including Freedmen)*   FIELD No. 3979

Dawes' Roll No.	NAME	Relationship to Person First Named	AGE	SEX	BLOOD	TRIBAL ENROLLMENT		
						Year	County	No.
IW 374	1 Harrell, Pious D 55		52	M	IW	1896	Atoka	14661
11148	2 " Selina 58	Wife	55	F	1/16	1896	"	5976
11149	3 " Pinkey 13	Dau	10	"	1/32	1896	"	5977
	4							
	5							
	6							
	7	ENROLLMENT OF NOS. 2 and 3 HEREON						
	8	APPROVED BY THE SECRETARY						
	9	OF INTERIOR MAR 10 1903						
	10	ENROLLMENT OF NOS. 1 HEREON						
	11	APPROVED BY THE SECRETARY						
	12	OF INTERIOR SEP 12 1903						
	13							
	14							
	15							
	16							
	17							

TRIBAL ENROLLMENT OF PARENTS

	Name of Father	Year	County	Name of Mother	Year	County
1	Samuel Harrell	Dead	Non Citz	Mahaley Harrell	Dead	Non Citz
2	Chas H Moran	"	" "	Eliz Moran		Blue
3	No1			No2		
4						
5						
6						
7						
8			No1 on 1896 roll as P. D. Harrold			
9			No2 " 1896 " " Salina Herald			
10			No3 " 1896 " " Pinkey "			
11						
12						
13						
14					Date of Application for Enrollment.	
15					Aug 28/99	
16						
17	P.O. Olney IT 11/12/02					

79

Choctaw By Blood Enrollment Cards 1898-1914

RESIDENCE:	Atoka	COUNTY.	**Choctaw Nation**	**Choctaw Roll** (Not Including Freedmen)	CARD NO.
POST OFFICE:	Atoka, I.T.				FIELD NO. 3980

Dawes' Roll No.	NAME		Relationship to Person First Named	AGE	SEX	BLOOD	TRIBAL ENROLLMENT		
							Year	County	No.
11150	1 Ward, John W	30	First Named	27	M	1/8	1896	Atoka	13943
11151	2 " Rachel A	5	Dau	1½	F	1/16			
I.W. 1336	3 " Rachel C	33	Wife	33	F	I.W.			
	4								
	5								
	6	ENROLLMENT							
	7	OF NOS. 1 and 2 APPROVED BY THE SECRETARY	HEREON						
	8	OF INTERIOR MAR 10 1903							
	9	ENROLLMENT							
	10	OF NOS. 3 APPROVED BY THE SECRETARY	HEREON						
	11	OF INTERIOR MAR 14 1905							
	12								
	13								
	14								
	15								
	16								
	17								

TRIBAL ENROLLMENT OF PARENTS

Name of Father	Year	County	Name of Mother	Year	County
1 Ed Ward	Dead	Atoka	Hamiah Ward	Dead	Non Citz
2 No 1			Rachel C Ward		" "
3 Daniel G. Brown		non-citizen	Rashel C Brown	Dead	" "
4					
5					
6					
7					
8					
9		No 1 on 1896 roll as Jno S. Ward			
10		No 2 Evidence of marriage of parents to be supplied:- Filed Dec 14/99			
11		No 1 As to marriage of parents see testimony of Julius C. Folsom.			
12		No 2 Affidavit of birth to be supplied:- Filed Dec 14/99			
13					Date of Application for Enrollment.
14	No.3 was placed on this card Dec 5, 1904, under an order of the Commission				
15	of that date holding that conclusive evidence had been submitted that				Aug 28/99
16	application was made for her enrollment as an intermarried citizen of				
17	the Choctaw Nation in August, 1899.				

Choctaw By Blood Enrollment Cards 1898-1914

RESIDENCE: Atoka **COUNTY.**
POST OFFICE: Atoka, I.T. **Choctaw Nation**

Choctaw Roll CARD NO.
(Not Including Freedmen) FIELD NO. 3981

Dawes' Roll No.	NAME	Relationship to Person First Named	AGE	SEX	BLOOD	TRIBAL ENROLLMENT Year	County	No.
11152	₁ Wright, Eliphalet N ⁴⁴	First Named	41	M	1/2	1896	Atoka	13947
I.W.375	₂ " Ida B ³⁷	Wife	34	F	IW			
11153	₃ " Muriel H ¹³	Dau	10	"	1/4	1896	Atoka	13948
11143	₄ " Gertrude I ⁷	"	4	"	1/4	1896	"	13949
	₅							
	₆							
	₇							
	₈	ENROLLMENT						
	₉	OF NOS. 1,3 and 4 HEREON						
	₁₀	APPROVED BY THE SECRETARY OF INTERIOR Mar 10 1903						
	₁₁	ENROLLMENT						
	₁₂	OF NOS. 2 HEREON APPROVED BY THE SECRETARY						
	₁₃	OF INTERIOR SEP 12 1903						
	₁₄							
	₁₅							
	₁₆							
	₁₇							

TRIBAL ENROLLMENT OF PARENTS

	Name of Father	Year	County	Name of Mother	Year	County
₁	Allen Wright	Dead	Atoka	Harriet N Wright	Dead	Non Citz
₂	S. C. Richards	"	Non Citz	Georgeina[sic]Richards	"	" "
₃	No1			No2		
₄	No1			No2		
₅						
₆						
₇						
₈						
₉	Certificate of marriage between Nos 1-2 exhibited,					
₁₀	and found satisfactory, but in in condition to be filed.					
₁₁	No1- As to marriage of parents, see					
₁₂	enrollment of sister, Clara E. Richards					
₁₃	No3 on 1896 roll as M. Hazel Wright					
₁₄	No4 " 1896 " " Gertrude "			Date of Application for Enrollment		
₁₅	No1- Admitted by Dawes Com, Case No 505 as Ida B Wright			Aug 28/99		
₁₆	No1 on 1896 roll as E. Nott Wright					
₁₇						

Olney 12/2/02

81

Choctaw By Blood Enrollment Cards 1898-1914

RESIDENCE: Atoka   COUNTY. **Choctaw Nation**   **Choctaw Roll** (Not Including Freedmen)   CARD NO.
POST OFFICE: Lehigh, I.T.   FIELD NO. **3982**

Dawes' Roll No.		NAME		Relationship to Person First Named	AGE	SEX	BLOOD	TRIBAL ENROLLMENT		
								Year	County	No.
11155	1	Harrison, John M	47	First Named	44	M	1/2	1896	Atoka	6004
I.W. 1009	2	" Rosa	33	Wife	30	F	I.W.	1896	"	14660
11156	3	" Cora	14	Dau	11	"	1/4	1896	Atoka	6005
	4									
	5									
	6									
	7	ENROLLMENT					ENROLLMENT			
	8	OF NOS. 1 and 3 HEREON APPROVED BY THE SECRETARY					OF NOS. ~~ 2 ~~~ HEREON APPROVED BY THE SECRETARY			
	9	OF INTERIOR Mar 10 1903					OF INTERIOR Oct 21 1904			
	10	Take no further action relative to enrollment of No2								
	11	Protest of Attys for Choctaw & Chickasaw Nations								
	12	Jan 23 '04								
	13									
	14									
	15									
	16									
	17									

TRIBAL ENROLLMENT OF PARENTS

	Name of Father	Year	County	Name of Mother	Year	County
1	Zeddick Harrison	Dead	Kiamitia	Eliz Harrison		Atoka
2	Norbon Cook	"	Non Citz	Rhoda Cook		Non Citz
3	No1			Bettie Harrison	Dau	" "
4						
5						
6						
7						
8						
9			No1 on 1896 roll as Jno. M. Harrison			
10			No2 As to marriage, see testimony of Henry C. LeFlore			
11			No3 As to marriage of parents, see			
12			testimony of Henry C. LeFlore			
13			No2 on 1896 roll as Rose Harris			
14						
15					Date of Application for Enrollment.	Aug 28/99
16			6/9/1904 P.O. No2 Coalgate I.T.			
17			No2 P.O. 310 E. Chestnut St. Denison Tex			
			No2 Coalgate I.T. 11/17/02			

Choctaw By Blood Enrollment Cards 1898-1914

Choctaw Nation

Choctaw Roll
(Not Including Freedmen)

CARD No.
FIELD No. 3983

Dawes' Roll No.	NAME	Relationship to Person	AGE	SEX	BLOOD	TRIBAL ENROLLMENT		
						Year	County	No.
I.W. 376	1 Richards, William W 72	First Named	69	M	IW			
	2							
	3							
	4							
	5							
	6							
	7							
	8							
	9							
	10							
	11							
	12							
	13							
	14							
	15							
	16							
	17							

ENROLLMENT
OF NOS. 1 HEREON
APPROVED BY THE SECRETARY
OF INTERIOR SEP 12 1903

TRIBAL ENROLLMENT OF PARENTS

	Name of Father	Year	County	Name of Mother	Year	County
1	Jas Richards	Dead	Non Citz	Aurena Richards	Dead	Non Citz
2						
3						
4						
5						
6						
7						
8	See Case No 642, Record of 1896, Dawes					
9	Com – Wm Richards Examine					
	papers and see if same person					
10						
11	No. 1 admitted as an intermarried citizen by					
12	Dawes Commission in 1896· Choctaw Case #642· No appeal					
13	No 1 is the husband of Cornelia Richards on Choctaw card #3886			Date of Application for Enrollment.		
14						
15				Aug 28/99		
16						
17						

Choctaw By Blood Enrollment Cards 1898-1914

RESIDENCE: Atoka	COUNTY.	Choctaw Nation	Choctaw Roll	CARD NO.
POST OFFICE: Atoka, I.T.			*(Not Including Freedmen)*	FIELD NO. **3984**

Dawes' Roll No.	NAME	Relationship to Person First Named	AGE	SEX	BLOOD	TRIBAL ENROLLMENT Year	County	No.
11157	₁ Richards, Clara E ²⁹	First Named	26	F	1/2	1896	Blue	10892
11158	₂ " Harriet C ⁸	Dau	5	"	1/4	1896	"	10893
DEAD	₃ " Ruth	"	3	"	1/4	1896	"	10960
	4							
	5							
	6	ENROLLMENT						
	7	OF NOS. 1 and 2 HEREON						
	8	APPROVED BY THE SECRETARY OF INTERIOR Mar 10 1903						
	9							
	10							
	11	No. 3 hereon dismissed under order of						
	12	the Commission to the Five Civilized						
	13	Tribes of March 31, 1905.						
	14							
	15							
	16							
	17							

TRIBAL ENROLLMENT OF PARENTS

	Name of Father	Year	County	Name of Mother	Year	County
1	Allen Wright	Dead	Atoka	Harriet Wright	Dead	Non Citz
2	W. L. Richards		Non Citz	No1		
3	" " "		" "	No1		
4						
5						
6						
7	As to marriage of parents of No1					
8	see testimony of Julius C. Folsom					
9						
10	No3 died Jany 14, 1901. Proof of death filed Nov 22, 1902.					
11						
12	For child of No1 see NB (Act Mar 3'05) Card #276					
13						
14					Date of Application for Enrollment.	
15					Aug 28/99	
16						
17						

Choctaw By Blood Enrollment Cards 1898-1914

RESIDENCE:	Atoka	COUNTY.								CARD NO.	
POST OFFICE:	Owl, I.T.		**Choctaw Nation**				Choctaw Roll *(Not Including Freedmen)*		FIELD NO.	**3985**	

Dawes' Roll No.	NAME	Relationship to Person First Named	AGE	SEX	BLOOD	TRIBAL ENROLLMENT		
						Year	County	No.
11159	1 Bond, Reed ³⁹		36	M	Full	1896	Atoka	1777
	2							
	3							
	4							
	5	ENROLLMENT						
	6	OF NOS. 1 HEREON APPROVED BY THE SECRETARY						
	7	OF INTERIOR Mar 10 1903						
	8							
	9							
	10							
	11							
	12							
	13							
	14							
	15							
	16							
	17							

TRIBAL ENROLLMENT OF PARENTS

	Name of Father	Year	County	Name of Mother	Year	County
1	Jesse Bond	Dead	Atoka	Sophie Bond	Dead	Atoka
2						
3						
4						
5						
6						
7	Wife and child on Chickasaw					
8	Card No 1533					
9						
10	No1 is now husband of No3 on #3717 Choctaw					
11						
12						
13						
14					Date of Application for Enrollment.	
15					Aug 28/99	
16						
17						

Choctaw By Blood Enrollment Cards 1898-1914

RESIDENCE: Jacks Fork	COUNTY. **Choctaw Nation**	**Choctaw Roll**	CARD No.
POST OFFICE: Stringtown, I.T.		*(Not Including Freedmen)*	FIELD No. **3986**

Dawes' Roll No.		NAME		Relationship to Person First Named	AGE	SEX	BLOOD	TRIBAL ENROLLMENT		
								Year	County	No.
I.W. 752	1	Hewitt Joseph C	⑥⓪	First Named	57	M	IW	1896	Jacks Fork	14662
11160	2	" Edna	39	Wife	36	F	3/8	1896	" "	6095
11161	3	" Mamie	18	Dau	15	"	3/16	1896	" "	6098
11162	4	" Phena	16	"	13	"	3/16	1896	" "	6099
11163	5	" Julia	14	"	11	"	3/16	1896	" "	6100
11164	6	" Minnie	12	"	9	"	3/16	1896	" "	6101
11165	7	" May	12	"	9	"	3/16	1896	" "	6102
11166	8	" Joseph G	10	Son	7	M	3/16	1896	" "	6104
11167	9	" Edna Jr	8	Dau	5	F	3/16	1896	" "	6103
11168	10	" Esther	6	"	1½	"	3/16			
11169	11	" George W	2	Son	2mo	M	3/16			
	12	No2 Evidence of marriage to								
	13	be supplied Recd Oct 7/99								
	14	No10 Affidavit of birth to be supplied – Recd Oct 7/99								
	15	ENROLLMENT			No1 See Decision of						
	16	OF NOS. 2,3,4,5,6,7,8,9,10 and 11 HEREON APPROVED BY THE SECRETARY		Mar 2 '04						
	17	OF INTERIOR Mar 10 1903								

TRIBAL ENROLLMENT OF PARENTS

	Name of Father	Year	County	Name of Mother	Year	County
1	George Hewit[sic]	Dead	Non Citz	Rachel Hewit	Dead	Non Citz
2	William Impson	"	Jacks Fork	Lucy Impson	"	Jack[sic] Fork
3	No1			No2		
4	No1			No2		
5	No1			No2		
6	No1			No2		
7	No1			No2		
8	No1			No2		
9	No1			No2		
10	No1			No2		
11	No.1			No.2		
12	No1 on 1896 roll as Joseph T Hewit – As to					
13	marriage, see his testimony					
14	No3 on 1896 roll as Mimie Hewitt			ENROLLMENT		Date of Application for Enrollment.
15	No4 " 1896 " " Finnie "			OF NOS. ~~3468 1 6666~~ HEREON APPROVED BY THE SECRETARY		Aug 28/99
16	No5 " 1896 " " Uria "			OF INTERIOR May -7 1904		
17	No7 " 1896 " " Mary "					
	No.11 Enrolled June 23, 1900					

Choctaw By Blood Enrollment Cards 1898-1914

RESIDENCE: Blue   COUNTY.

POST OFFICE: Boggy Depot I.T.   **Choctaw Nation**

Choctaw Roll
(Not Including Freedmen)

CARD No.

FIELD No. **3987**

Dawes' Roll No.	NAME		Relationship to Person First Named	AGE	SEX	BLOOD	TRIBAL ENROLLMENT		
							Year	County	No.
11170	₁ Maurer, Mary	54	First Named	51	F	1/4	1896	Blue	8780
11171	₂ Mullen Ada	25	Dau	22	F	1/8	1896	"	8782
11172	₃ Maurer Leonidas M	28	Son	25	M	1/8	1896	"	8781
11173	₄ Mullen, Joseph S Jr	2	Grand son	1mo	M	1/16			
I.W. 1128	₅ " Joseph S	24	Hus of No.2	24	M	I.W.			
	₆								
	₇								
	₈	ENROLLMENT							
	₉	OF NOS. 1,2,3 and 4 HEREON APPROVED BY THE SECRETARY							
	₁₀	OF INTERIOR Mar 10 1903							
	₁₁	ENROLLMENT							
	₁₂	OF NOS. ~~~ 5 ~~~ HEREON APPROVED BY THE SECRETARY							
	₁₃	OF INTERIOR Nov 16 1904							
	₁₄								
	₁₅								
	₁₆								
	₁₇								

TRIBAL ENROLLMENT OF PARENTS

	Name of Father	Year	County	Name of Mother	Year	County
₁	Robert Freeney	Dead	Non Citz	Sallie Freeney	Dead	Blue
₂	C. J. Maurer	"	" "	No1		
₃	" "	"	" "	No1		
₄	Joseph S. Mullen		Intermarried	No2		
₅	Jos P. Mullen		non citizen	Eliz. C. Mullen		non citizen
₆						
₇	No.2 is the wife of Joseph S Mullen on Choctaw card #D.532: March 6, 1901					
₈	No.4 Enrolled March 6th, 1901					
₉	For child of No⁵ 2&5, see NB (Apr 26, 1906) Card No. 61					
₁₀						
₁₁						
₁₂						
₁₃	No.5 transferred from Choctaw card #D-532 Oct 31, 1904: See Decision of Oct. 15, 1904					
₁₄					Date of Application for Enrollment.	
₁₅					Aug 28/99	
₁₆						
₁₇	No.5 P.O. Ardmore I.T. 12/4/99					

Choctaw By Blood Enrollment Cards 1898-1914

RESIDENCE: Blue   COUNTY. **Choctaw Nation**   **Choctaw Roll**   CARD NO.
POST OFFICE: Ego, I.T.   *(Not Including Freedmen)*   FIELD NO. 3988

Dawes' Roll No.	NAME		Relationship to Person	AGE	SEX	BLOOD	TRIBAL ENROLLMENT		
							Year	County	No.
11174	1 Wood, Sarah	56	First Named	53	F	1/4	1896	Blue	13887
11175	2 " Benjamin	16	Son	13	M	1/8	1896	"	13888
11176	3 " Mary	13	Dau	10	F	1/8	1896	"	13889
	4								
	5								
	6								
	7	ENROLLMENT OF NOS. 1,2 and 3 HEREON							
	8	APPROVED BY THE SECRETARY OF INTERIOR MAR 10 1903							
	9								
	10								
	11								
	12								
	13								
	14								
	15								
	16								
	17								

TRIBAL ENROLLMENT OF PARENTS

	Name of Father	Year	County	Name of Mother	Year	County
1	Robert Freeney	Dead	Non Citz	Sallie Freeney	Dead	Blue
2	Richard Wood		" "	No1		
3	" "		" "	No1		
4						
5						
6						
7	For child of No3, see NB (Apr 26-06) Card #419					
8						
9						
10						
11						
12						
13						
14						Date of Application for Enrollment.
15						Aug 28/99
16						
17						

Choctaw By Blood Enrollment Cards 1898-1914

RESIDENCE: Atoka COUNTY.
POST OFFICE: Coalgate, I.T.

Choctaw Nation

Choctaw Roll
(Not Including Freedmen)

CARD No.
FIELD No. 3989

Dawes' Roll No.	NAME	Relationship to Person First Named	AGE	SEX	BLOOD	TRIBAL ENROLLMENT		
						Year	County	No.
11177	₁ LeFlore, Henry C ⁶²	First Named	59	M	1/16	1896	Atoka	8328
11178	₂ " Ruby ⁴	Dau	1	F	1/32			
I.W. 1220	₃ " Josephine ³⁴	Wife	34	F	I.W.	1896	Atoka	14784
	4							
	5							
	6	ENROLLMENT						
	7	OF NOS. 1 and 2 APPROVED BY THE SECRETARY	HEREON					
	8	OF INTERIOR MAR 10 1903						
	9							
	10	ENROLLMENT						
	11	OF NOS. ~~~3~~~ APPROVED BY THE SECRETARY	HEREON					
	12	OF INTERIOR DEC 12 1904						
	₁₃ For child of Nos 1&3 see NB (Ap 26-06) Card #316							
	14							
	₁₅ No.3 admitted by Com. in 1896 Case #1246							
	₁₆ No.3 transferred from Choctaw card #D-384 Nov 26, 1904;							
	₁₇ See decision of Nov 31 1904							

TRIBAL ENROLLMENT OF PARENTS

	Name of Father	Year	County	Name of Mother	Year	County
₁	Brazil LeFlore	Dead	Kiamitia	Narcissa LeFlore	Dead	Kiamitia
₂	No1			Josephine LeFlore		white woman
₃	John Wright	dead	Non Citz	Charity Wright	dead	Non Citz
4						
5						
6						
7						
8						
9	No1 on 1896 roll as Henry LeFlore					
10	Wife, Josephine LeFlore, on Card					
11	No D384					
12						
13	No2 affidavit of birth to be					
14	supplied:- Recd Oct 7/99				Date of Application for Enrollment.	
15	See Case No. 1246 Dawes Com, Record of 1896, in which Josephine, [illegible]				Aug 28/99	
16	Rosa LeFlore appear. The two latter not known to have any					
17	relation to Josephine. License filed with Dawes Com, in 1896.					
	No.3 on 1896 roll as Jessee LeFlore					

No.3 originally listed for enrollment on Choctaw card #D-384 Aug 28/99

Choctaw By Blood Enrollment Cards 1898-1914

RESIDENCE:	Jacks Fork	COUNTY.
POST OFFICE:	Antlers, I.T.	

Choctaw Nation

Choctaw Roll *(Not Including Freedmen)*

CARD No.
FIELD No. 3990

Dawes' Roll No.	NAME		Relationship to Person	AGE	SEX	BLOOD	TRIBAL ENROLLMENT		
							Year	County	No.
11179	1 Wade, Wicy	37	First Named	34	F	1/2	1896	Atoka	13986
11180	2 " Eliza	12	Dau	9	"	1/2	1896	"	13987
11181	3 " Lissie	9	"	6	"	1/2	1896	"	13988
	4								
	5								
	6								
	7	ENROLLMENT							
	8	OF NOS. 1,2 and 3 HEREON APPROVED BY THE SECRETARY							
	9	OF INTERIOR MAR 10 1903							
	10								
	11								
	12								
	13								
	14								
	15								
	16								
	17								

TRIBAL ENROLLMENT OF PARENTS

	Name of Father	Year	County	Name of Mother	Year	County
1	John Tushka	Dead	Chick Roll	Louisa Durant	Dead	Atoka
2	Thomas Wade		Choctaw Roll	No1		
3	" "		" "	No1		
4						
5						
6			No2 on 1896 roll as Nicey Wade			
7						
8			Husband, Thomas Wade, on			
9			Chickasaw Card No 1534			
10						
11						
12						
13						
14					Date of Application for Enrollment.	
15					Aug 28/99	
16						
17						

Choctaw By Blood Enrollment Cards 1898-1914

Choctaw Nation

Choctaw Roll
(Not Including Freedmen)

CARD NO.
FIELD NO. 3991

Dawes' Roll No.	NAME	Relationship to Person First Named	AGE	SEX	BLOOD	TRIBAL ENROLLMENT		
						Year	County	No.
DEAD. 1	Moran, Reuben T		51	M	1/16	1896	Atoka	8825
2								
3								
4								
5								
6								
7								
8								
9								
10								
11								
12								
13								
14								
15								
16								
17								

No. 1 HEREON DISMISSED UNDER
ORDER OF THE COMMISSION TO THE FIVE
CIVILIZED TRIBES OF MARCH 31, 1905.

CANCELLED

Applicant cannot be identified on Choctaw-Chickasaw agreement Sept 25, 1902

TRIBAL ENROLLMENT OF PARENTS

	Name of Father	Year	County	Name of Mother	Year	County
1	C. H. Moran	Dead	Non Citz	Eliz. Moran		Blue
2						
3						
4						
5						
6		On 1896 roll as Reuben Moran				
7						
8		No 1 died June 26, 1920 — proof of death filed Nov 22, 1902				
9						
10						
11						
12						
13						
14					Date of Application	
15					for Enrollment.	
16					Aug 28/99	
17						

Choctaw By Blood Enrollment Cards 1898-1914

RESIDENCE:	Atoka	COUNTY.								
POST OFFICE:	Lehigh, I.T.									

Choctaw Nation   **Choctaw Roll** *(Not Including Freedmen)*   CARD NO. FIELD NO. **3992**

Dawes' Roll No.	NAME	Relationship to Person	AGE	SEX	BLOOD	TRIBAL ENROLLMENT		
						Year	County	No.
11182	1 Plummer, Charles W [35]	First Named	32	M	1/16	1896	Atoka	10540
I.W.377	2 " Sallie L [33]	Wife	31	F	IW			
11183	3 " Kittie E [5]	Dau	2	"	1/32			
11184	4 " Mary Christina [2]	Dau	4m	F	1/32			
	5							
	6							
	7							
	8	ENROLLMENT OF NOS. 1, 3 and 4 HEREON APPROVED BY THE SECRETARY OF INTERIOR MAR 10 1903						
	9							
	10							
	11	ENROLLMENT OF NOS. 2 HEREON APPROVED BY THE SECRETARY OF INTERIOR SEP 12 1903						
	12							
	13							
	14							
	15							
	16							
	17							

TRIBAL ENROLLMENT OF PARENTS

	Name of Father	Year	County	Name of Mother	Year	County
1	J. R. Plummer		Atoka	Mary S Plummer		Non Citz
2	W.J.B. Lloyd		Non Citz	Mattie Lloyd		" "
3	No1			No2		
4	No1			No2		
5						
6						
7			No1 on 1896 roll as Chas W. Plummer			
8			Was admitted by Act of Choctaw Council			
9			No39 – Approved Nov 8/95			
10			No2 Admitted by Dawes Com Case No 548			
11			No.4 Enrolled January 23, 1901			
12						
13						
14					#1 to 3	
15					Date of Application for Enrollment.	Aug 28/99
16						
17						

Choctaw By Blood Enrollment Cards 1898-1914

RESIDENCE: **Jacks Fork** COUNTY.
POST OFFICE: **Stringtown, IT**

Choctaw Nation

Choctaw Roll
(Not Including Freedmen)

CARD NO.
FIELD NO. **3993**

Dawes' Roll No.	NAME	Relationship to Person First Named	AGE	SEX	BLOOD	TRIBAL ENROLLMENT		
						Year	County	No.
DEAD	1 Bond, Sallie ~~DEAD~~		20	F	Full	1896	Jacks Fork	14086
11185	2 " Davis ¹	Son	7mo	M	3/4			
	3							
	4							
	5							
	6							
	7	ENROLLMENT OF NOS. 2 HEREON						
	8	APPROVED BY THE SECRETARY OF INTERIOR MAR 10 1903						
	9							
	10	No. 1 HEREON DISMISSED UNDER						
	11	ORDER OF THE COMMISSION TO THE FIVE CIVILIZED TRIBES OF MARCH 31, 1905.						
	12							
	13							
	14							
	15							
	16							
	17							

TRIBAL ENROLLMENT OF PARENTS

Name of Father	Year	County	Name of Mother	Year	County
1 Lewis Carnes	Dead	Jacks Fork	Levinsey Carnes	Dead	Jacks Fork
2 Calvin Bond	1896	Chickasaw roll Jacks Fork Co	No 1		
3					
4					
5					
6					
7 On 1896 roll as Sallie Williams					
8 No.1 is the wife of Calvin Bond on Chickasaw card #1047					
9 No.1 died Nov. 2, 1901: Proof of death filed Feby 13, 1902					
10 No.2 born July 5, 1901: Enrolled Feby 13, 1902					
11					
12					
13					
14			#1		
15			Date of Application for Enrollment	Aug 28/99	
16					
17					

Choctaw By Blood Enrollment Cards 1898-1914

RESIDENCE: Atoka   COUNTY. **Choctaw Nation**   **Choctaw Roll** *(Not Including Freedmen)*   CARD NO. FIELD NO. **3994**

POST OFFICE: Owl, I.T.

Dawes' Roll No.	NAME		Relationship to Person First Named	AGE	SEX	BLOOD	TRIBAL ENROLLMENT		
							Year	County	No.
11186	1 Frazier, Lymon	37	First Named	34	M	Full	1896	Atoka	4461
11187	2 " Caroline	43	Wife	40	F	"	1896	"	1778
11188	3 Harris, Jimson	18	S.Son	15	M	"	1896	"	6087
11189	4 " Martha	15	S.Dau	12	F	"	1896	"	6088
	5								
	6								
	7								
	8								
	9								
	10								
	11								
	12								
	13								
	14								
	15								
	16								
	17								

ENROLLMENT OF NOS. 1,2,3 and 4 HEREON APPROVED BY THE SECRETARY OF INTERIOR Mar 10 1903

TRIBAL ENROLLMENT OF PARENTS

	Name of Father	Year	County	Name of Mother	Year	County
1	Saminta Frazier	Dead	Jacks Fork	Waley Frazier	Dead	Jacks Fork
2	Alex McGee	"	Atoka	Elsie McGee	"	Atoka
3	Tulsom Harris	"	Tobucksy	No2		
4	" "	"	"	No2		
5						
6						
7						
8			No1 on 1896 roll as Limon Frazier			
9			No2 " 1896 " " Caroline Bond			
10			No3 " 1896 " " Jimmy Harris			
11						
12						
13						
14						
15				Date of Application for Enrollment	Aug 28/99	
16						
17						

Choctaw By Blood Enrollment Cards 1898-1914

RESIDENCE: Atoka COUNTY.
POST OFFICE: Stringtown, I.T.

Choctaw Nation
(Not Including Freedmen)

Choctaw .....

3995

Dawes' Roll No.	NAME	Relationship to Person First Named	AGE	SEX	BLOOD	TRIBAL ENROLLMENT		
						Year	County	No.
11190	₁ Cochran, Elizabeth ⁵¹		48	F	1/8	1896	Atoka	2941
11191	₂ Green, Charlie ¹⁶	Son	13	M	1/16	1896	"	2942
11192	₃ " Rosa B ¹²	Dau	9	F	1/16	1896	"	4977
	4							
	5							
	6							
	7	ENROLLMENT						
	8	OF NOS. 1,2 and 3 HEREON APPROVED BY THE SECRETARY						
	9	OF INTERIOR MAR 10 1903						
	10							
	11							
	12							
	13							
	14							
	15							
	16							
	17							

TRIBAL ENROLLMENT OF PARENTS

	Name of Father	Year	County	Name of Mother	Year	County
1	A. L. Pulcher	Dead	Non Citz	Phoebe Pulcher	Dead	Red River
2	John Green	"	" "	No 1		
3	" "	"	" "	No 1		
4						
5						
6						
7	No 1 on 1896 roll as Elizabeth Cocheron					
8	No 2 " 1896 " " Green Charley					
9	No 3 " 1896 " " Rena Belle Green					
10						
11						
12						
13						
14						
15				Date of Application for Enrollment.	Aug 28/99	
16						
17	No 3 P.O. Norman Okla 11/5/06					

95

Choctaw By Blood Enrollment Cards 1898-1914

RESIDENCE: Jacks Fork   COUNTY. **Choctaw Nation**   **Choctaw Roll**   CARD No.
POST OFFICE: Stringtown, I.T.   (Not Including Freedmen)   FIELD No. 3996

Dawes' Roll No.	NAME		Relationship to Person First Named	AGE	SEX	BLOOD	TRIBAL ENROLLMENT		
							Year	County	No.
I.W.147	1 Latimer, Byron H	32	First Named	29	M	IW			
11193	2 " Lula	21	Wife	18	F	1/4	1896	Jacks Fork	6097
11194	3 " Joseph B	4	Son	6mo	M	1/8			
11195	4 " Lulu Mattie	2	Dau	1mo	F	1/8			
	5								
	6								
	7								
	8	ENROLLMENT OF NOS. 2,3 and 4 HEREON							
	9	APPROVED BY THE SECRETARY							
	10	OF INTERIOR MAR 10 1903							
	11	ENROLLMENT OF NOS. 1 HEREON							
	12	APPROVED BY THE SECRETARY							
	13	OF INTERIOR JUN 13 1903							
	14								
	15								
	16								
	17								

TRIBAL ENROLLMENT OF PARENTS

	Name of Father	Year	County	Name of Mother	Year	County
1	A. H. Latimer		Non Citz	Mattie Latimer	Dead	Non Citz
2	J. C. Hewitt		" "	Edna Hewitt		Jacks Fork
3	No1			No2		
4	No1			No2		
5						
6						
7	No2 on 1896 roll as Lola Hewitt					
8	No3 Affidavit of birth to be					
9	supplied Recd Oct 7/99					
10	Evidence of marriage to be supplied:- Recd Oct 7/99					
11	See testimony of No1, as to marriage					
12	No.4 Enrolled January 3, 1901					
13						
14						
15				Date of Application for Enrollment.		Aug 28/99
16						
17						

Choctaw By Blood Enrollment Cards 1898-1914

RESIDENCE: Atoka COUNTY. **Choctaw Nation** | Choctaw Roll (Not Including Freedmen) | CARD NO.
POST OFFICE: Coalgate, I.T. | | FIELD NO. 3997

Dawes' Roll No.	NAME	Relationship to Person First Named	AGE	SEX	BLOOD	TRIBAL ENROLLMENT		
						Year	County	No.
I.W. 148	1 Ferrante, Sante 41		29	M	IW			
11196	2 " Isabinda 26	Wife	23	F	Full	1896	Atoka	13967
11197	3 " Otha 4	Son	6mo	M	1/2			
11198	4 " John 2	Son	3mo	M	1/2			
	5							
	6							
	7							
	8	ENROLLMENT						
	9	OF NOS. 2,3 and 4 HEREON APPROVED BY THE SECRETARY						
	10	OF INTERIOR MAR 10 1903						
	11	ENROLLMENT OF NOS. 1 HEREON						
	12	APPROVED BY THE SECRETARY						
	13	OF INTERIOR JUN 13 1903						
	14							
	15							
	16							
	17							

TRIBAL ENROLLMENT OF PARENTS

	Name of Father	Year	County	Name of Mother	Year	County
1	John Ferrante	Dead	Non Citz	Carolina Ferrante		Non Citz
2	Almon Wood		Atoka		Dead	Atoka
3	No1			No2		
4	No1			No2		
5						
6						
7			No2 On 1896 roll as Isabinda Woods			
8			No3 Affidavit of birth to be			
9			supplied:- Filed Nov 2/99			
10			No.4 Enrolled May 1, 1901			
11			For child of Nos 1&2 see NB (Apr 26-06) Card #323			
12			" " " " " " " Mar 3 '05) Card #277			
13						
14						
15				Date of Application for Enrollment.	Aug 28/99	
16	So McAlester I.T.					
17	P.O. Celestine IT 5/15/05					

97

Choctaw By Blood Enrollment Cards 1898-1914

RESIDENCE:	Atoka	COUNTY.	Choctaw Nation	Choctaw Roll	CARD NO.
POST OFFICE:	Owl, I.T.			(Not Including Freedmen)	FIELD NO. **3998**

Dawes' Roll No.	NAME	Relationship to Person First Named	AGE	SEX	BLOOD	TRIBAL ENROLLMENT Year	County	No.
11199	1 McGee, Thomas ³⁷	First Named	34	M	Full	1896	Gaines	9153
	2							
	3							
	4							
	5	ENROLLMENT OF NOS. 1 HEREON						
	6	APPROVED BY THE SECRETARY OF INTERIOR Mar 10 1903						
	7							
	8							
	9							
	10							
	11							
	12							
	13							
	14							
	15							
	16							
	17							

TRIBAL ENROLLMENT OF PARENTS

Name of Father	Year	County	Name of Mother	Year	County
1 Alex McGee	Dead	Atoka	Elsie McGee	Dead	Atoka
2					
3					
4					
5					
6					
7					
8					
9					
10					
11					
12					
13					
14					
15			Date of Application for Enrollment.	Aug 28/99	
16					
17					

Choctaw By Blood Enrollment Cards 1898-1914

RESIDENCE: Atoka COUNTY.
POST OFFICE: Atoka, I.T.

Choctaw Nation

Choctaw Roll
(Not Including Freedmen)

CARD NO.
FIELD NO. **3999**

Dawes' Roll No.	NAME	Relationship to Person First Named	AGE	SEX	BLOOD	TRIBAL ENROLLMENT Year	County	No.
11200	1 Frazier, Nicholas 36		33	M	Full	1896	Atoka	4459
11201	2 " Lina 49	Wife	46	F	"	1896	"	4460
DEAD	3 McGee, Sidney	Ward	17	M	"	1896	"	9430
	4							
	5							
	6							
	7	ENROLLMENT OF NOS. 1 and 2 HEREON						
	8	APPROVED BY THE SECRETARY						
	9	OF INTERIOR Mar 10 1903						
	10	No. 3 hereon dismissed under order of						
	11	the Commission to the Five Civilized						
	12	Tribes of March 31, 1905.						
	13							
	14							
	15							
	16							
	17							

TRIBAL ENROLLMENT OF PARENTS

	Name of Father	Year	County	Name of Mother	Year	County
1	Sam Frazier	Dead	Cedar	Kizzie Frazier	Dead	Jacks Fork
2	Jim Jerry	"	Atoka	Sally Jerry	"	Atoka
3	Chas McGee	"	Jackson	Mollie McGee	"	"
4						
5						
6						
7	No3 Died June 1902: proof of death filed Nov. 22, 1902					
8						
9						
10						
11						
12						
13						
14						Date of Application for Enrollment
15						Aug 28/99
16						
17	Lehigh I.T. 11/27/02					

99

Choctaw By Blood Enrollment Cards 1898-1914

RESIDENCE:	Atoka	COUNTY.					CARD NO.
POST OFFICE:	Ego, I.T.						FIELD NO. 4000

Choctaw Nation — Choctaw Roll (Not Including Freedmen)

Dawes' Roll No.	NAME		Relationship to Person First Named	AGE	SEX	BLOOD	TRIBAL ENROLLMENT Year	County	No.
11202	1 Freeny, Reuben	48	First Named	45	M	1/8	1896	Atoka	4464
I.W. 1421	2 " Mattie	41	Wife	35	F	IW	1896	"	14542
11203	3 " Robert	18	Son	15	M	1/16	1896	"	4465
11204	4 " Mary	16	Dau	13	F	1/16	1896	"	4468
11205	5 " Reuben Jr	14	Son	11	M	1/16	1896	"	4466
11206	6 " Belle	12	Dau	9	F	1/16	1896	"	4469
11207	7 " Pearl	10	"	7	"	1/16	1896	"	4470
11208	8 " Chock	8	"	5	"	1/16	1896	"	4471
11209	9 " Chick	7	"	4	"	1/16	1896	"	4472
11210	10 " Leota	4	"	1	"	1/16		ENROLLMENT	
11211	11 " Tokowa	2	Dau	2mo	"	1/16	OF NOS. ~~~ 2 ~~~~ HEREON APPROVED BY THE SECRETARY		
11212	12 " Indi Olia	1	Dau	5mo	F	1/16	OF INTERIOR Jun 12 1905		
	13	Surnames of all but No2							
	14	appear on 1896 roll as Freeney							
	15	No.12 Born Feb 1st 1902: Enrolled June 24th 1902							
	16	No.2 denied in 1896 by Dawes							
	17	Commission: Choctaw Case #468: No appeal							
		No2 1885 Blue No. 1237							

TRIBAL ENROLLMENT OF PARENTS

	Name of Father	Year	County	Name of Mother	Year	County	
1	Robert Freeny	Dead	Non Citz	Sallie Freeny	Dead	Blue	
2	John Laxton	"	" "	Dot Laxton	"	Non Citz	
3	No1	No2 restored to roll by		No2			
4	No1	Departmental authority		No2			
5	No1	of January 19,1909 (File 5-51)		No2		For child of No4 see NB (Apr 26'06) Card No 1303
6	No1			No2			For child of No1 see NB (Mar 8'05) Card No 578
7	No1	ENROLLMENT		No2			
8	No1	OF NOS. 1,3,4,5,6,7,8,9,10,11 and 12 HEREON APPROVED BY THE SECRETARY		No2			
9	No1	OF INTERIOR Mar 10 1903		No2			
10	No1			No2			
11	No1			No2			
12	No.1			No.2			
13	No2 Evidence of marriage to be			Dec 8/99 No2- See Dawes			
14	supplied: Filed Oct 26/99			Commission Record 1896		Date of Application for Enrollment
15	No2 = On 1896 roll as Martha C Freeny			Case 468 No11 enrolled 6/5/1900		Aug 28/99
16	No10-Affidavit of birth to be			For child of No.6 see NB (Apr 26-06) No 528		
17	supplied: Recd Dec 18/99 Irregular & returned for correction Filed Jany 17/04						

P.O. Fitzhugh IT 2/20/05 } Enrollment of No.2 cancelled by order of Department March 4 1907

Choctaw By Blood Enrollment Cards 1898-1914

RESIDENCE:	Atoka	COUNTY.	**Choctaw Nation**				**Choctaw Roll**	CARD No.	
POST OFFICE:	Owl, I.T.						*(Not Including Freedmen)*	FIELD No. **4001**	

Dawes' Roll No.	NAME		Relationship to Person First Named	AGE	SEX	BLOOD	TRIBAL ENROLLMENT		
							Year	County	No.
11213	1 Webster, Julius	30		27	M	Full	1896	Atoka	13920
11214	2 " Susanna	23	Wife	20	F	"	1896	Jacks Fork	7662
11215	3 " Ella	9	Dau	6	F	"	1896	Atoka	13922
DEAD	4 " Gracie		Dau	3mo	F	"			
	5								
	6								
	7								
	8	ENROLLMENT OF NOS. 1,2 and 3 HEREON							
	9	APPROVED BY THE SECRETARY OF INTERIOR Mar 10 1903							
	10								
	11	No. 4 hereon dismissed under order of							
	12	the Commission to the Five Civilized							
	13	Tribes of March 31, 1905.							
	14								
	15								
	16								
	17								

TRIBAL ENROLLMENT OF PARENTS

	Name of Father	Year	County	Name of Mother	Year	County
1	Francis Webster	Dead	Atoka	Eliz Webster	Dead	Atoka
2	Freeman Welch	"	Jacks Fork	Frances Honie		"
3	No1			Mattie Webster	Dead	"
4	No.1			No.2		
5						
6						
7	No2 on 1896 roll as Susianna Katiotubbi					
8						
9						
10	No4 died Aug 29, 1900: proof of death filed Nov. 25, 1902					
11						
12						
13						#1 to 3
14			No.4 Enrolled May 24, 1900.			Date of Application for Enrollment.
15						Aug 28/99
16						
17						

Choctaw By Blood Enrollment Cards 1898-1914

RESIDENCE: Atoka COUNTY. **Choctaw Nation** Choctaw Roll CARD NO.
POST OFFICE: Coalgate, I.T. *(Not Including Freedmen)* FIELD NO. **4002**

Dawes' Roll No.	NAME		Relationship to Person First Named	AGE	SEX	BLOOD	TRIBAL ENROLLMENT		
							Year	County	No.
11216	1 Gipson John	31	First Named	28	M	Full	1896	Atoka	4961
DEAD	2 " Liddie		Wife	32	F	"	1896	"	4962
11217	3 Wade Ransom	15	S.Son	12	M	"	1896	Tobucksy	612
	4								
	5								
	6								
	7	ENROLLMENT							
	8	OF NOS. 1 and 3 HEREON APPROVED BY THE SECRETARY							
	9	OF INTERIOR Mar 10 1903							
	10	No.2 hereon dismissed under order of							
	11	the Commission to the Five Civilized							
	12	Tribes of March 31, 1905.							
	13								
	14								
	15								
	16								
	17								

TRIBAL ENROLLMENT OF PARENTS

	Name of Father	Year	County	Name of Mother	Year	County
1	John Gipson	Dead	Jacks Fork	Mary Gipson	"	Jacks Fork
2	Martin Dick		Atoka	Mary Dick		Tobucksy
3	Bible Wade	Dead	Tobucksy	No2		
4						
5						
6						
7						
8						
9						
10	No.3 on 1893 Pay Roll, Page 71 No 612, Tobucksy					
11	Co., as Ransom Nale, also on 1896 roll					
12	Page 367 No 14001 as Samson Wade, Atoka Co.					
13	No2 died Nov 15, 1900, proof of death filed Nov 22, 1902					
14						
15					Date of Application for Enrollment	Aug 28/99
16						
17	No1 P.O Lehigh I.T. 11/19/02					

Choctaw By Blood Enrollment Cards 1898-1914

RESIDENCE: Atoka COUNTY.								
POST OFFICE: Coalgate, I.T.	**Choctaw Nation**			Choctaw Roll (Not Including Freedmen)	CARD NO. FIELD NO. **4003**			

Dawes' Roll No.	NAME	Relationship to Person First Named	AGE	SEX	BLOOD	TRIBAL ENROLLMENT		
						Year	County	No.
11218	1 James, Edward 30		27	M	Full	1896	Atoka	7318
11219	2 Lucy DIED PRIOR TO SEPTEMBER 25 2690 2	Wife	23	F	"	1896	Sans Bois	27
	3							
	4							
	5							
	6 ENROLLMENT							
	7 OF NOS. 1 and 2 HEREON APPROVED BY THE SECRETARY							
	8 OF INTERIOR Mar 10 1903							
	9							
	10							
	11							
	12							
	13							
	14							
	15							
	16							
	17							

TRIBAL ENROLLMENT OF PARENTS

	Name of Father	Year	County	Name of Mother	Year	County
1	Alex James	Dead	Atoka	E-ma-to-na	Dead	Atoka
2	Jas. Adams		Sans Bois	Liza Adams		Sans Bois
3						
4						
5						
6	No2 on 1896 roll as Lucy Adams					
7	No.2 also on 1896 roll, page 180, #7319 as Alonzo James, June 7,1900					
8	No.2 died Dec – 1901: Enrollment cancelled by Department July 8, 1904					
9						
10						
11						
12						
13						
14					Date of Application for Enrollment.	
15					Aug 28/99	
16						
17						

Choctaw By Blood Enrollment Cards 1898-1914

RESIDENCE:	Blue	COUNTY.	**Choctaw Nation**			Choctaw Roll	CARD NO.	
POST OFFICE:	Ego, I.T.					*(Not Including Freedmen)*	FIELD NO. 4004	

Dawes' Roll No.	NAME		Relationship to Person	AGE	SEX	BLOOD	TRIBAL ENROLLMENT		
							Year	County	No.
I.W. 1129	1 Hattox, John W	31	First Named	28	M	IW			
11220	2 " Stella	20	Wife	17	F	1/16	1896	Atoka	4467
11221	3 " Azile	2	Dau	3mo	F	1/32			
11222	4 " Francis Cleo	1	Dau	1mo	F	1/32			
	5								
	6								
	7								
	8	ENROLLMENT							
	9	OF NOS. 2,3 and 4 HEREON APPROVED BY THE SECRETARY							
	10	OF INTERIOR MAR 10 1903							
	11								
	12	ENROLLMENT							
	13	OF NOS. 1 HEREON APPROVED BY THE SECRETARY							
	14	OF INTERIOR NOV 16 1904							
	15								
	16								
	17								

TRIBAL ENROLLMENT OF PARENTS

	Name of Father	Year	County	Name of Mother	Year	County
1	Philip Hattox		Non Citz	Frances C. Hattox		Non Citz
2	Reuben Freeny		Atoka	Mattie Freeny		Intermarried
3	No.1			No.2		
4	No 1			No 2		
5						
6						
7	No2- As to marriage of parents, see					
8	enrollment of father, Reuben Freeny					
9	No2 on 1896 roll as Stella Freeney					
10	No.3 Enrolled November 28th, 1900					
	No.4 Born June 24th 1902; Enrolled July 14th 1902					
11	Affidavit Nos 1 and 2 as to residence on date of their marriage filed May 6, 1903					
12						
13	For child of Nos 1&2 see NB (Apr 26-06) Card #504				#1&2	
14					Date of Application for Enrollment	
15					Aug 28/99	
16						
17	P.O. Fitzhugh I.T.					

7/14/02

Choctaw By Blood Enrollment Cards 1898-1914

RESIDENCE:	Atoka	COUNTY.			
POST OFFICE:	Owl, I.T.				

Choctaw Nation

Choctaw Roll (Not Including Freedmen)

CARD NO.

FIELD NO. **4005**

Dawes' Roll No.	NAME	Relationship to Person First Named	AGE	SEX	BLOOD	TRIBAL ENROLLMENT		
						Year	County	No.
11223	1 Harris, Elias 21		18	M	Full	1896	Atoka	6086
	2							
	3							
	4							
	5							
	6							
	7							
	8							
	9							
	10							
	11							
	12							
	13							
	14							
	15							
	16							
	17							

ENROLLMENT
OF NOS. 1 HEREON
APPROVED BY THE SECRETARY
OF INTERIOR Mar 10 1903

TRIBAL ENROLLMENT OF PARENTS

	Name of Father	Year	County	Name of Mother	Year	County
1	Tulsom Harris	Dead	Tobucksy	Caroline Harris		Atoka
2						
3						
4						
5			on 1896 roll as Ely Harris			
6						
7						
8						
9						
10						
11						
12						
13						
14						
15				Date of Application for Enrollment.	Aug 28/99	
16						
17						

PO Blanco IT 6/13/05

Choctaw By Blood Enrollment Cards 1898-1914

RESIDENCE: Chickasaw Nation COUNTY.   **Choctaw Nation**   **Choctaw Roll** (Not Including Freedmen)   CARD NO.

POST OFFICE: Hart, I.T.   FIELD NO. **4006**

Dawes' Roll No.	NAME	Relationship to Person First Named	AGE	SEX	BLOOD	Year	County	No.
DEAD.	1 Lowery, William J		50	M	1/16	1896	Atoka	8303
I.W. 980	2 Pollock, Eliza J ⁴²	Wife	39	F	IW	1896	"	14785
11224	3 Lowery, Benjamin H ²²	Son	19	M	1/32	1896	"	8305
11225	4 " Franklin ¹⁸	"	15	"	1/32	1896	"	8306
11226	5 " Ida M ¹³	Dau	10	F	1/32	1896	"	8307
11227	6 " Myrtle ¹¹	"	8	"	1/32	1896	"	8308
11228	7 " Ola ⁹	"	6	"	1/32	1896	"	8309
	8 No 1 HEREON DISMISSED UNDER							
	9 ORDER OF THE COMMISSION TO THE FIVE							
	10 CIVILIZED TRIBES OF MARCH 31, 1905.							
	11 ENROLLMENT							
	12 OF NOS. 3,4,5,6 and 7 HEREON APPROVED BY THE SECRETARY							
	13 OF INTERIOR MAR 10 1903							
	14 For child of No4 see NB (Apr 26-06) Card #913							
	15 " " " " 2 " " " " " #1102							
	16							
	17 See Petition No W 26							

TRIBAL ENROLLMENT OF PARENTS

	Name of Father	Year	County	Name of Mother	Year	County
1	B. H. Lowery	Dead	Non Citz	Lucy Lowery	Dead	Sans Bois
2	Jas Turnbull	"	" "	Mary Turnbull		Non Citz
3	No1			No2		
4	No1			No2		
5	No1			No2		
6	No1			No2		
7	No1			No2		
8	No1 on 1896 roll as W. J. Lowery					
9	No2 " 1896 " " Eliza J Laurery					
10	No3 " 1896 " " Bennie Lowery					
11	As to marriage of No1-2, see testimony of Emiline Krebbs			ENROLLMENT OF NOS. 2 ~ HEREON APPROVED BY THE SECRETARY		
12	No.2 admitted by Dawes Commission in 1896, as			OF INTERIOR SEP 22 1904		
13	an intermarried citizen, Choctaw case #853; no appeal					
14	Nº2 is now the wife of T. J. Pollock, Noncitizen; Evidence of marriage filed Nov. 1, 1902					
15	Nº1 Died Dec. 29, 1899: Proof of death filed Nov. 1, 1902			Date of Application for Enrollment. Aug 28/99		
16						
17	No.2- Speed I.T. 6/2/08					

Choctaw By Blood Enrollment Cards 1898-1914

RESIDENCE:	Atoka	COUNTY.		
POST OFFICE:	Atoka, I.T.			

Choctaw Nation

Choctaw Roll CARD NO.
(Not Including Freedmen) FIELD NO. 4007

Dawes' Roll No.	NAME	Relationship to Person First Named	AGE	SEX	BLOOD	TRIBAL ENROLLMENT		
						Year	County	No.
11229	1 Jones, Cornelius A 52		49	M	Full	1896	Atoka	7290
	2							
	3							
	4	ENROLLMENT						
	5	OF NOS. 1 HEREON APPROVED BY THE SECRETARY						
	6	OF INTERIOR MAR 10 1903						
	7							
	8							
	9							
	10							
	11							
	12							
	13							
	14							
	15							
	16							
	17							

TRIBAL ENROLLMENT OF PARENTS

	Name of Father	Year	County	Name of Mother	Year	County
1	Sampson Jones	Dead	Blue	Hul-ba-hoke	Dead	Blue
2						
3						
4						
5						
6						
7						
8						
9						
10						
11						
12						
13						
14					Date of Application for Enrollment	
15					Aug 28/99	
16						
17						

Choctaw By Blood Enrollment Cards 1898-1914

RESIDENCE: **Blue**   COUNTY. **Choctaw Nation**   **Choctaw Roll** CARD NO.

POST OFFICE: **Boggy Depot, I.T.**   *(Not Including Freedmen)*   FIELD NO. **4008**

Dawes' Roll No.		NAME		Relationship to Person First Named	AGE	SEX	BLOOD	TRIBAL ENROLLMENT Year	County	No.
14387	1	Krebbs, John W	25	First Named	22	M	1/8			
14388	2	" Benjamin	19	Bro	16	"	1/8			
14389	3	" May	15	Sister	12	F	1/8			
14390	4	" John Odus	1	Son	5mo	M	1/16			
14391	5	" John	1	Nephew	13mo	M	1/16			
15844	6	" Hubert		Son	1	M	1/16			
I.W. 1477	7	" Provie Lee	18	Wife	18	F	I.W.			
	8									
	9	ENROLLMENT								
	10	OF NOS. 1,2,3,4 and 5 HEREON APPROVED BY THE SECRETARY OF INTERIOR Apr 11 1903								
	11	ENROLLMENT								
	12	OF NOS. ~~~ 6 ~~~ HEREON APPROVED BY THE SECRETARY								
	13	OF INTERIOR Jun 12 1905			For child of No2 see NB (Apr 26-06) Card #416						
	14				No.7 placed on this card May 15, 1905 in						
	15				accordance with order of Commission holding						
	16	For child of No2 see NB (Mar 3'05) Card #279			application was made in time under act 7/1,1902						
	17	" " " Nos 1&7 " " " " #1152									

ENROLLMENT OF NOS. seven HEREON APPROVED BY THE SECRETARY OF INTERIOR Aug 22 1905

TRIBAL ENROLLMENT OF PARENTS

	Name of Father	Year	County	Name of Mother	Year	County
1	J. W. Krebbs	Dead	Choctaw	Eliza Krebbs	Dead	Non Citz
2	" " "	"	"	" "	"	" " "
3	" " "	"	"	" "	"	" " "
4	No.1			Provi Lee Krebbs		" "
5	Nº2			Susie Bell Krebbs		" "
6	No 1			Provi Lee Krebbs		non citizen
7						
8						
9	Admitted by Dawes Com, Case No 1202 No appeal					
10	No1 was admitted as John W. Krebbs Jr.					
11	No2 " " " Bennie "					
12	No.1 is now the husband of Provi Lee Kribbs[sic] a non citizen. Evidence of marriage filed Dec. 13, 1901					
13	No.4 born July 15, 1901: Enrolled Dec. 13, 1901				#1 to 4	
14	Nº2 is now the husband of Susie Bell Krebbs a noncitizen			Date of Application for Enrollment.		
15	Evidence of marriage filed Aug. 21, 1902; Now on Choctaw card #5990			Aug 28/99		
16	Nº5 Born July 20, 1901: enrolled Aug 21, 1902					
17	No6 was born Sept. 15, 1902: Application received April 25, 1905					
	P.O. Folsom I.T. 4/18/03					

For child of No.3 see NB (March 3, 1905) #1151

Choctaw By Blood Enrollment Cards 1898-1914

RESIDENCE: Chickasaw Nation ~~COUNTY~~.
POST OFFICE: Hart, I.T.

Choctaw Nation

Choctaw Roll
(Not Including Freedmen)

CARD NO.
FIELD NO. 4009

Dawes' Roll No.	NAME	Relationship to Person First Named	AGE	SEX	BLOOD	TRIBAL ENROLLMENT		
						Year	County	No.
11230	1 Chocklen Mary ²⁴	First Named	21	F	1/32	1896	Tobucksy	11300
11231	2 Shockley, Lemuel G ³	Son	4mo	M	1/64			
	3							
	4							
	5							
	6	ENROLLMENT						
	7	OF NOS. 1 and 2 HEREON APPROVED BY THE SECRETARY						
	8	OF INTERIOR MAR 10 1903						
	9							
	10							
	11							
	12							
	13							
	14							
	15							
	16							
	17							

TRIBAL ENROLLMENT OF PARENTS

	Name of Father	Year	County	Name of Mother	Year	County
1	W. G. Lowery		Tobucksy	Mary A Lowery		Intermarried
2	Jesse Schockley[sic]		Non Citz	No1		
3						
4						
5						
6						
7						
8		As to marriage of parents of No1, see				
9		enrollment of father, W. G. Lowery				
10						
11						
12		No2 Affidavit of birth to be				
13		supplied.- Received and filed March 15th, 1900				
14		The father on No.2 seems to have been Andrew Schockley; see letter attached			Date of Application for Enrollment.	
15		For child of No2[sic] see NB (Apr 26'06) #899 M[sic]			Aug 28/99	
16						
17						

Choctaw By Blood Enrollment Cards 1898-1914

Dawes' Roll No.	NAME		Relationship to Person	AGE	SEX	BLOOD	TRIBAL ENROLLMENT		
							Year	County	No.
11232	1 Moran, John W	31	First Named	28	M	1/16	1896	Jackson	8740
I.W.378	2 " Emma	24	Wife	21	F	IW	1896	"	14827
11233	3 " Thomas	6	Son	3	M	1/32	1896	"	8741
DEAD	4 " Willie M		Dau	1½	F	1/32			
11234	5 " Anna Laura	1	Dau	2mo	F				
	6								
	7								
	8	ENROLLMENT OF NOS. 1,3 and 5 HEREON							
	9	APPROVED BY THE SECRETARY OF INTERIOR MAR 10 1903							
	10	ENROLLMENT							
	11	OF NOS. 2 HEREON							
	12	APPROVED BY THE SECRETARY OF INTERIOR SEP 12 1903							
	13								
	14	No. 4 HEREON DISMISSED UNDER ORDER OF THE COMMISSION TO THE FIVE							
	15	CIVILIZED TRIBES OF MARCH 31, 1905.							
	16	No4 died April 21, 1902; proof of death filed Dec 2, 1902							
	17								

TRIBAL ENROLLMENT OF PARENTS

Name of Father	Year	County	Name of Mother	Year	County
1 Marmaduke Moran		Chick Dist	Catherine Moran	Dead	Non Citz
2 John Ray		Non Citz	Tennessee Ray	"	" "
3 No1			No2		
4 No1			No2		
5 No1			No2		
6 No1- Admitted by Act of Choctaw Council,					
7 Approved Nov 3/79					
8					
9 No2- Admitted by Dawes Com					
10 Case No 365					
11					
12 No4- Affidavit of birth to be					
13 supplied:- Filed Oct 26/99				#1 to
14 No5 born Oct 24 1901: Enrolled Dec. 4, 1901				Date of Applic for Enrollm
15 For child of Nos 1&2 see NB (Apr 26'06) Card #1213				Aug 28
16 " " " " " " (Mar 3'05) " #1237				
17 P.O. Valliant, I.T.				

11/28/02

110

RESIDENCE: Atoka	COUNTY.	**Choctaw Nation**	Choctaw Roll	CARD No.
POST OFFICE: Owl, I.T.			*(Not Including Freedmen)*	FIELD No. **4011**

Dawes' Roll No.	NAME	Relationship to Person First Named	AGE	SEX	BLOOD	TRIBAL ENROLLMENT		
						Year	County	No.
11235	1 Harkins, Giles W ⁴¹		38	M	1/2	1896	Atoka	5967
I.W.571	2 " Mollie ³¹	Wife	27	F	I.W.	1896	"	14652
11236	3 " Charley C ¹¹	Son	8	M	1/4	1896	Atoka	5968
11237	4 " Allington T ⁹	"	6	"	1/4	1896	"	5969
11238	5 " "Erle" ¹	"	1	M	1/4			
	6							
	7							
	8							
	9	ENROLLMENT OF NOS. 1, 3, 4 and 5 HEREON APPROVED BY THE SECRETARY OF INTERIOR Mar 10 1903						
	10							
	11							
	12							
	13	ENROLLMENT OF NOS. 2 HEREON APPROVED BY THE SECRETARY OF INTERIOR Feb 8 1904						
	14							
	15							
	16							
	17							

TRIBAL ENROLLMENT OF PARENTS

	Name of Father	Year	County	Name of Mother	Year	County
1	G. W. Harkins	Dead	Blue	Sophie Harkins	Dead	Blue
2	Jno Sharp	"	Non Citz	Mary Sharp		Non Citz
3	No1			No2		
4	No1			No2		
5	No1			No2		
6						
7			No1 on 1896 roll as G. W. Harkins			
8						
9			No2- Evidence of marriage to			
10			be supplied:- Supplied 9/15/1899			
11			No3 on 1896 roll as Charley Harkins			
12			No4 " 1896 " " Linton "			
			No2 " 1896 " " Money "			
13			No5 Born Aug 5, 1901: Enrolled Nov. 22, 1902			
14			For child of Nos 1&2 see NB (Mar 3, 1905) #665			Date of Application for Enrollment.
15						Aug 28/99
16						
17			P.O. Coalgate I.T.	11/17/02		

Choctaw By Blood Enrollment Cards 1898-1914

RESIDENCE: Atoka   COUNTY. **Choctaw Nation**   **Choctaw Roll** C
POST OFFICE: Lehigh, I.T.   *(Not Including Freedmen)*   FIELD NO. 4012

Dawes' Roll No.	NAME	Relationship to Person First Named	AGE	SEX	BLOOD	TRIBAL ENROLLMENT Year	County	No.
11239	1 Keel, Charlie 70	First Named	67	M	Full	1896	Atoka	7637
11240	2 " Sumela 35	Wife	32	F	"	1896	"	7638
11241	3 " Josiah 10	Son	7	M	"	1896	"	7639
11242	4 " Annie 8	Dau	5	F	"	1896	"	7641
11243	5 " Arfus 7	Son	4	M	"	1896	"	7640
~~DEAD.~~	6 ~~" Sylvester DEAD.~~	"	~~7mo~~	"	"			
11244	7 Stanford, Rebecca 16	S.Dau	13	F	"	1896	Atoka	11620
11245	8 Keel, Charley 1	Son	6wks	M	"			
	9							
	10							
	11							
	12							
	13							
	14							
	15							

No. 6 HEREON DISMISSED UNDER ORDER OF THE COMMISSION TO THE FIVE CIVILIZED TRIBES OF MARCH 31, 1905.

ENROLLMENT OF NOS. 1,2,3,4,5,7 and 8 HEREON APPROVED BY THE SECRETARY OF INTERIOR MAR 10 1903

TRIBAL ENROLLMENT OF PARENTS

	Name of Father	Year	County	Name of Mother	Year	County
1	Allen Keel	Dead	Chick Dist		Dead	in Mississippi
2	Jackson Ahchehubbee	"	Kiamitia	Sally Ahchehubbee	"	Kiamitia
3	No1			No2		
4	No1			No2		
5	No1			No2		
6	~~No1~~			~~No2~~		
7	David Stanford	Dead	Jacks Fork	No2		
8	No.1			No.2		
9						
10						
11			No2 on 1896 roll as Sumner Keel			
12			No3 " 1896 " " Jonit "			
13			No4 " 1896 " " Junie "			#1 to 7
14			No6 Affidavit of birth to be supplied:- Recd			Date of Application for Enrollment.
15			No.8 born Nov. 9, 1901: Enrolled Dec. 27, 1901			Aug 28/99
16			~~No6 Died Oct 12, 1900: evidence of death filed Nov 22, 1902~~			
17			P.O. Coalgate, I.T.			

11/17/02

112

Choctaw By Blood Enrollment Cards 1898-1914

RESIDENCE: Atoka   COUNTY. **Choctaw Nation**   Choctaw Roll   CARD NO.
POST OFFICE: Coalgate, I.T.   *(Not Including Freedmen)*   FIELD NO. **4013**

Dawes' Roll No.	NAME	Relationship to Person First Named	AGE	SEX	BLOOD	TRIBAL ENROLLMENT Year	County	No.
11246	1 Ott, Samuel A ²⁶	First Named	23	M	Full	1896	Atoka	10024
11247	2 " Rhoda ³⁰	Wife	27	F	"	1896	"	10025
11248	3 Folsom, Felix ¹³	S.Son	10	M	"	1896	"	4478
11249	4 " Adam ¹¹	"	8	"	"	1896	"	4479
	5							
	6							
	7							
	8	ENROLLMENT OF NOS. 1,2,3 and 4 HEREON APPROVED BY THE SECRETARY OF INTERIOR Mar 10 1903						
	9							
	10							
	11							
	12							
	13							
	14							
	15							
	16							
	17							

TRIBAL ENROLLMENT OF PARENTS

	Name of Father	Year	County	Name of Mother	Year	County
1	Johnson Ott		Atoka	Vicey Ott		Atoka
2	Lymom[sic] Homma	Dead		Pash-homma	Dead	Tobucksy
3	Mitchell Folsom	"	Tobucksy	No2		
4	" "	"	"	No2		
5						
6						
7						
8	No1 On 1896 roll as S. A. Ott					
9						
10	No1 obtained divorce from No2 and married Rosa A. Lawrence on Choctaw card #3961.					
11						
12						
13						
14				Date of Application for Enrollment.		
15				Aug 28/99		
16						
17						

Choctaw By Blood Enrollment Cards 1898-1914

RESIDENCE:	Chickasaw Natn	~~COUNTY.~~	**Choctaw Nation**				**Choctaw Roll** *(Not Including Freedmen)*		CARD NO. **4014**
POST OFFICE:	Wapanucka I.T.								FIELD NO.

Dawes' Roll No.	NAME	Relationship to Person	AGE	SEX	BLOOD	TRIBAL ENROLLMENT		
						Year	County	No.
11250	1 Mosely William ³³ ✓	First Named	30	M	1/2	1893	Atoka	802
	2							
	3							
CITIZENSHIP CERTIFICATE ISSUED FOR NO 1	4							
	5 MAR 21 1903							
	6							
	7							
	8							
	9							
	10							
	11							
	12							
	13							
	14							
	15 ENROLLMENT OF NOS. 1 HEREON							
	16 APPROVED BY THE SECRETARY							
	17 OF INTERIOR MAR 10 1903							

TRIBAL ENROLLMENT OF PARENTS

	Name of Father	Year	County	Name of Mother	Year	County
1	George William	Dead	Creek Roll	Casaline William		Chick
2						
3						
4						
5						
6						
7	On 1893 Pay Roll, page 77, No 802, Atoka Co					
8	as William Mosly [sic]					
9						
10	Wife and family on Chickasaw Card					
11	No 1536					
12						
13						
14						
15						Aug 28/99
16						
17						

Choctaw By Blood Enrollment Cards 1898-1914

RESIDENCE:	Atoka	COUNTY.	**Choctaw Nation**			**Choctaw Roll** *(Not Including Freedmen)*		CARD NO.	
POST OFFICE:	Atoka, I.T.							FIELD NO.	4015

Dawes' Roll No.	NAME	Relationship to Person First Named	AGE	SEX	BLOOD	TRIBAL ENROLLMENT		
						Year	County	No.
11251	1 Peter, William 63		60	M	Full	1896	Atoka	10550
	2							
	3							
	4							
	5	ENROLLMENT						
	6	OF NOS. 1 HEREON APPROVED BY THE SECRETARY						
	7	OF INTERIOR MAR 10 1903						
	8							
	9							
	10							
	11							
	12							
	13							
	14							
	15							
	16							
	17							

TRIBAL ENROLLMENT OF PARENTS

	Name of Father	Year	County	Name of Mother	Year	County
1		Dead	in Mississippi		Dead	in Mississippi
2						
3						
4						
5						
6						
7						
8						
9						
10						
11						
12						
13						
14						
15				Date of Application for Enrollment.	Aug 28/99	
16						
17						

Choctaw By Blood Enrollment Cards 1898-1914

RESIDENCE: Atoka   COUNTY. **Choctaw Nation**   **Choctaw Roll**   CARD No.
POST OFFICE: Atoka, I.T.   *(Not Including Freedmen)*   FIELD No. 4016

Dawes' Roll No.	NAME	Relationship to Person	AGE	SEX	BLOOD	TRIBAL ENROLLMENT		
						Year	County	No.
11252	1 Williams, Austin 70	First Named	67	M	Full	1896	Atoka	14060
11253	2 " Wicey 64	Wife	61	F	"	1896	"	14061
	3							
	4							
	5							
	6	ENROLLMENT						
	7	OF NOS. 1 and 2 HEREON						
	8	APPROVED BY THE SECRETARY OF INTERIOR MAR 10 1903						
	9							
	10							
	11							
	12							
	13							
	14							
	15							
	16							
	17							

TRIBAL ENROLLMENT OF PARENTS

	Name of Father	Year	County	Name of Mother	Year	County
1	Fe-lih-nu-tubbee	Dead	Towson	Ok-la-te-ma	Dead	Atoka
2	A-pa-sho-ha	"	Jacks Fork	Bicey	"	Jacks Fork
3						
4						
5						
6						
7	No1 on 1896 roll as Oston Williams					
8						
9						
10						
11						
12						
13						
14						
15					Date of Application for Enrollment.	Aug 28/99
16						
17	P.O. Lehigh I.T. 7/18/07					

Choctaw By Blood Enrollment Cards 1898-1914

Choctaw Nation

Choctaw Roll
(Not Including Freedmen)

CARD NO.
FIELD NO. 4017

Dawes' Roll No.	NAME	Relationship to Person First Named	AGE	SEX	BLOOD	TRIBAL ENROLLMENT		
						Year	County	No.
11254	1 Smallfield, Ellen 49	Named	46	F	3/8	1896	Atoka	11648
11255	2 Belt, Malinda 26	Dau	23	"	3/16	1896	"	1847
11256	3 Smallfield, John 16	Son	13	M	3/16	1896	"	11649
11257	4 McDonald, Eli Jackson 2	G. Son	3m	M	3/32			
	5							
	6							
	7							
	8	ENROLLMENT OF NOS. 1,2,3 and 4 HEREON APPROVED BY THE SECRETARY OF INTERIOR MAR 10 1903						
	9							
	10							
	11							
	12							
	13							
	14							
	15							
	16							
	17							

TRIBAL ENROLLMENT OF PARENTS

	Name of Father	Year	County	Name of Mother	Year	County
1	Haley Wilson	Dead	Gaines	Malinda Wilson	Dead	Gaines
2	Fred Smallfield	"	Non Citz	No1		
3	" "	"	" "	No1		
4	Wm McDonald			No.2		
5						
6						
7	No2 on 1896 roll as Melinda Bell					
8						
9	No3 on 1896 roll as Jno Smallfield					
10	No.4 Enrolled January 17, 1901					
11	No2 is the wife of J.B. Gardner, a non-citizen. Evidence of					
12	marriage filed Jany 26, 1903					
	For children of No.2 see NB (March 3,1905) #1267					
13						
14					Date of Application for Enrollment.	
15					Aug 28/99	
16						
17						

Choctaw By Blood Enrollment Cards 1898-1914

RESIDENCE: **Atoka**   COUNTY. **Choctaw Nation**   **Choctaw Roll**   CARD No.

POST OFFICE: **Stringtown, I.T.**   *(Not Including Freedmen)*   FIELD No. **4018**

Dawes' Roll No.		NAME	Relationship to Person First Named	AGE	SEX	BLOOD	TRIBAL ENROLLMENT Year	TRIBAL ENROLLMENT County	TRIBAL ENROLLMENT No.
11258	1	Shults, Winnie ³⁹	First Named	36	F	3/8	1896	Atoka	11650
	2								
	3								
	4								
	5	ENROLLMENT							
	6	OF NOS. 1 HEREON APPROVED BY THE SECRETARY							
	7	OF INTERIOR MAR 10 1903	.						
	8								
	9								
	10								
	11								
	12								
	13								
	14								
	15								
	16								
	17								

TRIBAL ENROLLMENT OF PARENTS

	Name of Father	Year	County	Name of Mother	Year	County
1	John Shults	Dead	Non Citz	Polly Shults	Dead	Atoka
2						
3						
4						
5						
6						
7						
8						
9						
10						
11						
12						
13						
14						
15				Date of Application for Enrollment.		Aug 28/99
16						
17						

118

Choctaw By Blood Enrollment Cards 1898-1914

RESIDENCE: Jacks Fork COUNTY.								
POST OFFICE: Stringtown, I.T.			**Choctaw Nation**			**Choctaw Roll** (Not Including Freedmen)	CARD NO. FIELD NO. 4019	

Dawes' Roll No.	NAME	Relationship to Person First Named	AGE	SEX	BLOOD	TRIBAL ENROLLMENT		
						Year	County	No.
11259	1 Peter, Elizabeth 56		53	F	Full	1896	Jacks Fork	10594
11260	2 " Ellis 14	Ward	11	M	"	1896	" "	10595
	3							
	4							
	5							
	6	ENROLLMENT						
	7	OF NOS. 1 and 2 HEREON APPROVED BY THE SECRETARY						
	8	OF INTERIOR MAR 10 1903						
	9							
	10							
	11							
	12							
	13							
	14							
	15							
	16							
	17							

TRIBAL ENROLLMENT OF PARENTS

	Name of Father	Year	County	Name of Mother	Year	County
1	Fisher	Dead	Skullyville	Elsie Fisher	Dead	Skullyville
2	Lohn[sic] Lewis	"	Atoka		"	Atoka
3						
4						
5						
6						
7	No1 on 1896 roll as Ishmatona Peter					
8	No2 " 1896 " Alice Peter					
9	No.1 is now the wife of Jimson Cole, Choctaw card #4129					
10					11/17/02	
11						
12						
13					Date of Application for Enrollment.	
14						
15					Aug 28/99	
16						
17						

119

Choctaw By Blood Enrollment Cards 1898-1914

RESIDENCE:	Atoka	COUNTY.	Choctaw Nation		Choctaw Roll	CARD NO.	
POST OFFICE:	Atoka, I.T.				(Not Including Freedmen)	FIELD NO. 4020	

Dawes' Roll No.	NAME	Relationship to Person First Named	AGE	SEX	BLOOD	TRIBAL ENROLLMENT		
						Year	County	No.
DEAD.	1 Sexton, Sillen		71	F	Full	1896	Atoka	11624
	2							
	3							
	4							
	5							
	6							
	7							
	8							
	9							
	10							
	11							
	12							
	13							
	14							
	15	No. 1 HEREON DISMISSED UNDER						
	16	ORDER OF THE COMMISSION TO THE FIVE						
	17	CIVILIZED TRIBES OF MARCH 31, 1905.						

TRIBAL ENROLLMENT OF PARENTS

Name of Father	Year	County	Name of Mother	Year	County
1 Ish-tom-bey	Dead	in Mississippi	Jennie Bell	Dead	in Mississippi
2					
3					
4					
5					
6					
7	On 1896 roll as Sillam Sexton				
8					
9					
10					
11	No1 died in 1901; proof of death filed Nov 26, 1902				
12					
13					
14					
15				Date of Application for Enrollment.	Aug 28/99
16					
17					

Choctaw By Blood Enrollment Cards 1898-1914

RESIDENCE: Atoka COUNTY. **Choctaw Nation** Choctaw Roll CARD NO.
POST OFFICE: Stringtown, I.T. (Not Including Freedmen) FIELD NO. 4021

Dawes' Roll No.	NAME	Relationship to Person First Named	AGE	SEX	BLOOD	TRIBAL ENROLLMENT		
						Year	County	No.
11261	1 McDonald, Minnie 32		29	F	3/16	1896	Atoka	9454
11262	2 " Ada L 8	Dau	5	"	3/32	1896	"	9455
11263	3 " Alice M 6	"	3	"	3/32			
11264	4 " William A 3	Son	3mo	M	3/32			
11265	5 " Nora Bell 1	Dau	4mo	F	3/32			
	6							
	7							
	8							
	9	ENROLLMENT						
	10	OF NOS. 1,2,3,4 and 5 HEREON APPROVED BY THE SECRETARY						
	11	OF INTERIOR MAR 10 1903						
	12							
	13							
	14							
	15							
	16							
	17							

TRIBAL ENROLLMENT OF PARENTS

	Name of Father	Year	County	Name of Mother	Year	County
1	Fred Smallfield	Dead	Non Citz	Ellen Smallfield		Atoka
2	E. J. McDonald		" "	No1		
3	" " "		" "	No1		
4	" " "		" "	No1		
5	" " "		" "	Nº1		
6						
7						
8	No1 on 1896 roll as Minnie McDonnal					
9	No2 " 1896 " " Addie "					
10	No3 Affidavit of birth to be supplied: Filed Oct 26/99					
11	Nº5 Born Jany 17, 1902: enrolled June 10, 1902					
12						
13					#1 to 3 inc	
14					Date of Application for Enrollment.	
15					Aug 28/99	
16					No4 enrolled Dec 14/99	
17						

Choctaw By Blood Enrollment Cards 1898-1914

RESIDENCE: Atoka   COUNTY. **Choctaw Nation**   Choctaw Roll   CARD NO.
POST OFFICE: Atoka, I.T.   *(Not Including Freedmen)*   FIELD NO. **4022**

Dawes' Roll No.	NAME	Relationship to Person First Named	AGE	SEX	BLOOD	TRIBAL ENROLLMENT Year	County	No.
11266	1 Robinson, Lina 43	First Named	40	F	Full	1893	Jackson	420
~~11267~~	~~2 DIED PRIOR TO SEPTEMBER 25, 23902 Lovina~~	Dau	~~20~~	"	"	~~1893~~	"	~~421~~
15941	3 Carnes, Mary Ann	Dau of No.2	1	"	3/4			
	4							
	5	*Notify L. D. Harton Boswell I.T. of approval of No3*						
	6							
	7	ENROLLMENT						
	8	OF NOS. 1 and 2 HEREON APPROVED BY THE SECRETARY						
	9	OF INTERIOR Mar 10 1903						
	10	ENROLLMENT						
	11	OF NOS. ~~~ 3 ~~~ HEREON APPROVED BY THE SECRETARY						
	12	OF INTERIOR Nov 24 1905						
	13							
	14							
	15							
	16							
	17							

TRIBAL ENROLLMENT OF PARENTS

	Name of Father	Year	County	Name of Mother	Year	County
1	Ma-loh-nubbee	Dead		Wicey	Dead	Jacks Fork
2	~~Geo. Robinson~~	"	~~Atoka~~	~~No1~~		
3	Jackson Carnes	1896	Blue	No.2		
4						
5						
6						
7						
8	No1 on 1893 Pay Roll, Page 46, No 420, Jackson Co., as Liney Joe.					
9	No2 on 1893 Pay Roll, Page 46, No 421					
10	Jackson Co., as Leviney Robinson					
11	No.2 died May 4, 1902: Enrollment cancelled by Department July 8, 1904					
12	N°2 was married to Jackson Carnes Choctaw card #1853 March 11, 1901					
13	No 3 was born January 23d, 1902; application received and name placed on this card					
	March 25, 1905 under provision of Act of Congress approved March 3, 1905 #1&2					
14					Date of Application for Enrollment.	
15					Aug 28/99	
16						
17						

Choctaw By Blood Enrollment Cards 1898-1914

RESIDENCE: Atoka	COUNTY.							
POST OFFICE: Owl, I.T.	**Choctaw Nation**			**Choctaw Roll** (Not Including Freedmen)		CARD No. FIELD NO. **4023**		

Dawes' Roll No.	NAME		Relationship to Person First Named	AGE	SEX	BLOOD	TRIBAL ENROLLMENT		
							Year	County	No.
11268	1 Byington, Eliza	48	First Named	45	F	Full	1896	Atoka	6023
11269	2 Hayes Mary	23	Dau	20	"	"	1896	"	6024
11270	3 " Sallie	18	"	15	"	"	1896	"	6025
11271	4 " Nellie	10	"	7	"	"	1896	"	6026
	5								
	6								
	7								
	8	ENROLLMENT							
	9	OF NOS. 1,2,3 and 4 HEREON APPROVED BY THE SECRETARY							
	10	OF INTERIOR Mar 10 1903							
	11								
	12								
	13								
	14								
	15								
	16								
	17								

TRIBAL ENROLLMENT OF PARENTS

	Name of Father	Year	County	Name of Mother	Year	County
1	Josie Chitto	Dead	Atoka	Pe-sa-ha-ma	Dead	Atoka
2	Stephen Hayes	"	"	No1		
3	" "	"	"	No1		
4	" "	"	"	No1		
5						
6						
7	No1- On 1896 roll as Eliza Hayes					
8						
9	No.1 wife of Sampson Roberts, Choctaw card #4211					
10	No.2 is now the wife of Calvin Bond, Choctaw card #5411					
	No.3 is now the wife of Jackson McIntosh Choctaw card #4036					
11						
12						
13						
14						
15			Date of Application for Enrollment.	Aug 28/99		
16						
17						

Choctaw By Blood Enrollment Cards 1898-1914

RESIDENCE: Atoka	COUNTY. **Choctaw Nation**	**Choctaw Roll** (Not Including Freedmen)	CARD NO.
POST OFFICE: Lehigh, I.T.			FIELD NO. 4024

Dawes' Roll No.	NAME	Relationship to Person	AGE	SEX	BLOOD	TRIBAL ENROLLMENT		
						Year	County	No.
11272	1 Long, Lucy ⁵³	First Named	50	F	Full	1896	Atoka	8276
11273	2 Nowabbi, Charlie ¹⁷	G.Son	14	M	"	1896	"	9852
	3							
	4							
	5							
	6	ENROLLMENT						
	7	OF NOS. 1 and 2 HEREON APPROVED BY THE SECRETARY						
	8	OF INTERIOR MAR 10 1903						
	9							
	10							
	11							
	12							
	13							
	14							
	15							
	16							
	17							

TRIBAL ENROLLMENT OF PARENTS

	Name of Father	Year	County	Name of Mother	Year	County
1	Josie	Dead	Atoka		Dead	Atoka
2	Joe Nowabbi	"	"	Elizabeth	"	"
3						
4						
5						
6						
7	No2 is a male. Sex changed under Departmental authority of Jan 17, 1907 (I.T.D.					
8	#814-1907) DC 4187-1907					
9	No2 on 1896 roll as Susa Long					
	No3 " 1896 " " Charlie Nowabbee					
10						
11						
12						
13						
14						
15				Date of Application for Enrollment.		Aug 28/99
16						
17						

Choctaw By Blood Enrollment Cards 1898-1914

RESIDENCE: Jackson COUNTY. **Choctaw Nation** **Choctaw Roll** CARD NO.
POST OFFICE: Mayhew, I.T. *(Not Including Freedmen)* FIELD NO. 4025

Dawes' Roll No.	NAME	Relationship to Person First Named	AGE	SEX	BLOOD	TRIBAL ENROLLMENT		
						Year	County	No.
11274	1 Harkins, Limsey		40	F	Full	1896	Jackson	5812
11275	2 " Willis	Son	6	M	"	1896	"	5813
	3							
	4							
	5							
	6							
	7	ENROLLMENT OF NOS. 1 and 2 HEREON						
	8	APPROVED BY THE SECRETARY OF INTERIOR MAR 10 1903						
	9							
	10							
	11							
	12							
	13							
	14							
	15							
	16							
	17							

DIED PRIOR TO SEPTEMBER 25 1902

TRIBAL ENROLLMENT OF PARENTS

	Name of Father	Year	County	Name of Mother	Year	County
1	Ke-las-by	Dead		Salen	Dead	Atoka
2	Wallace Harkins	"	Jackson	No1		
3						
4						
5						
6						
7			No1 on 1896 roll as Linsey Harkins			
8			No. 1 died Sept 23, 1899. Enrollment cancelled by Department July 8, 1904			
9						
10						
11						
12						
13						
14					Date of Application for Enrollment	
15					Aug 28/99	
16						
17						

Choctaw By Blood Enrollment Cards 1898-1914

| RESIDENCE: | Atoka | COUNTY. | **Choctaw Nation** | **Choctaw Roll** | CARD NO. |
| POST OFFICE: | Atoka, I.T. | | | *(Not Including Freedmen)* | FIELD NO. 4026 |

Dawes' Roll No.		NAME	Relationship to Person First Named	AGE	SEX	BLOOD	TRIBAL ENROLLMENT Year	County	No.
DEAD.	1	Lewis, Susan	Named	48	F	Full	1896	Atoka	8246
11276	2	" Culberson [21]	Son	18	M	"	1896	"	8247
	3								
	4								
	5								
	6	ENROLLMENT							
	7	OF NOS. 2 HEREON APPROVED BY THE SECRETARY							
	8	OF INTERIOR MAR 10 1903							
	9								
	10	NO. 1 HEREON DISMISSED UNDER ORDER OF THE COMMISSION TO THE FIVE							
	11	CIVILIZED TRIBES OF MARCH 31, 1905.							
	12								
	13								
	14								
	15								
	16								
	17								

TRIBAL ENROLLMENT OF PARENTS

	Name of Father	Year	County	Name of Mother	Year	County
1	John Forester	Dead	Atoka	Nellie Forester	Dead	Atoka
2	Sampson Lewis	"	"	No1		
3						
4						
5						
6						
7						
8			No1 died February 10, 1900; proof of death filed Nov 25, 1902			
9						
10						
11						
12						
13						
14					Date of Application for Enrollment	Aug 28/99
15						
16						
17						

Choctaw By Blood Enrollment Cards 1898-1914

RESIDENCE:	Atoka	COUNTY.	**Choctaw Nation**		**Choctaw Roll**		CARD NO.	
POST OFFICE:	Coalgate, I.T.				*(Not Including Freedmen)*		FIELD NO. 4027	

Dawes' Roll No.	NAME		Relationship to Person First Named	AGE	SEX	BLOOD	TRIBAL ENROLLMENT		
							Year	County	No.
11277	1 Cobb, Micy	61		58	F	Full	1896	Atoka	2921
	2								
	3								
	4								
	5	ENROLLMENT							
	6	OF NOS. 1 HEREON APPROVED BY THE SECRETARY							
	7	OF INTERIOR MAR 10 1903							
	8								
	9								
	10								
	11								
	12								
	13								
	14								
	15								
	16								
	17								

TRIBAL ENROLLMENT OF PARENTS

	Name of Father	Year	County	Name of Mother	Year	County
1	John Forester	Dead	Atoka	Nellie Forester	Dead	Atoka
2						
3						
4			On 1896 roll as Nicy Cobb			
5						
6						
7						
8						
9						
10						
11						
12						
13						
14						
15				Date of Application for Enrollment.	Aug 28/99	
16						
17						

Choctaw By Blood Enrollment Cards 1898-1914

RESIDENCE:	Atoka	COUNTY.							CARD	
POST OFFICE:	Atoka, I.T.		**Choctaw Nation**		Choctaw Roll *(Not Including Freedmen)*				FIELD NO. 4028	

Dawes' Roll No.	NAME		Relationship to Person First Named	AGE	SEX	BLOOD	TRIBAL ENROLLMENT		
							Year	County	No.
11278	1 Jacob, Avey	46	First Named	43	F	Full	1896	Atoka	7243
	2								
	3								
	4								
	5	ENROLLMENT OF NOS. 1 HEREON							
	6	APPROVED BY THE SECRETARY OF INTERIOR MAR 10 1903							
	7								
	8								
	9								
	10								
	11								
	12								
	13								
	14								
	15								
	16								
	17								

TRIBAL ENROLLMENT OF PARENTS

	Name of Father	Year	County	Name of Mother	Year	County
1	Ah-lo-bo-tuby	Dead	Atoka	Ish-te-nu-a-hoke	Dead	Atoka
2						
3						
4						
5						
6						
7						
8						
9						
10						
11						
12						
13						
14					Date of Application for Enrollment.	
15					Aug 28/99	
16						
17						

Choctaw By Blood Enrollment Cards 1898-1914

RESIDENCE: Atoka COUNTY.
POST OFFICE: Atoka, I.T.

Choctaw Nation

Choctaw Roll
(Not Including Freedmen)

CARD NO.
FIELD NO. 4029

Dawes' Roll No.	NAME	Relationship to Person First Named	AGE	SEX	BLOOD	TRIBAL ENROLLMENT		
						Year	County	No.
11279	1 Carnes, Emily ~~DIED PRIOR TO SEPTEMBER 25, 1902~~	First Named	33	F	Full	1896	Atoka	2940
	2							
	3							
	4							
	5	ENROLLMENT						
	6	OF NOS. 1 HEREON APPROVED BY THE SECRETARY						
	7	OF INTERIOR MAR 10 1903						
	8							
	9							
	10							
	11							
	12							
	13							
	14							
	15							
	16							
	17							

TRIBAL ENROLLMENT OF PARENTS

	Name of Father	Year	County	Name of Mother	Year	County
1	Forbis Carnes	Dead	Atoka	Betsy McGee	Dead	Blue
2						
3						
4						
5						
6			On 1896 roll as Emily Carn			
7			Nº1 Died April 14, 1902; proof of death Jany 24, 1903			
8			No.1 died April 14, 1902. Enrollment cancelled by Department July 8, 1904			
9						
10						
11						
12						
13						
14					Date of Application for Enrollment.	
15					Aug 28/99	
16						
17						

Choctaw By Blood Enrollment Cards 1898-1914

RESIDENCE: Atoka   COUNTY. **Choctaw Nation**   **Choctaw Roll**   CARD NO.
POST OFFICE: Lehigh, I.T.   *(Not Including Freedmen)*   FIELD NO. 4030

Dawes' Roll No.	NAME	Relationship to Person First Named	AGE	SEX	BLOOD	TRIBAL ENROLLMENT		
						Year	County	No.
11280	₁ Wilson, Lucy ⁶⁶	First Named	63	F	Full	1896	Atoka	13971
11281	₂ Noah, Sarah ²²	G.Dau	19	"	"	1896	"	9835
	3							
	4							
	5							
	6	ENROLLMENT						
	7	OF NOS. 1 and 2 HEREON APPROVED BY THE SECRETARY						
	8	OF INTERIOR MAR 10 1903						
	9							
	10							
	11							
	12							
	13							
	14							
	15							
	16							
	17							

TRIBAL ENROLLMENT OF PARENTS

	Name of Father	Year	County	Name of Mother	Year	County
1	Riley Roberts	Dead	Kiamitia		Dead	Kiamitia
2	Elisha Noah	"	Atoka	Elizabeth Noah	"	Atoka
3						
4						
5						
6			No2 on 1896 roll as Sarah Nowa			
7						
8						
9						
10						
11						
12						
13						
14				Date of Application for Enrollment.		Aug 28/99
15						Aug 28/99
16						
17						

130

Choctaw By Blood Enrollment Cards 1898-1914

RESIDENCE:	Atoka	COUNTY.	**Choctaw Nation**				Choctaw Roll	CARD No.	
POST OFFICE:	Lehigh, I.T.		*(Not Including Freedmen)*					FIELD No.	4031

Dawes' Roll No.	NAME		Relationship to Person First Named	AGE	SEX	BLOOD	TRIBAL ENROLLMENT		
							Year	County	No.
11282	1 Beams, Eliza	41		38	F	Full	1896	Atoka	1858
	2								
	3								
	4								
	5	ENROLLMENT							
	6	OF NOS. 1 HEREON APPROVED BY THE SECRETARY							
	7	OF INTERIOR MAR 10 1903							
	8								
	9								
	10								
	11								
	12								
	13								
	14								
	15								
	16								
	17								

TRIBAL ENROLLMENT OF PARENTS

	Name of Father	Year	County	Name of Mother	Year	County
1	Gilbert Beams	Dead	Jacks Fork	Annie Beams	Dead	Jacks Fork
2						
3						
4						
5						
6						
7						
8						
9						
10						
11						
12						
13						
14						Date of Application for Enrollment
15						Aug 28/99
16						
17						

131

Choctaw By Blood Enrollment Cards 1898-1914

RESIDENCE:	Atoka	COUNTY.			CARD NO.
POST OFFICE:	Coalgate, I.T.	**Choctaw Nation**	**Choctaw Roll** (Not Including Freedmen)	FIELD NO.	4032

Dawes' Roll No.	NAME		Relationship to Person	AGE	SEX	BLOOD	TRIBAL ENROLLMENT		
							Year	County	No.
11283	1 Harvey, Bicy	36	First Named	33	F	Full	1896	Atoka	1772
	2								
	3								
	4								
	5								
	6								
	7	ENROLLMENT OF NOS. 1 HEREON							
	8	APPROVED BY THE SECRETARY OF INTERIOR MAR 10 1903							
	9								
	10								
	11								
	12								
	13								
	14								
	15								
	16								
	17								

TRIBAL ENROLLMENT OF PARENTS

	Name of Father	Year	County	Name of Mother	Year	County
1	Harvey	Dead	Jacks Fork	Ish-ta-o-na	Dead	Jacks Fork
2						
3						
4						
5						
6						
7	On 1896 roll as Lysee Byington					
8						
9						
10						
11						
12						
13						
14						
15				Date of Application for Enrollment.	Aug 28/99	
16						
17						

Choctaw By Blood Enrollment Cards 1898-1914

Dawes' Roll No.	NAME	Relationship to Person First Named	AGE	SEX	BLOOD	TRIBAL ENROLLMENT		
						Year	County	No.
11284	1 Frazier, Betsy 65		62	F	Full	1896	Atoka	4483
11285	2 " Sweeney 15	Son	12	M	"	1896	"	4484
	3							
	4							
	5							
	6	ENROLLMENT						
	7	OF NOS. 1 and 2 HEREON APPROVED BY THE SECRETARY						
	8	OF INTERIOR MAR 10 1903						
	9							
	10							
	11							
	12							
	13							
	14							
	15							
	16							
	17							

TRIBAL ENROLLMENT OF PARENTS

	Name of Father	Year	County	Name of Mother	Year	County
1	William	Dead	Atoka	Mollie	Dead	Atoka
2	Stanton Frazier	"	"	No 1		
3						
4						
5						
6						
7		No2 on 1896 roll as Freeney Frazier				
8						
9						
10						
11						
12						
13						
14						
15				Date of Application for Enrollment.	Aug 28/99	
16						
17						

Choctaw By Blood Enrollment Cards 1898-1914

Dawes' Roll No.	NAME		Relationship to Person First Named	AGE	SEX	BLOOD	TRIBAL ENROLLMENT		
							Year	County	No.
11286	1 Peter, Sarah	23	First Named	20	F	Full	1893	Atoka	294
11287	2 Sunny, Dora	4	Dau	1	"	'			
11288	3 Peter, Simon	2	Son	4m	M	"			
	4								
	5								
	6								
	7	ENROLLMENT OF NOS. 1,2 and 3 HEREON							
	8	APPROVED BY THE SECRETARY OF INTERIOR Mar 10 1903							
	9								
	10								
	11								
	12								
	13								
	14								
	15								
	16								
	17								

TRIBAL ENROLLMENT OF PARENTS

	Name of Father	Year	County	Name of Mother	Year	County
1	Stanton Frazier	Dead	Atoka	Betsy Frazier		Atoka
2	Dunaway Sunny	"	"	No1		
3	Thompson Peter	1893	"	No1		
4						
5						
6			No1 on 1893 Pay Roll, Page 28, No 294, Atoka			
7			as Sarah Frazier			
8			No1 also on 1896 census roll, Choctaw nation[sic]			
9			For child of No.1 see NB (March 3, 1905) #1369 as Celey Frazier: page 108, #44641			Mar. 27, 1900
10			No1 is now the wife of Thompson Peter			
11			on Choctaw Card #4115, March 25, 1901. Evidence of			
12			marriage to be supplied,			
13			No.3 Enrolled March 25, 1901			#1&2
14						Date of Application for Enrollment.
15						Aug 28/99
16						
17						

RESIDENCE:	Atoka	COUNTY.								

Choctaw Nation   **Choctaw Roll** *(Not Including Freedmen)*

POST OFFICE: Lehigh, I.T.

CARD NO. FIELD NO. **4035**

Dawes' Roll No.	NAME	Relationship to Person First Named	AGE	SEX	BLOOD	TRIBAL ENROLLMENT		
						Year	County	No.
DEAD	1 Gibson, Jincy		40	F	Full	1896	Atoka	4940
11289	2 " Wesley 14	Son	11	M	"	1896	"	4941
11290	3 " Peter 11	"	8	"	"	1896	"	4942
11291	4 " Molly 8	Dau	5	F	'	1896	"	4943
	5							
	6							
	7	ENROLLMENT OF NOS. 2, 3 and 4 HEREON APPROVED BY THE SECRETARY OF INTERIOR Mar 10 1903						
	8							
	9							
	10							
	11	No.1 hereon dismissed under order of the Commission to the Five Civilized Tribes of March 31, 1905.						
	12							
	13							
	14							
	15							
	16							
	17							

TRIBAL ENROLLMENT OF PARENTS

	Name of Father	Year	County	Name of Mother	Year	County
1	Joel Vance	Dead	Jacks Fork	Wicey Williams		Atoka
2	Cephus Gibson		Atoka	No1		
3	" "		"	No1		
4	" "		"	No1		
5						
6						
7						
8						
9						
10						
11	Surnames appear on 1896 roll as Gipson Atoka					
12	No2 on 1896 roll Blue Co. Page 121 #4965					
13	No3 " 1896 " " " " 121 #4966					
14	No4 " 1896 " " " " 121 #4967					
15	No1 died Sept 18, 1902 proof of death filed Nov 22, 1902					
16	Correct age of No2 is 21 years. See testimony relative thereto of May 24, 1903					
17	For child of No.1 see NB (Mar 3, 1905) #625					

Date of Application for Enrollment.   Aug 28/99

Choctaw By Blood Enrollment Cards 1898-1914

Dawes' Roll No.	NAME		Relationship to Person First Named	AGE	SEX	BLOOD	TRIBAL ENROLLMENT		
							Year	County	No.
11292	1 Byington, Simpson	38	First Named	35	M	Full	1896	Jacks Fork	1913
11293	2 " Annie	31	Wife	28	F	"	1896	" "	1914
11294	3 " Silas	14	Son	11	M	"	1896	" "	6125
11295	4 " Jackson	10	"	7	M	"	1896	" "	1916
11296	5 McIntosh, Jackman	19	S.Son	16	M	"	1896	" "	1915
11297	6 " Chostin	14	"	11	M	"	1896	" "	9459
11298	7 Byington, Cilian	2	Dau	4mo	F	"			
	8								
	9								
	10								
	11	ENROLLMENT							
	12	OF NOS. 1,2,3,4,5,6 and 7 HEREON APPROVED BY THE SECRETARY							
	13	OF INTERIOR Mar 10 1903							
	14								
	15								
	16								
	17								

TRIBAL ENROLLMENT OF PARENTS

	Name of Father	Year	County	Name of Mother	Year	County
1	Alfred Byington		Eagle	Lizzie Byington	Dead	Eagle
2	John Gibson	Dead	Jacks Fork	Ok-la-hu-na	"	Jacks Fork
3	No 1			Miney Byington	"	" "
4	No 1			No 2		
5	Joe McIntosh	Dead	Jacks Fork	No 2		
6	" "	"	" "	No 2		
7	No.1			No.2		
8						
9						
10						
11	No3 on 1896 roll as Silas Holson					
12	No5 " 1896 " " Jackman Byington					
13	No6 " 1896 " " Chartin McIntosh				#1 to 6 inc	
14	No.7 Enrolled November 12th, 1900 No.5 husband of No.3 on Choctaw card #4023				Date of Application for Enrollment.	
15	For child of Nos 1 and 2 see NB (March 3, 1905) #1293				Aug 28/99	
16						
17						

Choctaw By Blood Enrollment Cards 1898-1914

RESIDENCE: Jackson COUNTY.							CARD NO.	
POST OFFICE: Mayhew, I.T.	**Choctaw Nation** *(Not Including Freedmen)*			**Choctaw Roll**			FIELD NO. 4037	

Dawes' Roll No.	NAME	Relationship to Person First Named	AGE	SEX	BLOOD	TRIBAL ENROLLMENT		
						Year	County	No.
11299	1 Christie, Adam 46		43	M	Full	1896	Jackson	2805
	2							
	3							
	4							
	5 ENROLLMENT							
	6 OF NOS. 1 HEREON APPROVED BY THE SECRETARY							
	7 OF INTERIOR MAR 10 1903							
	8							
	9							
	10							
	11							
	12							
	13							
	14							
	15							
	16							
	17							

TRIBAL ENROLLMENT OF PARENTS

	Name of Father	Year	County	Name of Mother	Year	County
1	Te-ho-cubbee	Dead	Bok Tuklo	Se-bi-tey	Dead	Bok Tuklo
2						
3						
4						
5						
6						
7						
8						
9						
10						
11						
12						
13						
14					Date of Application for Enrollment.	
15					Aug 28/99	
16						
17						

137

Choctaw By Blood Enrollment Cards 1898-1914

RESIDENCE:	Jacks Fork	COUNTY.	Choctaw Nation		Choctaw Roll	CARD NO.	
POST OFFICE:	Stringtown, I.T.				(Not Including Freedmen)	FIELD NO. 4038	

Dawes' Roll No.	NAME	Relationship to Person First Named	AGE	SEX	BLOOD	TRIBAL ENROLLMENT Year	TRIBAL ENROLLMENT County	TRIBAL ENROLLMENT No.
DEAD.	1 Paine, Lola	Named	59	F	Full	1896	Atok.	10587
	2							
	3							
	4							
	5							
	6							
	7							
	8 No. 1 HEREON DISMISSED UNDER ORDER OF THE COMMISSION TO THE FIVE							
	9 CIVILIZED TRIBES OF MARCH 31, 1905.							
	10							
	11							
	12							
	13							
	14							
	15							
	16							
	17							

TRIBAL ENROLLMENT OF PARENTS

	Name of Father	Year	County	Name of Mother	Year	County
1	Tom Spain	Dead	Jacks Fork	Ho-key	Dead	Jacks Fork
2						
3						
4						
5						
6						
7						
8	On 1896 roll as Lottie Pain					
9						
10						
11	No1 Died in December, 1900; proof of death filed Nov. 25, 1902					
12						
13						
14						Date of Application for Enrollment.
15						Aug 28/99
16						
17						

138

Choctaw By Blood Enrollment Cards 1898-1914

RESIDENCE:	Jackson	COUNTY.								
POST OFFICE:	Mayhew, I.T.		**Choctaw Nation**				**Choctaw Roll** *(Not Including Freedmen)*		FIELD NO.	

Dawes' Roll No.	NAME		Relationship to Person First Named	AGE	SEX	BLOOD	TRIBAL ENROLLMENT		
							Year	County	No.
11300	1 Drew, Sallie A	35	First Named	32	F	Full	1893	Jackson	169
11301	2 Chubbee, Moses	10	Son	7	M	"	1893	"	170
	3								
	4								
	5								
	6	ENROLLMENT							
	7	OF NOS. 1 and 2 HEREON							
	8	APPROVED BY THE SECRETARY OF INTERIOR MAR 10 1903							
	9								
	10								
	11								
	12								
	13								
	14								
	15								
	16								
	17								

TRIBAL ENROLLMENT OF PARENTS

	Name of Father	Year	County	Name of Mother	Year	County
1	Lynn Drew	Dead	Jackson	Silway Drew	Dead	Jackson
2	Davison Chubbee	"	"	No 1		
3						
4						
5						
6						
7			No 1 on 1893 Pay Roll, Page 18, No 169, Jackson			
8			Co as Salliean Drew			
9			No 2 on 1893 Pay Roll Page 18, No 170 Jackson			
10			Co, as Mosses Chubbie			
			For child of No. 1 see NB (Mar 3, 1904) #468			
11						
12						
13						
14					Date of Application for Enrollment.	Aug 28/99
15						
16						
17	P.O. Caddo Okla					

139

Choctaw By Blood Enrollment Cards 1898-1914

RESIDENCE: Atoka	COUNTY.					CARD NO.
POST OFFICE: Coalgate, I.T.	**Choctaw Nation**		**Choctaw Roll** *(Not Including Freedmen)*			FIELD NO. **4040**

Dawes' Roll No.	NAME	Relationship to Person First Named	AGE	SEX	BLOOD	TRIBAL ENROLLMENT		
						Year	County	No.
11302	1 Dwight, Solomon 36	First Named	33	M	Full	1893	Kiamitia	96
	2							
	3							
	4							
	5	ENROLLMENT OF NOS. 1 HEREON APPROVED BY THE SECRETARY OF INTERIOR Mar 10 1903						
	6							
	7							
	8							
	9							
	10							
	11							
	12							
	13							
	14							
	15							
	16							
	17							

TRIBAL ENROLLMENT OF PARENTS

Name of Father	Year	County	Name of Mother	Year	County
1 Sha-lih-tubbee	Dead	Atoka		Dead	
2					
3					
4					
5					
6					
7		On 1893 Pay roll, Page 120, No 96, Kiamitia			
8		Co, as Sol Chukmubbe			
9					
10		No. 1 also on 1896 census roll as Solomon Hachubbe			
11		#5378		May 16, 1900	
12					
13		No1 is now husband of Salena Peterson		Date of Application for Enrollment.	
14		Choctaw Card #4129			
15				Aug 28/99	
16					
17					

Choctaw By Blood Enrollment Cards 1898-1914

RESIDENCE:	Jackson	COUNTY.	**Choctaw Nation**		Choctaw Roll	CARD NO.	
POST OFFICE:	Mayhew, I.T.				*(Not Including Freedmen)*	FIELD NO. **4041**	

Dawes' Roll No.	NAME		Relationship to Person First Named	AGE	SEX	BLOOD	TRIBAL ENROLLMENT		
							Year	County	No.
11303	1 Billy, Mary	43	First Named	40	F	Full	1896	Atoka	1863
11304	2 Cravatt, Ward	17	Son	14	M	"	1893	"	49
11305	3 Billy Salena	9	Dau	6	F	"	1896	"	4989
16051	4 Oshter, Bakie		Dau	1	F	"			
	5								
	6								
	7	ENROLLMENT							
	8	OF NOS. 1,2 and 3 HEREON APPROVED BY THE SECRETARY							
	9	OF INTERIOR Mar 10 1903							
	10								
	11								
	12								
	13								
	14	ENROLLMENT							
	15	OF NOS. ~~~ 4 ~~~ HEREON APPROVED BY THE SECRETARY							
	16	OF INTERIOR Aug 22 1906							
	17								

TRIBAL ENROLLMENT OF PARENTS

	Name of Father	Year	County	Name of Mother	Year	County
1	Billy Abaltubbee	Dead	Kiamitia	Ellen	Dead	Kiamitia
2	Benson Cravatt		Jackson	No1		
3	Cephus Gibson		Atoka	No1		
4	Isham Oshter		Choctaw Roll#11893	No1		
5						
6						
7			No2 on 1893 Pay Roll, Page 5, No 49, Atoka Co., as			
8			Ward Billy			
9			No3 on 1896 roll as Selina Gibson			
10						
11	Application for enrollment of No4 received March 4,1905 under act of Congress of March					
12	3,1905. No.4 placed on this card February 21 1906					
13						#1 to 3
14					Date of Application for Enrollment.	
15					Aug 28/99	
16			No.4 Granted			
17	P.O. Boswell, I.T.		Jun 13 1906			

141

Choctaw By Blood Enrollment Cards 1898-1914

RESIDENCE: Jackson COUNTY. **Choctaw Nation** Choctaw Roll CARD NO.
POST OFFICE: Mayhew, I.T. (Not Including Freedmen) FIELD NO. 4042

Dawes' Roll No.	NAME	Relationship to Person	AGE	SEX	BLOOD	TRIBAL ENROLLMENT		
						Year	County	No.
11306	1 Stewart, Wicy 46	First Named	43	F	Full	1896	Jackson	375
	2							
	3							
	4							
	5 ENROLLMENT OF NOS. 1 HEREON							
	6 APPROVED BY THE SECRETARY OF INTERIOR MAR 10 1903							
	7							
	8							
	9							
	10							
	11							
	12							
	13							
	14							
	15							
	16							
	17							

TRIBAL ENROLLMENT OF PARENTS

	Name of Father	Year	County	Name of Mother	Year	County
1	Thos. Roberts	Dead	Kiamitia	Winnie Roberts	Dead	Kiamitia
2						
3						
4						
5						
6						
7	On 1896 roll as Witchie Anchubbe					
8						
9						
10						
11						
12						
13						
14					Date of Application for Enrollment.	
15					Aug 28/99	
16						
17						

Choctaw By Blood Enrollment Cards 1898-1914

RESIDENCE:	Atoka	COUNTY.							
POST OFFICE:	Coalgate, I.T.								

Choctaw Nation

Choctaw Roll *(Not Including Freedmen)*

CARD NO.

FIELD NO. 4043

Dawes' Roll No.	NAME	Relationship to Person First Named	AGE	SEX	BLOOD	TRIBAL ENROLLMENT		
						Year	County	No.
11307	1 Willis, Jincy ¹⁹	First Named	16	F	Full	1896	Atoka	13924
	2							
	3							
	4							
	5 ENROLLMENT							
	6 OF NOS. 1 HEREON APPROVED BY THE SECRETARY							
	7 OF INTERIOR Mar 10 1903							
	8							
	9							
	10							
	11							
	12							
	13							
	14							
	15							
	16							
	17							

TRIBAL ENROLLMENT OF PARENTS

	Name of Father	Year	County	Name of Mother	Year	County
1	Sarphin Willis	Dead	Tobucksy	Mollie Janes	Dead	Atoka
2						
3						
4						
5						
6						
7						
8						
9						
10						
11						
12						
13						
14					Date of Application for Enrollment	
15					Aug 28/99	
16						
17						

Choctaw By Blood Enrollment Cards 1898-1914

RESIDENCE: Atoka   COUNTY. **Choctaw Nation**   **Choctaw Roll**   CARD NO.
POST OFFICE: Owl, I.T.   *(Not Including Freedmen)*   FIELD NO. **4044**

Dawes' Roll No.		NAME		Relationship to Person First Named	AGE	SEX	BLOOD	TRIBAL ENROLLMENT Year	County	No.
I.W. 379	1	McCarter, Andrew L	41	First Named	37	M	IW	1896	Jacks Fork	14879
11308	2	" Mattie	27	Wife	24	F	1/4	1896	" "	9462
11309	3	" Elmer W	11	Son	8	M	1/8	1896	" "	9463
11310	4	" Emmet P	7	"	4	"	1/8	1896	" "	9465
11311	5	" Ethel B	4	Dau	1½	F	1/8			
11312	6	" Edgar C	1	Son	3 wks	M	1/8			
	7									
	8									
	9									
	10	ENROLLMENT OF NOS. 2,3,4,5 and 6 HEREON								
	11	APPROVED BY THE SECRETARY								
	12	OF INTERIOR MAR 10 1903								
	13	ENROLLMENT OF NOS. 1 HEREON								
	14	APPROVED BY THE SECRETARY								
	15	OF INTERIOR SEP 12 1903								
	16									
	17									

TRIBAL ENROLLMENT OF PARENTS

	Name of Father	Year	County	Name of Mother	Year	County
1	John McCarter	Dead	Non Citz	Jane McCarter	Dead	Non Citz
2	Tony Maytubby	"	Chick Roll	Lucinda Maytubby	"	Kiamitia
3	No1			No2		
4	No1			No2		
5	No1			No2		
6	No1			No2		
7						
8						
9						
10	No1 on 1896 roll as A. L. McCarter					
11	No3 " 1896 " " E W "					
12	No4 " 1896 " " Emmett P "					
13	No5 Affidavit of birth to be supplied:- Filed Oct 26/99					
14	No.6 Enrolled September 3, 1901				Date of Application for Enrollment.	
15	For child of Nos 1&2 see NB (Act Mar 3 '05) Card #280				Aug 29/99	
16						
17						

144

RESIDENCE: Atoka   COUNTY.
POST OFFICE: Owl, I.T.

Choctaw Nation

Choctaw Roll
(Not Including Freedmen)

CARD NO.
FIELD NO. 4045

Dawes' Roll No.	NAME		Relationship to Person First Named	AGE	SEX	BLOOD	TRIBAL ENROLLMENT		
							Year	County	No.
I.W. 380	₁ Wallace, John	49		37	M	IW	1896	Jacks Fork	15192
11313	₂ " Minerva J	34	Wife	31	F	1/8	1896	" "	14088
11314	₃ " Mattie M	14	Dau	11	"	1/16	1896	" "	14089
11315	₄ " Clarence E	9	Son	6	M	1/16	1896	" "	14090
11316	₅ " May M	7	Dau	4	F	1/16	1896	" "	14091
11317	₆ " Viola G	4	"	5mo	"	1/16			
	₇								
	₈								
	₉								
	₁₀	ENROLLMENT							
	₁₁	OF NOS. 2,3,4,5 and 6 HEREON APPROVED BY THE SECRETARY							
	₁₂	OF INTERIOR MAR 10 1903							
	₁₃	ENROLLMENT							
	₁₄	OF NOS. 1 HEREON APPROVED BY THE SECRETARY							
	₁₅	OF INTERIOR SEP 12 1903							
	₁₆								
	₁₇								

TRIBAL ENROLLMENT OF PARENTS

	Name of Father	Year	County	Name of Mother	Year	County
₁	John Wallace		Non Citz	Eliza Wallace	Dead	Non Citz
₂	John McCoy	Dead	Kiamitia	Lucinda McCoy	"	Jacks Fork
₃	No1			No2		
₄	No1			No2		
₅	No1			No2		
₆	No1			No2		
₇						
₈						
₉						
₁₀			No2 on 1896 roll as Minervy Wallace			
₁₁			No3 " 1896 " " Mattly "			
₁₂			No4 " 1896 " " Elrena "			
₁₃			No5 " 1896 " " Mary M "			
₁₄			No6 Affidavit of birth to be supplied:- Filed Oct 26/99		Date of Application for Enrollment	
₁₅			No1- Evidence of marriage to be supplied:-		Aug 29/99	
₁₆	Child of No3 on NB (Apr 26-06) Card #301					
₁₇	" " Nos 1&2 see NB (Mar 3-05) Card #281					

Choctaw By Blood Enrollment Cards 1898-1914

Dawes' Roll No.	NAME		Relationship to Person	AGE	SEX	BLOOD	TRIBAL ENROLLMENT		
							Year	County	No.
11318	1 Plummer, Raymond	37	First Named	34	M	1/8	1896	Atoka	10572
I.W. 381	2 " Laura B	28	Wife	24	F	IW			
11319	3 " Joe R	8	Dau	5	"	1/16	1896	Atoka	10573
11320	4 " Frank E	5	Son	2	M	1/16			
11321	5 " Dawes R	3	"	2mo	"	1/16			
	6								
	7								
	8	No4 Affidavit of birth to							
	9	be supplied:- Recd Oct 26/99							
	10	For child of Nos 1&2 see NB (Mar 3-05) #912							
	11								
	12	ENROLLMENT							
	13	OF NOS. 1,3,4 and 5 HEREON APPROVED BY THE SECRETARY							
	14	OF INTERIOR MAR 10 1903							
	15	ENROLLMENT							
	16	OF NOS. 2 HEREON APPROVED BY THE SECRETARY							
	17	OF INTERIOR SEP 12 1903							

TRIBAL ENROLLMENT OF PARENTS

	Name of Father	Year	County	Name of Mother	Year	County
1	J. R. Plummer		Atoka	Mary S Plummer		Non Citz
2	John Crabtree	Dead	Non Citz		Dead	" "
3	No1			No2		
4	No1			No2		
5	No1			No2		
6						
7						
8						
9	No1 on 1896 roll as Raymon Plummer					
10	Was also admitted by Act of Choctaw Council No 39, Approved Nov 8/95					
11	No3 on 1896 roll as Joe Plummer — Was					
12	also admitted by Act of Choctaw Council, No					
13	39, Approved Nov 8/95, as Joe A Plummer					
14	No2- Was admitted by Dawes Com. Case No 580					Date of Application for Enrollment.
15	No1- As to marriage of parents, see					Aug 29/99
16	enrollment of Joseph R Plummer.					nrolled Dec 16
17						

Choctaw By Blood Enrollment Cards 1898-1914

RESIDENCE: Atoka COUNTY.
POST OFFICE: Lehigh, I.T.

Choctaw Nation

Choctaw Roll
(Not Including Freedmen)

CARD NO.
FIELD NO. 4047

Dawes' Roll No.	NAME	Relationship to Person First Named	AGE	SEX	BLOOD	TRIBAL ENROLLMENT		
						Year	County	No.
11322	1 Reagan, Mary G 40		37	F	1/8	1896	Atoka	10990
11323	2 Mann, Stella 19	Dau	16	"	1/16	1896	"	10992
11324	3 Reagan, Thomas B 11	Son	8	M	1/16	1896	"	10991
	4							
	5							
	6							
	7	ENROLLMENT OF NOS. 1,2 and 3 HEREON APPROVED BY THE SECRETARY OF INTERIOR MAR 10 1903						
	8							
	9							
	10							
	11							
	12							
	13							
	14							
	15							
	16							
	17							

TRIBAL ENROLLMENT OF PARENTS

	Name of Father	Year	County	Name of Mother	Year	County
1	J. R. Plummer		Atoka	Mary S Plummer		Non Citz
2	Earl V. Reagan	Dead	Non Citz	No1		
3	" " "	"	" "	No1		
4						
5						
6						
7						
8						
9						
10		No1 on 1896 roll as Mollie Reagan- was				
11		also admitted by Act of Choctaw Council				
12		No 39, Approved Nov 8/95				
13		No2-3 were also admitted by same Act.				
14		No1 - As to marriage of parents, see			Date of Application for Enrollment:	
15		enrollment of Joseph R. Plummer			Aug 29/99	
16		No2 is now wife of Jewel Mann; evidence of marriage filed Dec 13, 1902				
17	P.O. Nixon I.T.	For child of No2 see NB (Mar 3 1905) #559				

10/13/02

147

Choctaw By Blood Enrollment Cards 1898-1914

RESIDENCE: Atoka	COUNTY. **Choctaw Nation**	**Choctaw Roll** (Not Including Freedmen)	CARD No.
POST OFFICE: Atoka, I.T.			FIELD No. 4048

Dawes' Roll No.	NAME		Relationship to Person First Named	AGE	SEX	BLOOD	TRIBAL ENROLLMENT		
							Year	County	No.
I.W.**382**	1 Conlan, Michael	43	First Named	40	M	IW	1896	Atoka	14422
11325	2 " Czarina	32	Wife	29	F	1/4	1896	"	2917
11326	3 " Lottie A	7	Dau	4	"	1/8	1896	"	2918
	4								
	5								
	6								
	7	ENROLLMENT OF NOS. 2 and 3 HEREON							
	8	APPROVED BY THE SECRETARY							
	9	OF INTERIOR MAR 10 1903							
	10	ENROLLMENT OF NOS 1 HEREON							
	11	APPROVED BY THE SECRETARY OF INTERIOR SEP 12 1903							
	12								
	13								
	14								
	15								
	16								
	17								

TRIBAL ENROLLMENT OF PARENTS

	Name of Father	Year	County	Name of Mother	Year	County
1	Michael Conlan	Dead	Non Citz	Anna Conlan		Non Citz
2	James Colbert	"	Chick Roll	Athenias Colbert		Atoka
3	No1			No2		
4						
5						
6						
7						
8						
9	Surname of all on 1896 roll, Conlen					
10	No1 on 1896 roll as Michael Conlin					
11	All enrolled on 1896 roll under name of Conlin					
12	No1- Evidence of marriage to be					
13	supplied:- Filed Oct 26/99					
14	No.1 admitted by Dawes Commission in 1896 as an intermarried citizen; Choctaw case #695; no appeal					
15			Date of Application for Enrollment.		Aug 29/99	
16						
17						

148

Choctaw By Blood Enrollment Cards 1898-1914

RESIDENCE: Atoka   COUNTY.   **Choctaw Nation**   **Choctaw Roll**   CARD No.

POST OFFICE: Lehigh, I.T.   *(Not Including Freedmen)*   FIELD NO. **4049**

Dawes' Roll No.		NAME		Relationship to Person	AGE	SEX	BLOOD	TRIBAL ENROLLMENT		
								Year	County	No.
11327	1	Plummer Joseph R	69	First Named	66	M	1/4	1896	Atoka	10565
I.W. 383	2	" Mary S	65	Wife	62	F	I.W.			
11328	3	" John E	31	Son	28	M	1/8	1896	Atoka	10571
I.W. 673	4	" Ella Pearl	23	Wife of No3	23	F	I.W.			
	5									
	6									
	7	ENROLLMENT OF NOS. 1 and 3 HEREON APPROVED BY THE SECRETARY OF INTERIOR Mar 10 1903								
	8									
	9									
	10	ENROLLMENT OF NOS. 2 HEREON APPROVED BY THE SECRETARY OF INTERIOR Sep 12 1903								
	11									
	12									
	13	ENROLLMENT OF NOS. 4 HEREON APPROVED BY THE SECRETARY OF INTERIOR Mar 26 1904								
	14									
	15									
	16									
	17									

TRIBAL ENROLLMENT OF PARENTS

	Name of Father	Year	County	Name of Mother	Year	County
1	J. R. Plummer	Dead	Non Citz	Ann V. Plummer	Dead	Choctaw
2	G. W. Spruill	"	" " "	Eliz. Spruill	"	Non Citz
3	No1			No2		
4	Thos. B. Seal		non citizen	Permelia Seal		non citizen
5						
6	No.4 transferred from Choctaw card D562, January 25, 1904					
7	See decision of January 7, 1904					
8	No1 was admitted by Act of Choctaw					
9	Council. Approved November 2, 1883					
10	No2 was admitted by Dawes Com, Cae No 459					
11	No3 on 1896 roll as J. E. Plummer					
12	was also admitted by Act of Choctaw					
13	Council No 39 Approved No 8/95. As					
14	J. E. Plummer					Date of Application for Enrollment.
15	No.3 is now married to Ellen Pearl Plummer on Choctaw card D.562					
16	For child of Nos 3&4 see N B (Apr 26 '06) Card #266					Aug 29/99
17						

149

Choctaw By Blood Enrollment Cards 1898-1914

RESIDENCE: Atoka   COUNTY. **Choctaw Nation**   Choctaw Roll   CARD NO.

POST OFFICE: Atoka, I.T.   *(Not Including Freedmen)*   FIELD NO. **4050**

Dawes' Roll No.	NAME	Relationship to Person First Named	AGE	SEX	BLOOD	TRIBAL ENROLLMENT Year	County	No.
11329	1 Wilson, Charles ⁹¹	First Named	88	M	Full	1896	Atoka	14053
DEAD.	2 " Lucy	Wife	70	F	"	1896	"	14054
	3							
	4							
	5							
	6							
	7	ENROLLMENT OF NOS. 1 HEREON APPROVED BY THE SECRETARY						
	8	OF INTERIOR MAR 10 1903						
	9							
	10							
	11	No. 2 HEREON DISMISSED UNDER						
	12	ORDER OF THE COMMISSION TO THE FIVE						
	13	CIVILIZED TRIBES OF MARCH 31, 1905.						
	14							
	15							
	16							
	17							

TRIBAL ENROLLMENT OF PARENTS

	Name of Father	Year	County	Name of Mother	Year	County
1	Ma-sha-cha	Dead	Cedar	E-la-te-ka	Dead	Cedar
2	Jefferson Sexton	"	Atoka	Winnie Sexton	"	Atoka
3						
4						
5						
6						
7	No2 died March 24, 1900; proof of death filed Nov 25, 1902					
8						
9						
10						
11						
12						
13						
14					Date of Application for Enrollment.	
15					Aug 29/99	
16						
17						

Choctaw By Blood Enrollment Cards 1898-1914

RESIDENCE: **Jacks Fork** COUNTY. **Choctaw Nation**   **Choctaw Roll** CARD NO.
POST OFFICE: **Stringtown, I.T.**   *(Not Including Freedmen)* FIELD NO. **4051**

Dawes' Roll No.	NAME	Relationship to Person First Named	AGE	SEX	BLOOD	TRIBAL ENROLLMENT		
						Year	County	No.
11330	1 Bond, Moses ⁷¹		68	M	Full	1896	Jacks Fork	1882
~~11331~~	2 " ~~Harrison~~ ⁴	~~Son~~	~~1~~	"	"			
	3							
	4							
	5							
	6	ENROLLMENT						
	7	OF NOS. 1 and 2 HEREON APPROVED BY THE SECRETARY						
	8	OF INTERIOR Mar 10 1903						
	9							
	10							
	11							
	12							
	13							
	14							
	15							
	16							
	17							

TRIBAL ENROLLMENT OF PARENTS

	Name of Father	Year	County	Name of Mother	Year	County
1	Bond	Dead	in Mississippi	Ish-te-mi-ah	Dead	Gaines
2	~~No1~~			~~Narsie Bond~~	"	~~Jacks Fork~~
3						
4						
5						
6	No2 is duplicate of Harrison Bond on Choctaw card #4845					
7	His enrollment opposite #11331 cancelled under Departmental instructions of September 26, 1903					
8						
9						
10						
11						
12						
13						
14						
15				Date of Application for Enrollment.	Aug 29/99	
16						
17						

Choctaw By Blood Enrollment Cards 1898-1914

RESIDENCE:	Atoka	COUNTY.								CARD NO.	
POST OFFICE:	Lehigh I.T.		**Choctaw Nation** *(Not Including Freedmen)*				**Choctaw Roll**			FIELD NO. **4052**	

Dawes' Roll No.	NAME		Relationship to Person	AGE	SEX	BLOOD	TRIBAL ENROLLMENT		
							Year	County	No.
11332	1 Beams, Simon	59	First Named	56	M	1/2	1896	Atoka	1746
11333	2 " Elsie	7	Dau	4	F	3/4	1896	"	1747
	3								
	4								
	5								
	6	ENROLLMENT							
	7	OF NOS. 1 and 2 HEREON APPROVED BY THE SECRETARY							
	8	OF INTERIOR Mar 10 1903							
	9								
	10								
	11								
	12								
	13								
	14								
	15								
	16								
	17								

TRIBAL ENROLLMENT OF PARENTS

	Name of Father	Year	County	Name of Mother	Year	County
1	Gilbert Beams	Dead	Jacks Fork	Iney Beams	Dead	Jacks Fork
2	No1			Eliz. Beams	"	Atoka
3						
4						
5						
6	No1 on 1896 roll as Simeon Beams					
7	No2 " 1896 " " Elsey "					
8						
9						
10						
11						
12						
13						
14				Date of Application for Enrollment.	Aug 29/99	
15						
16						
17						

RESIDENCE: Atoka   COUNTY.   **Choctaw Nation**   **Choctaw Roll**   CARD No.

POST OFFICE: Legal, I.T.   *(Not Including Freedmen)*   FIELD No. **4053**

Dawes' Roll No.	NAME	Relationship to Person First Named	AGE	SEX	BLOOD	TRIBAL ENROLLMENT Year	County	No.
11334	1 King, Anderson 61	Named	58	M	Full	1896	Atoka	7643
11335	2 " Louvina 68	Wife	65	F	1/4	1896	"	4433
11336	3 " McGee 15	Son	12	M	Full	1896	"	7645
11337	4 " Anderson Jr 13	"	10	"	"	1896	"	7646
11338	5 Jones, Dora 15	G.Dau	12	F	"	1893	Gaines	287
15473	6 " Julia 6	"	3	"	"			
	7							
	8							
	9							
	10							
	11							
	12							
	13							
	14							
	15							
	16							
	17							

ENROLLMENT
OF NOS. 1,2,3,4 and 5 HEREON
APPROVED BY THE SECRETARY
OF INTERIOR Mar 10 1903

ENROLLMENT
OF NOS. ~~~~ 6 ~~~~ HEREON
APPROVED BY THE SECRETARY
OF INTERIOR May 9 1904

N°6 Born Sept 28th 1896 proof of birth
filed March 14, 1904

TRIBAL ENROLLMENT OF PARENTS

	Name of Father	Year	County	Name of Mother	Year	County
1	James King	Dead	Sans Bois	Pikey King	Dead	Skullyville
2	Calvin Campbell	"	Non Citz	Mary Campbell	"	Kiamitia
3	No1			Lizzie King	"	Atoka
4	No1			" "	"	"
5	Jamison Jones	Dead	Gaines	Adaline Jones	"	Gaines
6	" "	"	"	" "	"	"
7						
8						
9				Adaline Jones 1893 Gaines Page 30 No 286		
10			No2 on 1896 roll as Lovina Franklin			
11			No4 " 1896 " " Anderson King			
12		Gaines Co	No5 on 1893 Pay Roll, Page 30, No 287			
13			Mother of Nos 5-6 is dead. No			
14			physician present at birth of No6			Date of Application for Enrollment.
15			N°5 is wife of W.S. Smith non-citizen -- evidence of			Aug 29/99
16			marriage filed Jany 23, 1903			
17			For child of No5 see NB (Mar 3-05) Card #1357			
			" " " " (Apr 26-06) " #436			

No5 PO Guertie IT 4/27/05

Choctaw By Blood Enrollment Cards 1898-1914

RESIDENCE: Atoka   COUNTY.
POST OFFICE: Atoka, I.T.

Choctaw Nation

Choctaw Roll (Not Including Freedmen)

CARD No.
FIELD No. 4054

Dawes' Roll No.	NAME	Relationship to Person First Named	AGE	SEX	BLOOD	TRIBAL ENROLLMENT		
						Year	County	No.
11339	1 James, Cephus ⁵⁴	First Named	51	M	Full	1896	Atoka	7312
11340	2 " Louisiana ⁴⁵	Wife	42	F	"	1896	"	8844
	3							
	4							
	5	ENROLLMENT						
	6	OF NOS. 1 and 2 HEREON APPROVED BY THE SECRETARY						
	7	OF INTERIOR MAR 10 1903						
	8							
	9							
	10							
	11							
	12							
	13							
	14							
	15							
	16							
	17							

TRIBAL ENROLLMENT OF PARENTS

	Name of Father	Year	County	Name of Mother	Year	County
1	Wilham James	Dead	Atoka	E-sha-to-na	Dead	Atoka
2	John Steele	"	"	Netsey Steele	"	"
3						
4						
5						
6						
7	No2 on 1896 roll as Louisiana More					
8						
9						
10						
11						
12						
13						
14					Date of Application for Enrollment.	
15					Aug 29/99	
16						
17						

RESIDENCE:	Atoka	COUNTY.							
POST OFFICE:	Lehigh I.T.	**Choctaw Nation**		**Choctaw Roll** *(Not Including Freedmen)*			CARD NO. FIELD NO. **4055**		

Dawes' Roll No.		NAME	Relationship to Person First Named	AGE	SEX	BLOOD	TRIBAL ENROLLMENT		
							Year	County	No.
11341	1	Goings, Susan		40	F	1/2	1896	Atoka	4945
11342	2	" James	Son	13	M	3/4	1896	"	4946
11343	3	" John L	"	9	"	1/4	1896	"	4947
11344	4	" Rena	Dau	6	F	1/4	1896	"	4949
11345	5	" Mike	Son	3	M	1/4	1896	"	4948
	6								
	7								
	8								
	9	CITIZENSHIP CERTIFICATE ISSUED FOR NO. 1-2-3-4 & 5							
	10	AUG 14 1903							
	11								
	12								
	13								
	14	ENROLLMENT OF NOS. 1-2-3-4-5 HEREON							
	15	APPROVED BY THE SECRETARY							
	16	OF INTERIOR MAR 10 1903							
	17								

TRIBAL ENROLLMENT OF PARENTS

	Name of Father	Year	County	Name of Mother	Year	County
1	Bill Goer	Dead	Non Citz	Susan Goer	Dead	Kiamitia
2	Jos Roberson	"	Atoka	No1		
3	Ransom Goings		Non Citz	No1		
4	" "		" "	No1		
5	" "		" "	No1		
6						
7						
8	No1 on 1896 roll as Sarah Goings					
9	No2 " 1896 " " Jim "					
10	No3 " 1896 " " John "					
11						
12						
13						
14						
15						
16					Aug 29/99	
17						

Choctaw By Blood Enrollment Cards 1898-1914

RESIDENCE: **Blue** COUNTY. **Choctaw Nation** **Choctaw Roll** CARD NO.
POST OFFICE: **Caddo, I.T.** *(Not Including Freedmen)* FIELD NO. **4056**

Dawes' Roll No.	NAME	Relationship to Person First Named	AGE	SEX	BLOOD	TRIBAL ENROLLMENT Year	County	No.
DEAD	1 Jefferson, Thomas	First Named	67	M	Full	1896	Blue	7214
11346	2 " Mollie 50	Wife	47	F	"	1896	"	7215
11347	3 " Abraham 16	Son	13	M	"	1896	"	7216
DEAD	4 " Thomas E	"	11	!	"	1896	"	7217
DEAD	5 Nail, Melissa	S.Dau	28	F	"	1896	"	9804
11348	6 Byington, Mary A 20	Ward	17	"	"	1896	"	403
11349	7 Anderson, John 18	"	15	M	"	1896	"	419
11350	8 Honey, Simon 10	"	7	"	"	1896	"	5878
11351	9 Byington, Jesse 1	Son of N°6	4mo	M	"			
	10							

No1 died May 1901: proof of death filed Nov. 22, 1902
No4 died Dec. 16, 1900: proof of death filed Nov 22, 1902
No5 died May 8, 1901: proof of death filed Nov. 22, 1902

ENROLLMENT
OF NOS. 2,3,6,7,8 and 9 HEREON
APPROVED BY THE SECRETARY
OF INTERIOR Mar 10 1903

TRIBAL ENROLLMENT OF PARENTS

	Name of Father	Year	County	Name of Mother	Year	County
1	Ah-lo-ma	Dead	Jackson	Cah-lo-na	Dead	Blue
2	Ik-sa-ho-pi-ye	"	Atoka	Betsey	"	
3	No1			No2		
4	No1			No2		
5	Min-te-hi-ya	Dead	Blue	No2		
6	William Anderson	"	"	Mary Anderson	Dead	Blue
7	" "	"	"	" "	"	"
8	Josephus Honey	"	"	Jincey Honey	"	"
9	Alonzo Byington	1896	Atoka	N°6		
10	No4 on 1896 roll as Thomas Jefferson					
11	No6 " 1896 " " Mary Anderson					
12	No7 " 1896 " " Johnny "					
13	N°6 is now the wife of Alonzo Byington on Choctaw card #3380. Evidence of marriage filed Oct. 23, 1902.					#1 to 8
14	N°9 Born June 15, 1902, enrolled Oct. 23, 1902					Date of Application for Enrollment.
15	No1, 4 and 5 hereon dismissed under order of the Commission to the Five Civilized Tribes of March 31, 1905.					Aug 29/99

156

Choctaw By Blood Enrollment Cards 1898-1914

RESIDENCE: Atoka   COUNTY. **Choctaw Nation**   Choctaw Roll   CARD NO.

POST OFFICE: Atoka, I.T.   *(Not Including Freedmen)*   FIELD NO. 4057

Dawes' Roll No.	NAME		Relationship to Person First Named	AGE	SEX	BLOOD	TRIBAL ENROLLMENT		
							Year	County	No.
11352	1 LeFlore, Greenwood	42	First Named	39	M	1/8	1896	Atoka	8316
I.W. 384	2 " Marion	37	Wife	29	F	IW	1896	"	14789
11353	3 " Nola	15	Dau	12	"	1/16	1896	Atoka	8317
11354	4 " Louie	13	Dau	10	F	1/16	1896	"	8318
11355	5 " Corrinn	7	Dau	4	F	1/16	1896	"	8319
11356	6 " James	13	Nephew	10	M	1/16	1896	"	8320
	7								
	8								
	9								
	10	ENROLLMENT OF NOS. 1,3,4,5 and 6 HEREON							
	11	APPROVED BY THE SECRETARY							
	12	OF INTERIOR MAR 10 1903							
	13	ENROLLMENT OF NOS. 2 HEREON							
	14	APPROVED BY THE SECRETARY							
	15	OF INTERIOR SEP 12 1903							
	16								
	17								

TRIBAL ENROLLMENT OF PARENTS

	Name of Father	Year	County	Name of Mother	Year	County
1	J. D. LeFlore	Dead	in Mississippi	Fannie N. LeFlore	Dead	Non Citz
2	Jas. Hudson	"	Non Citz		"	" "
3	No1			No2		
4	No1			No2		
5	No1			No2		
6	Chas. Trimble		Non Citz	Fannie L Trimble	Dead	in Mississippi
7						
8						
9	No4 on 1896 roll as Louisa LeFlore			Nos 1,3 and 4 admitted by act of Choctaw		
10	No5 " 1896 " " C. "			Council of Oct. 26, 1893		
11	No6 " 1896 " " Jim T "					
12	No1 as to marriage of parents					
13	see his testimony					
14	No2 on 1896 roll as Mary A. LeFlore					
15	All but No1 were admitted by Dawes Com,				Date of Application for Enrollment.	
	Case No 1226, as La Flore Error Nos 2,5&6 admitted					
16	No.4 Sex changed under Departmental instructions of				Aug 29/99	
	March 1, 1904 (D.C. #7217-1904)					
17	P.O. S McAlester I.T.					

12/30/02

157

Choctaw By Blood Enrollment Cards 1898-1914

									CARD NO.		
							Choctaw Roll		FIELD NO. 4058		
							(Not Including Freedmen)				

Dawes' Roll No.	NAME		Relationship to Person	AGE	SEX	BLOOD	TRIBAL ENROLLMENT			
							Year	County		No.
11357	1 King, Lucinda	53	First Named	50	F	Full	1896	Atoka		7649
11358	2 " Nelson	7	Son	4	M	"	1896	"		7650
	3									
	4									
	5									
	6	ENROLLMENT								
	7	OF NOS. 1 and 2 HEREON APPROVED BY THE SECRETARY								
	8	OF INTERIOR MAR 10 1903								
	9									
	10									
	11									
	12									
	13									
	14									
	15									
	16									
	17									

TRIBAL ENROLLMENT OF PARENTS

	Name of Father	Year	County	Name of Mother	Year	County
1	Silas Pusley	Dead	Gaines		Dead	Gaines
2	Campbell King	"	Atoka	No1		
3						
4						
5						
6						
7						
8						
9						
10						
11						
12						
13						
14						
15				Date of Application for Enrollment.		Aug 29/99
16						
17						

Choctaw By Blood Enrollment Cards 1898-1914

RESIDENCE: Blue COUNTY. **Choctaw Nation** **Choctaw Roll** CARD NO.
POST OFFICE: Boggy Depot, I.T. *(Not Including Freedmen)* FIELD NO. **4059**

Dawes' Roll No.	NAME	Relationship to Person First Named	AGE	SEX	BLOOD	TRIBAL ENROLLMENT		
						Year	County	No.
DEAD	1 Perkins, David	Named	30	M	Full	1896	Blue	10516
11359	2 " Serena 25	Wife	22	F	"	1896	"	1680
	3							
	4							
	5							
	6 ENROLLMENT							
	7 OF NOS. 2 HEREON APPROVED BY THE SECRETARY							
	8 OF INTERIOR Mar 10 1903							
	9 No.1 hereon dismissed under order of							
	10 the Commission to the Five Civilized							
	11 Tribes of March 31, 1905.							
	12							
	13							
	14							
	15							
	16							
	17							

TRIBAL ENROLLMENT OF PARENTS

	Name of Father	Year	County	Name of Mother	Year	County
1	David Perkins	Dead	Blue	Elsie Perkins	Dead	Blue
2	James Billy	"	"	Mebina Billy	"	Kiamitia
3						
4						
5						
6						
7	No2 on 1896 roll as Serena Billy					
8	No1 died Dec. 30, 1901, proof of death filed Nov. 22, 1902					
9	N°2 is now wife of N. A. Perkins, Choctaw card #3437 11/17/02					
10						
11						
12						
13						
14						
15					Date of Application for Enrollment.	Aug 29/99
16						
17						

Choctaw By Blood Enrollment Cards 1898-1914

RESIDENCE: Atoka   COUNTY. **Choctaw Nation**   **Choctaw Roll**   CARD NO.
POST OFFICE: Atoka, I.T.   *(Not Including Freedmen)*   FIELD NO. 4060

Dawes' Roll No.		NAME		Relationship to Person	AGE	SEX	BLOOD	TRIBAL ENROLLMENT			
								Year	County		No.
11360	1	Wilson, Marcus	43	First Named	40	M	Full	1896	Atoka		14051
	2										
	3										
	4										
	5	ENROLLMENT									
	6	OF NOS. 1 HEREON APPROVED BY THE SECRETARY									
	7	OF INTERIOR MAR 10 1903									
	8										
	9										
	10										
	11										
	12										
	13										
	14										
	15										
	16										
	17										

TRIBAL ENROLLMENT OF PARENTS

	Name of Father	Year	County	Name of Mother	Year	County
1	Chas Wilson		Atoka	Tik-ba-te-ma	Dead	Atoka
2						
3						
4						
5						
6						
7						
8						
9						
10						
11						
12						
13						
14						
15				Date of Application for Enrollment.	Aug 29/99	
16						
17						

160

Choctaw By Blood Enrollment Cards 1898-1914

RESIDENCE: Kiamitia COUNTY.			**Choctaw Nation**			**Choctaw Roll** *(Not Including Freedmen)*	CARD NO.	
POST OFFICE: Goodland, I.T.							FIELD NO. **4061**	

Dawes' Roll No.	NAME		Relationship to Person First Named	AGE	SEX	BLOOD	TRIBAL ENROLLMENT		
							Year	County	No.
11361	1 Carnes, Annie	22		19	F	Full	1896	Kiamitia	11014
11362	2 Carnes, Malina	1	Dau	4mo	F	"			
	3								
	4								
	5								
	6	ENROLLMENT							
	7	OF NOS. 1 and 2 HEREON APPROVED BY THE SECRETARY							
	8	OF INTERIOR Mar 10 1903							
	9								
	10								
	11								
	12								
	13								
	14								
	15								
	16								
	17								

TRIBAL ENROLLMENT OF PARENTS

	Name of Father	Year	County	Name of Mother	Year	County
1	Battiest Robinson	Dead	Towson	Ellen Samuel		Kiamitia
2	Anderson Carnes	1896	Atoka	No.1		
3						
4						
5						
6						
7	No. 1 is now the wife of Anderson Carnes on Choctaw Card #4278. See letter of					
8	A. Tellea filed Aug. 13, 1901					
9	No2 Enrolled Aug 13, 1901					
10	For child of No.1 see NB (Apr 26, 1906) Card No. 148					
11						
12						
13						
14					#1	
15				Date of Application for Enrollment	Aug 29/99	
16						
17						

Choctaw By Blood Enrollment Cards 1898-1914

RESIDENCE:	Atoka	COUNTY.							
POST OFFICE:	Atoka I.T.								

Choctaw Nation — Choctaw Roll *(Not Including Freedmen)*

CARD NO. / FIELD NO. **4062**

Dawes' Roll No.	NAME	Relationship to Person First Named	AGE	SEX	BLOOD	TRIBAL ENROLLMENT Year	County	No.
11363	1 Bays, Emma ²⁴	First Named	21	F	1/4	1893	Atoka	260
11364	2 Crowley Narne ⁶	Son	3	M	1/8			
DEAD	3 " Mattie	"[sic]	8mo	F	1/8			
11365	4 Bays, John Henry ¹	Son	4mo	M	1/8			
	5							
	6							
	7							
	8							
	9							
	10							
	11							
	12							
	13							
	14							
	15							
	16							
	17							

ENROLLMENT OF NOS. 1,2 and 4 HEREON APPROVED BY THE SECRETARY OF INTERIOR Mar 10 1903

No.3 hereon dismissed under order of the Commission to the Five Civilized Tribes of March 31, 1905.

TRIBAL ENROLLMENT OF PARENTS

	Name of Father	Year	County	Name of Mother	Year	County
1	Henry Frazier	Dead	Atoka	Lottie Frazier		Non Citz
2	Geo. Crowley		Non Citz	No1		
3	" "		" "	No1		
4	J. L. Bays		" "	No.1		
5						
6	No2 is a male. Sex changed under Departmental authority of Jan. 17, 1907 (L.T.D					
7	812-1907) D.C 4186-1907					
8	No1 is now wife of J. L. Bays, a non citizen; evidence of marriage filed Dec. 22, 1902					
9	No1 On 1893 Pay Roll, Page 25, No 260, Atoka Co, as Emly Frazier					
10	For child of No1 see NB (Mar 3 '05) #1335					
11	Nos 2-3 Affidavits of birth to be supplied. Filed Oct 26/99					
12	Evidence of divorce of No1 from her former husband filed Feby 16, 1903					
13	No1- As to marriage of parents, see					
14	testimony of Louvina King.					
15	No3 died Oct. 31, 1899: proof of death filed Nov. 22, 1902					
16	No4 Born Aug 5 1902: enrolled Dec 22, 1901					
17	P.O. No1 Coalgate I.T.					

Date of Application for Enrollment. Aug 29/99

11/19/02

162

Choctaw By Blood Enrollment Cards 1898-1914

RESIDENCE:	Jackson	COUNTY.							
POST OFFICE:	Mayhew, I.T.							CARD NO. FIELD NO.	**4063**

Choctaw Nation

Choctaw Roll *(Not Including Freedmen)*

Dawes' Roll No.	NAME		Relationship to Person First Named	AGE	SEX	BLOOD	TRIBAL ENROLLMENT		
							Year	County	No.
DEAD	1 Tully, Silas	64		61	M	Full	1896	Jackson	12373
11366	2 " Jincy	33	Wife	30	F	"	1893	Wade	65
DEAD	3 " Isabelle	17	Dau	14	"	"	1896	Jackson	12375
11367	4 " Molsey	10	"	7	"	"	1896	"	12376
11368	5 " Canada	4	Son	9mo	M	"			
11369	6 Jones, Grayson	7	S.Son	4	"	"			
11370	7 Tully, Emma	2	Dau	9mo	F	"			
	8								
	9	ENROLLMENT							
	10	OF NOS. 2,4,5,6 and 7 HEREON APPROVED BY THE SECRETARY							
	11	OF INTERIOR Mar 10 1903							
	12	No1 died Feb, 1901: proof of							
	13	death filed Dec. 6, 1902							
	14	No.3 died in 1901: proof of death filed Dec 6, 1902							
	15	No.1 and 3 hereon dismissed under							
	16	order of the Commission to the Five							
	17	Civilized Tribes of March 31, 1905.							

TRIBAL ENROLLMENT OF PARENTS

Name of Father	Year	County	Name of Mother	Year	County
1 Ta-le-ho-ma	Dead	Jackson	Sally Homma	Dead	Jackson
2 Ellis Bohanan		Wade		"	Wade
3 No1			Ellen Tully	"	Jackson
4 No1			" "	"	"
5 No1			No2		
6 Willis Jones		Jackson	No2		
7 No.1			No.2		
8					
9 No4 on 1896 roll as Malissa Tully					
10 No2 on 1893 Pay roll, Page 8, No 65,					
11 Wade Co, as Jincy Bohanan					
12 Nos 5-6 Affidavits of birth to be supplied:-					
13 No2 also on 1896 roll, Page 176, No 7158,					#1 to 6
14 as Jincy Jones, Jackson Co					Date of Application for Enrollment.
15 No7, Enrolled Sept. 4, 1901					Aug 29/99
16					
17					

Choctaw By Blood Enrollment Cards 1898-1914

RESIDENCE:	Atoka	COUNTY.		
POST OFFICE:	Coalgate, IT			

Choctaw Nation

Choctaw Roll (*Not Including Freedmen*)

CARD NO.
FIELD NO. **4064**

Dawes' Roll No.	NAME	Relationship to Person First Named	AGE	SEX	BLOOD	TRIBAL ENROLLMENT		
						Year	County	No.
11371	1 James Louisiana 33 ✓	First Named	30	F	Full	1893	Cedar	266
11372	2 Patterson Mary A 4 ✓	Dau	1	"	"			
15845	3 Gipson, Jincey ✓	"	1	F	"			
SHIP CERTIFICATE OR NO 1 & 2 MAY 15 1903	4							
	6							
	7							
	8							
	9							
	10							
CERTIFICATE NO ~~ 31 ~~ 24 1905	ENROLLMENT OF NOS. ~~ 3 ~~ HEREON APPROVED BY THE SECRETARY OF INTERIOR JUN 12 1905							
	13							
	14	ENROLLMENT OF NOS. 1 - 2 HEREON APPROVED BY THE SECRETARY OF INTERIOR MAR 10 1903						
	15							
	16							
	17							

TRIBAL ENROLLMENT OF PARENTS

	Name of Father	Year	County	Name of Mother	Year	County
1	Thompson James	Dead	Towson	Hullit James	Dead	Bok Tuklo
2	John Patterson		Jacks Fork	No 1		
3	John Gipson		Choctaw	No 1		
4						
5						
6						
7						
8	No 1 on 1896 Choctaw Roll Jacks Fork County, page 270					
9	No 10599 as Louisiana Patterson					
10	No 1 on 1893 Pay Roll, Page 25 No 266 Cedar Co					
11	No 3 was born Sept 25, 1902, application first received March 4, 1905 and No.3 placed on this card, under act of Congress approved March 3, 1905					
12	Father of No.3 on Choctaw card No 4002, No. 1 thereon					
13						
14						
15						Aug 29/99
16						
17						

164

Choctaw By Blood Enrollment Cards 1898-1914

RESIDENCE:	Atoka	COUNTY.	**Choctaw Nation**	**Choctaw Roll**	CARD NO.
POST OFFICE:	Legal, I.T.			*(Not Including Freedmen)*	FIELD NO. 4065

Dawes' Roll No.	NAME	Relationship to Person First Named	AGE	SEX	BLOOD	TRIBAL ENROLLMENT		
						Year	County	No.
11373	1 Cunnish, Webster 25	First Named	22	M	1/8	1896	Atoka	7659
	2							
	3							
	4							
	5	ENROLLMENT						
	6	OF NOS. 1 HEREON APPROVED BY THE SECRETARY						
	7	OF INTERIOR MAR 10 1903						
	8							
	9							
	10							
	11							
	12							
	13							
	14							
	15							
	16							
	17							

TRIBAL ENROLLMENT OF PARENTS

Name of Father	Year	County	Name of Mother	Year	County
1 Cunnish Maytubby	Dead	Chick Roll	Louvina King		Atoka
2					
3					
4					
5			.		
6 No1 Husband of Martha Anderson on Choctaw Card #3281; Evidence of marriage filed Dec 26 1902					
7 On 1896 roll as Webster Kernish					
8 For child of No.1 see NB (March 3, 1905) #1447					
9					
10					
11					
12					
13					Date of Application for Enrollment:
14					
15					Aug 29/99
16					
17 P.O. Lehigh I.T. 12/26/02					

Choctaw By Blood Enrollment Cards 1898-1914

RESIDENCE:	Atoka	COUNTY.	**Choctaw Nation**	**Choctaw Roll**	CARD NO.
POST OFFICE:	Coalgate, I.T.			*(Not Including Freedmen)*	FIELD NO. 4066

Dawes' Roll No.	NAME	Relationship to Person First Named	AGE	SEX	BLOOD	TRIBAL ENROLLMENT		
						Year	County	No.
I.W. 385	1 LeFlore, Anne Mary 57	First Named	54	F	IW	1896	~~Atoka~~	~~14753~~
	2						Blue	14776
	3							
	4							
	5							
	6							
	7							
	8							
	9							
	10							
	11							
	12							
	13							
	14							
	15							
	16							
	17							

ENROLLMENT
OF NOS. 1 HEREON
APPROVED BY THE SECRETARY
OF INTERIOR SEP 12 1903

TRIBAL ENROLLMENT OF PARENTS

Name of Father	Year	County	Name of Mother	Year	County
1 F. J. Maurer	Dead	Non Citz	Annie M Maurer	Dead	Non Citz
2					
3					
4					
5					
6					
7	~~On 1896 roll as Arley M LeFlore, also on~~				
8	~~1896 roll as~~ Mary LeFlore, Page 393, ~~No 14776~~				
9	~~Atoka~~				
10					
11					
12					
13					
14					
15				Date of Application for Enrollment.	Aug 29/99	
16					
17	P.O. Lehigh I.T.				

11/17/02

Choctaw By Blood Enrollment Cards 1898-1914

RESIDENCE: Atoka   COUNTY.
POST OFFICE: Atoka, I.T.

Choctaw Nation

Choctaw Roll *(Not Including Freedmen)*

CARD NO.
FIELD NO. **4067**

Dawes' Roll No.	NAME		Relationship to Person First Named	AGE	SEX	BLOOD	TRIBAL ENROLLMENT		
							Year	County	No.
11374	₁ Folsom, Don J	36	First Named	33	M	1/16	1896	Atoka	4452
I.W.386	₂ " Deborah	31	Wife	28	F	IW	1896	"	14541
11375	₃ " Daphne	14	Dau	11	"	1/32	1896	Atoka	4455
11376	₄ " Robinson	13	Son	10	M	1/32	1896	"	4453
11377	₅ " Ethel	12	Dau	9	F	1/32	1896	"	4456
11378	₆ " Blanche	10	"	7	"	1/32	1896	"	4457
11379	₇ " Henry H	9	Son	6	M	1/32	1896	"	4454
11380	₈ " Alice	7	Dau	4	F	1/32	1896	"	4458
11381	₉ " Ruth	4	"	2	"	1/32			
11382	₁₀ " Adelaide	3	"	2mo	"	1/32			
11383	₁₁ " Christine	2	Dau	2½mo	F	1/32			
	₁₂ Affidavit as to No 9 filed								
	₁₃ Nov 2/99								
	₁₄ No.2 admitted by Dawes Commission in 1896								
	₁₅ as an intermarried citizen: Choctaw case #445								
	no appeal								
	₁₆ No.11 Enrolled December 15, 1900.								
	₁₇								

TRIBAL ENROLLMENT OF PARENTS

	Name of Father	Year	County	Name of Mother	Year	County
₁	Julius C Folsom		Atoka	Nettie Folsom	Dead	Atoka
₂	J. R. Brown		Non Citz	Emma Brown		Non Citz
₃	No1			No2		
₄	No1			No2		
₅	No1			No2		
₆	No1			No2		
₇	No1			No2		
₈	No1			No2		
₉	No1			No2		
₁₀	No1			No2		
₁₁	No.1			No.2		
₁₂	No2- As to marriage, see testimony of					
₁₃	Julius C Folsom					
₁₄	No9-10 Affidavits of birth to be supplied Filed Oct 26/ 99					
	No3 On 1896 roll as Dolphine Folsom					
₁₅	No5 " 1896 " " Eshel "					
₁₆	No6 " 1896 " " Maggie "					
₁₇	No2 " 1896 " " Debrott Fulson					

ENROLLMENT OF NOS. 1,3,4,5,6,7,8,9,10 and 11 HEREON APPROVED BY THE SECRETARY OF INTERIOR MAR 10 1903

ENROLLMENT OF NOS 2 HEREON APPROVED BY THE SECRETARY OF INTERIOR SEP 12 1903

#1 to 10 inc

Date of Application for Enrollment. Aug 29/99

P.O. Lindsey I.T. 11/20/02

Choctaw By Blood Enrollment Cards 1898-1914

Dawes' Roll No.	NAME	Relationship to Person	AGE	SEX	BLOOD	TRIBAL ENROLLMENT		
						Year	County	No.
I.W. 387	1 Perry, Adolphus E 35	First Named	32	M	I.W.			
11384	2 " Carrie M 28	Wife	25	F	1/8	1896	Atoka	10582
	3							
	4							
	5							
	6	ENROLLMENT						
	7	OF NOS. 2 HEREON APPROVED BY THE SECRETARY						
	8	OF INTERIOR MAR 10 1903						
	9	ENROLLMENT						
	10	OF NOS. 1 HEREON APPROVED BY THE SECRETARY						
	11	OF INTERIOR SEP 12 1903						
	12							
	13							
	14							
	15							
	16							
	17							

TRIBAL ENROLLMENT OF PARENTS

Name of Father	Year	County	Name of Mother	Year	County
1 Edward Perry		Non Citz	Melanie Perry		Non Citz
2 Forbis LeFlore	Dead	Blue	Annie M LeFlore		" "
3					
4					
5					
6		No2- On 1896 roll as Clora Perry- As to			
7		marriage of parents, see enrollment of			
8		mother, Annie M. LeFlore			
9					
10		No.1 admitted in 1896 as an intermarried citizen by			
11		Dawes Commission, Choctaw Case #575. No appeal.			
12					
13					
14					
15			Date of Application for Enrollment.	Aug 29/99	
16					
17					

Choctaw By Blood Enrollment Cards 1898-1914

	RESIDENCE: Atoka COUNTY.				

RESIDENCE: Atoka COUNTY. **Choctaw Nation** **Choctaw Roll** (Not Including Freedmen) CARD NO.
POST OFFICE: Allen, I.T. FIELD NO. 4069

Dawes' Roll No.	NAME	Relationship to Person First Named	AGE	SEX	BLOOD	TRIBAL ENROLLMENT Year	County	No.
I.W.388	1 Bentley, John M 35	First Named	29	M	IW			
11385	2 " Lucy 30	Wife	27	F	1/8	1896	Blue	8182
11386	3 " John W E 3	Son	5mo	M	1/16			
11387	4 " Ellis LeFlore 1	Son	1mo	M	1/16			
	5							
	6							
	7	ENROLLMENT						
	8	OF NOS. 2,3 and 4 HEREON APPROVED BY THE SECRETARY						
	9	OF INTERIOR Mar 10 1903						
	10	ENROLLMENT						
	11	OF NOS. 1 HEREON APPROVED BY THE SECRETARY						
	12	OF INTERIOR SEP 12 1903						
	13							
	14							
	15							
	16							
	17							

TRIBAL ENROLLMENT OF PARENTS

	Name of Father	Year	County	Name of Mother	Year	County
1	Ellis R Bentley		Non Citz	Marra A Bentley	Dead	Non Citz
2	Forbis LeFlore	Dead	Blue	Annie M LeFlore		Intermarried
3	No1			No2		
4	No.1			No.2		
5						
6						
7			No2- As to marriage of parents, see			
8		enrollment of mother, Annie M. LeFlore				
9		No3- Affidavit of birth to be				
10		supplied:- Filed Oct 26/99				
11		No2 on 1896 roll as Lucy LeFlore				
12		No.4 Born Feby 28, 1902: enrolled March 31, 1902.				
13						
14				Date of Application for Enrollment.		
15				Aug 29/99		
16						
17						

169

Choctaw By Blood Enrollment Cards 1898-1914

RESIDENCE: **Atoka** COUNTY. **Choctaw Nation** **Choctaw Roll** CARD NO.
POST OFFICE: **Limestone, I.T.** *(Not Including Freedmen)* FIELD NO. **4070**

Dawes' Roll No.	NAME		Relationship to Person First Named	AGE	SEX	BLOOD	TRIBAL ENROLLMENT		
							Year	County	No.
11388	1 LeFlore. Charles	61	First Named	58	M	1/8	1896	Atoka	8288
I.W. 389	2 " Louisa F	25	Wife	23	F	IW	1896	"	14783
	3								
	4								
	5								
	6	ENROLLMENT							
	7	OF NOS. 1 HEREON APPROVED BY THE SECRETARY							
	8	OF INTERIOR MAR 10 1903							
	9	ENROLLMENT							
	10	OF NOS. 2 HEREON APPROVED BY THE SECRETARY							
	11	OF INTERIOR SEP 12 1903							
	12								
	13								
	14								
	15								
	16								
	17								

TRIBAL ENROLLMENT OF PARENTS

	Name of Father	Year	County	Name of Mother	Year	County
1	Forbis LeFlore	Dead	Blue	Rebecca LeFlore	Dead	Blue
2	R. L. Patrick	"	Non Citz	Lucy M Patrick	"	Non Citz
3						
4						
5						
6	No1 on 1896 roll as Chas A LeFlore					
7	Both admitted by Dawes Com. Case					
8	No 1212 Application in this case was only for wife					
9	No1 was admitted as Chas LaFlore					
	No2 " " " Louisa Frances					
10	LaFlore					
11	Right name of No2 is "Louisa".					
12						
13						
14						
15				Date of Application for Enrollment.	Aug 29/99	
16						
17	P.O. Limestone Ind Ter					

Choctaw By Blood Enrollment Cards 1898-1914

RESIDENCE: **Jackson** COUNTY. **Choctaw Nation** **Choctaw Roll** CARD NO.
POST OFFICE: **Mayhew, I.T.** (Not Including Freedmen) FIELD NO. **4071**

Dawes' Roll No.	NAME	Relationship to Person First Named	AGE	SEX	BLOOD	TRIBAL ENROLLMENT		
						Year	County	No.
11389	1 Frazier, Mary 66	First Named	63	F	Full	1896	Jackson	4308
	2							
	3							
	4							
	5	ENROLLMENT						
	6	OF NOS. 1 HEREON APPROVED BY THE SECRETARY						
	7	OF INTERIOR MAR 10 1903						
	8							
	9							
	10							
	11							
	12							
	13							
	14							
	15							
	16							
	17							

TRIBAL ENROLLMENT OF PARENTS

	Name of Father	Year	County	Name of Mother	Year	County
1	Cha-fa-tubbee	Dead	Kiamitia		Dead	Chick Disr
2						
3						
4						
5						
6						
7						
8						
9						
10						
11						
12						
13						
14						
15				Date of Application for Enrollment.		Aug 29/99
16						
17						

Choctaw By Blood Enrollment Cards 1898-1914

RESIDENCE:	Atoka	COUNTY.						CARD NO.
POST OFFICE:	Stringtown, I.T.	**Choctaw Nation**		**Choctaw Roll** *(Not Including Freedmen)*			FIELD NO.	**4072**

Dawes' Roll No.	NAME	Relationship to Person	AGE	SEX	BLOOD	TRIBAL ENROLLMENT		
						Year	County	No.
11390	1 Welch, Frances 48	First Named	45	F	Full	1896	Jacks Fork	6111
	2							
	3							
	4							
	5	ENROLLMENT OF NOS. 1 HEREON APPROVED BY THE SECRETARY OF INTERIOR Mar 10 1903						
	6							
	7							
	8							
	9							
	10							
	11							
	12							
	13							
	14							
	15							
	16							
	17							

TRIBAL ENROLLMENT OF PARENTS

	Name of Father	Year	County	Name of Mother	Year	County
1	Ya-hom-bey	Dead	Jacks Fork	Mollie	Dead	Jacks Fork
2						
3						
4						
5						
6	On 1896 roll as Phillissie Home					
7						
8						
9						
10						
11						
12						
13						
14						
15					Date of Application for Enrollment.	Aug 29/99
16						
17						

Choctaw By Blood Enrollment Cards 1898-1914

				COUNTY.				CARD NO.	

Choctaw Nation

Atoka COUNTY.

POST OFFICE: Coalgate, I.T.

Choctaw Roll *(Not Including Freedmen)*

CARD NO. FIELD NO. **4073**

Dawes' Roll No.		NAME	Relationship to Person First Named	AGE	SEX	BLOOD	TRIBAL ENROLLMENT		
							Year	County	No.
DEAD.	1	Andrews, John		45	M	IW			
11391	2	" Maggie 28	Wife	25	F	3/4	1896	Atoka	12473
11392	3	" Marie 5	Dau	1	"	3/8			
11393	4	Thompson, Bun 6	S.Son	3	M	3/8	1896	Atoka	2971
	5								
	6								
	7								
	8	ENROLLMENT							
	9	OF NOS. 2,3, and 4 HEREON APPROVED BY THE SECRETARY							
	10	OF INTERIOR MAR 10 1903							
	11	No. 1 HEREON DISMISSED UNDER							
	12	ORDER OF THE COMMISSION TO THE FIVE							
	13	CIVILIZED TRIBES OF MARCH 31, 1905.							
	14								
	15								
	16								
	17								

TRIBAL ENROLLMENT OF PARENTS

	Name of Father	Year	County	Name of Mother	Year	County
1	Andrews	Dead	Non Citz	Millie Andrews		Non Citz
2	Thompson	"	Blue	Sarah Thompson	Dead	Blue
3	No1			No2		
4	Thompson		Non Citz	No2		
5						
6						
7			No2 on 1896 roll as Maggie Thompson			
8			No4 " 1896 " " Ed. Colton			
9			Nos 3-4 Affidavits of birth to be			
10			supplied:- Affidavit as to No3 filed Oct 26/99. As to No4 filed Nov 2/99			
11			No1 died July 1, 1902; proof of death filed Nov 26, 1902			
12			For child of No.2 see NB (Mar 3'05) #590			
13						
14						
15					Date of Application for Enrollment.	Aug 29/99
16						
17	No1 PO Newberry I.T. 3/28/05					

Choctaw By Blood Enrollment Cards 1898-1914

	RESIDENCE:	Atoka	COUNTY.			
	POST OFFICE:	Kiowa, I.T.				

Choctaw Nation

Choctaw Roll *(Not Including Freedmen)*

CARD NO. FIELD NO. **4074**

Dawes' Roll No.	NAME	Relationship to Person First Named	AGE	SEX	BLOOD	TRIBAL ENROLLMENT Year	TRIBAL ENROLLMENT County	TRIBAL ENROLLMENT No.
11394	1 Benjamin, Charlie	Named	57	M	Full	1896	Atoka	1828
11395	2 " Josephine	Wife	27	F	"	1896	"	1829
	3							
	4							
	5							
	6							
	7							
	8							
	9							
	10							
	11							
	12							
	13							
	14							
	15							
	16							
	17							

ENROLLMENT
OF NOS. 1 and 2 HEREON
APPROVED BY THE SECRETARY
OF INTERIOR MAR 10 1903

TRIBAL ENROLLMENT OF PARENTS

Name of Father	Year	County	Name of Mother	Year	County
1 Ma-ko-chubbee	Dead	Towson	Ok-li-ye-hema	Dead	Towson
2 James Collins	"	Atoka	Mary Collins	"	Atoka
3					
4					
5					
6					
7					
8					
9					
10					
11					
12					
13					
14				Date of Application for Enrollment.	
15				Aug 29/99	
16					
17					

			RESIDENCE: Atoka COUNTY.				

RESIDENCE: Atoka   **COUNTY.**

POST OFFICE: Coalgate, I.T.

Choctaw Nation

Choctaw Roll
(Not Including Freedmen)

CARD NO.

FIELD NO. 4075

Dawes' Roll No.	NAME	Relationship to Person First Named	AGE	SEX	BLOOD	TRIBAL ENROLLMENT		
						Year	County	No.
I.W. 390	1 Rushing, Annie 40		38	F	IW			
	2							
	3							
	4							
	5							
	6							
	7							
	8	ENROLLMENT						
	9	OF NOS. 1 HEREON						
	10	APPROVED BY THE SECRETARY OF INTERIOR SEP 12 1903						
	11							
	12							
	13							
	14							
	15							
	16							
	17							

TRIBAL ENROLLMENT OF PARENTS

	Name of Father	Year	County	Name of Mother	Year	County
1	Hugh Sherwood	Dead	Non Citz	Eliz Sherwood	Dead	Non Citz
2						
3						
4						
5						
6	Admitted by Dawes Com Case No 655.					
7						
8						
9						
10						
11						
12						
13						
14						
15				Date of Application for Enrollment	Aug 29/99	
16	Tupelo Okla 11/30/10					
17						

Waupanucka[sic] 11/19/02

175

Choctaw By Blood Enrollment Cards 1898-1914

RESIDENCE:	Jackson	COUNTY.	**Choctaw Nation**		Choctaw Roll	CARD NO.	
POST OFFICE:	Mayhew, I.T.				*(Not Including Freedmen)*	FIELD NO. **4076**	

Dawes' Roll No.	NAME		Relationship to Person First Named	AGE	SEX	BLOOD	TRIBAL ENROLLMENT		
							Year	County	No.
11396	1 Colbert, Aaron	41	First Named	38	M	1/2	1896	Jackson	2809
DEAD	2 " Tennessee		Wife	28	F	Full	1896	"	2810
11397	3 " Eliza	14	Dau	11	"	3/4	1896	"	2811
11398	4 Thompson, Marful	17	Ward	14	M	Full	1896	"	12377
11399	5 " Sissy	13	"	10	F	"	1896	"	12378
11400	6 " Jincy	11	"	8	"	"	1896	"	12379
	7								
	8								
	9								
	10	ENROLLMENT OF NOS. 1,3,4,5 and 6 HEREON APPROVED BY THE SECRETARY							
	11	OF INTERIOR Mar 10 1903							
	12								
	13	No. 2 hereon dismissed under order of							
	14	the Commission to the Five Civilized							
	15	Tribes of March 31, 1905.							
	16								
	17								

TRIBAL ENROLLMENT OF PARENTS

	Name of Father	Year	County	Name of Mother	Year	County
1	Philip Colbert	Dead	Chick Roll		Dead	Kiamitia
2	Ca-no-un-tubbee	"	Jackson	Ish-tu-na	"	Jackson
3	No 1			Tennessee Colbert		"
4	Robert Thompson	Dead	Jackson	Nicey Thompson	Dead	"
5	" "	"	"	" "	"	"
6	" "	"	"	" "	"	"
7						
8	No.2 died March 1900; proof of death filed Nov. 22, 1902					
9	For child of No.3 see NB (Apr 26, 1906) Card no. 25					
10	" " " " 1 " " (Mar 3, 1905) " " 458					
11						
12						
13						
14					Date of Application for Enrollment	
15					Aug 29/99	
16						
17			P.O. Boswell, I.T.			

4/22/02

Choctaw By Blood Enrollment Cards 1898-1914

RESIDENCE: **Atoka** COUNTY. **Choctaw Nation** **Choctaw Roll** CARD NO.

POST OFFICE: **Lehigh, I.T.** (Not Including Freedmen) FIELD NO. **4077**

Dawes' Roll No.	NAME		Relationship to Person First Named	AGE	SEX	BLOOD	TRIBAL ENROLLMENT		
							Year	County	No.
11401	1 Vinson, Charles S	59	First Named	56	M	1/4	1896	Atoka	12626
11402	2 " Mary A	58	Wife	55	F	3/4	1896	"	12627
11403	3 " Rhoda	16	Dau	13	"	3/8	1893	Jacks Fork	570
	4								
	5								
	6								
	7	ENROLLMENT							
	8	OF NOS. 1,2 and 3 HEREON APPROVED BY THE SECRETARY							
	9	OF INTERIOR MAR 10 1903							
	10								
	11								
	12								
	13								
	14								
	15								
	16								
	17								

TRIBAL ENROLLMENT OF PARENTS

	Name of Father	Year	County	Name of Mother	Year	County
1	Hiram Vinson	Dead	Non Citz	Malinda Vinson	Dead	Blue
2	Benj James	"	Bok Tuklo	Mary James	"	"
3	No1			Rachel Nelson	"	Kiamitia
4						
5						
6						
7						
8	No1 on 1896 roll as Charlie Vinson					
9	No3 on 1893 Pay Roll, Page 64, No 270,					
10	Jacks Fork Co, also on 1896 roll, Page 2[?]0, No 9878 as Rhoda Nelson					
11	For child of No.3 see NB (March 3 1905) #1[?]01					
12						
13						
14					Date of Application for Enrollment.	
15					Aug 29/99	
16						
17						

Choctaw By Blood Enrollment Cards 1898-1914

RESIDENCE:	Atoka	COUNTY.							CARD NO.	
POST OFFICE:	Lehigh, I.T.		Choctaw Nation			Choctaw Roll *(Not Including Freedmen)*			FIELD NO.	4078

Dawes' Roll No.	NAME		Relationship to Person	AGE	SEX	BLOOD	TRIBAL ENROLLMENT			
							Year	County		No.
11404	1 Shinn, Mary	36	First Named	33	F	3/8	1896	Atoka		11659
11405	2 " Rena E	11	Dau	8	"	3/16	1896	"		11661
11406	3 " Charley	9	Son	6	M	3/16	1896	"		11660
11407	4 " Henry	6	"	3	"	3/16				
	5									
	6									
	7									
	8	ENROLLMENT OF NOS. 1,2,3 and 4 HEREON								
	9	APPROVED BY THE SECRETARY								
	10	OF INTERIOR MAR 10 1903								
	11									
	12									
	13									
	14									
	15									
	16									
	17									

TRIBAL ENROLLMENT OF PARENTS

	Name of Father	Year	County	Name of Mother	Year	County
1	Dull Sanders	Dead	Cherokee	Kiziah Battiest		Jackson
2	William Shinn	"	Non Citz	No1		
3	" "	"	" "	No1		
4	" "	"	" "	No1		
5						
6						
7			No4 Affidavit of birth to be			
8			supplied:- Filed Nov 2/99			
9						
10						
11						
12						
13						
14						Date of Application for Enrollment.
15						Aug 29/99
16						
17						

178

Choctaw By Blood Enrollment Cards 1898-1914

RESIDENCE: Chickasaw Nation ~~COUNTY~~.
POST OFFICE: Healdton, I.T.
Choctaw Nation
Choctaw Roll
(Not Including Freedmen)
CARD NO.
FIELD NO. **4079**

Dawes' Roll No.	NAME	Relationship to Person First Named	AGE	SEX	BLOOD	TRIBAL ENROLLMENT		
						Year	County	No.
11408	1 Bennett, Lucy E 30	First Named	27	F	1/8	1896	Atoka	1805
11409	2 " William F 11	Son	8	M	1/16	1896	"	1806
11410	3 " Joseph C 8	"	5	"	1/16	1896	"	1807
11411	4 " Margaret V 7	Dau	4	F	1/16	1896	"	1808
DEAD.	5 " ~~Minerva E~~	"	~~1~~	"	~~1/16~~			
	6							
	7							
	8							
	9	ENROLLMENT						
	10	OF NOS. 1,2,3 and 4 HEREON APPROVED BY THE SECRETARY						
	11	OF INTERIOR MAR 10 1903						
	12	No. 5 HEREON DISMISSED UNDER						
	13	ORDER OF THE COMMISSION TO THE FIVE CIVILIZED TRIBES OF MARCH 31, 1905.						
	14							
	15							
	16							
	17							

TRIBAL ENROLLMENT OF PARENTS

	Name of Father	Year	County	Name of Mother	Year	County
1	Thos. Lowery		Chick Dist	Margaret Lowery	Dead	Non Citz
2	Thos. Bennett		Non Citz	No 1		
3	" "		" "	No 1		
4	" "		" "	No 1		
5	" "		" "	~~No 1~~		
6						
7	No 1 on 1896 roll as Lucy M Bennett					
8	No 2 " 1896 " " Wᵐ T. "					
9						
10	No 1- Evidence of marriage of parents					
11	to be supplied					
12						
13	No 5 Affidavit of birth to be					
14	supplied:- Filed Oct 26/99				Date of Application for Enrollment	
15	No.5 Died Dec, 1899. Proof of death filed Nol. 1, 1902 ~~For child of No 1 see NB (Apr 26-06) Card #438~~				Aug 29/99	
16	" children " " " (Mar 3-05) " #1223					
17						

179

Choctaw By Blood Enrollment Cards 1898-1914

RESIDENCE: Atoka	COUNTY.	**Choctaw Nation**	**Choctaw Roll**	CARD NO.
ICE: Atoka, I.T.			*(Not Including Freedmen)*	FIELD NO. 4080

NAME		Relationship to Person	AGE	SEX	BLOOD	TRIBAL ENROLLMENT		
						Year	County	No.
1 Jones, Noel	62	First Named	59	M	Full	1896	Atoka	7279
2 Wilson, Narcissa	17	Dau	14	F	"	1896	"	7283
3 Jones, Edward	15	Son	12	M	"	1896	"	7281
4 " Israel	22	"	19	"	"	1896	"	7282
5 Wilson, Clarence Monroe	2	Grand Son	2m	M	1/2			
6 " Walter Green	1	Grand Son	1mo	M	1/2			
7								
8								
9								
10								
11								
12								
13								
14								
15								
16								
17								

ENROLLMENT
OF NOS. 1,2,3,4,5 and 6   HEREON
APPROVED BY THE SECRETARY
OF INTERIOR   MAR 10 1903

TRIBAL ENROLLMENT OF PARENTS

Name of Father	Year	County	Name of Mother	Year	County
1 Solomon Jones	Dead	Blue		Dead	Bok Tuklo
2 No1			Mary Jones	"	Blue
3 No1			" "	"	"
4 No1			" "	"	"
5 S.W. Wilson		non citizen	No2		
6 " "		" "	Nº2		
7					
8 No2 on 1896 roll as Narcissus Jones					
9 No2 is now the wife of S. W. Wilson a non citizen					
10 Evidence of marriage filed February 5, 1901					
No.5 Enrolled February 5, 1901					
11 Nº6 Born Aug 28, 1902. Enrolled Sept. 25, 1902.					
12 For child of No.2 see NB (March 3, 1905) #1128					
13					
14				#1 to 4 inc	
15			Date of Application for Enrollment.	Aug 29/99	
16					
17					

RESIDENCE:	Atoka	COUNTY.							

Choctaw Nation

Choctaw Roll (Not Including Freedmen)

POST OFFICE: Atoka, I.T.

CARD No.
FIELD No. 4081

Dawes' Roll No.	NAME		Relationship to Person First Named	AGE	SEX	BLOOD	TRIBAL ENROLLMENT		
							Year	County	No.
11418	1 Jacob, Austin	63		60	M	Full	1896	Atoka	7244
11419	2 " Eastman	26	Son	23	"	"	1896	"	7250
11420	3 " Nelson	23	"	20	"	"	1896	"	7246
11421	4 " Eliza	21	Dau	18	F	"	1896	"	7248
11422	5 Jacob Wilson	16	Son	13	M	"	1896	"	7247
11423	6 " Sillen	3	Dau	10	F	"	1896	"	7249
11424	7 Armstrong, Edmond	1	Gr. Son	6mo	M	"			
	8								
	9								
	10								
	11	ENROLLMENT							
	12	OF NOS. 1,2,3,4,5,6 and 7 HEREON APPROVED BY THE SECRETARY							
	13	OF INTERIOR M 10 1903							
	14								
	15								
	16								
	17								

TRIBAL ENROLLMENT OF PARENTS

	Name of Father	Year	County	Name of Mother	Year	County
1	Jacob	Dead	Towson		Dead	Towson
2	No1			Sealey A Jacob	"	Atoka
3	No1			" " "	"	"
4	No1			" " "	"	"
5	No1			" " "	"	"
6	No1			" " "	"	"
7	Lewis Armstrong	1896	Atoka	No.4		
8	No4 on 1896 roll as Liza Jacob					
9	No6 " 1896 " " Sillum "					
10	No.4 is now the wife of Lewis Armstrong on Choctaw card #4363. Evidence of marriage filed April 2, 1902.					
11	No.7 Born Oct 7, 1901; enrolled April 2, 1902					
12	No. [?] now the husband of Mary Frazier No2 on 7-3481 8/14/1911					
13	No.2 is now the husband of Sina Armstrong, Choctaw card #4088 11/17/02					
14	No.1 is husband of Sarah Lewis on Choctaw card #4089 11/20/02 1 to 6 inc					
15	For child of No4 see NB (Act Mar 3-05) Card #282				Date of Application for Enrollment.	
16	" " " " 2 " " " " " " " 283				Aug 29/99	
17	P.O. #2 Bennington Okla 8/14/11					

181

Choctaw By Blood Enrollment Cards 1898-1914

RESIDENCE:	Atoka	COUNTY.	**Choctaw Nation**	Choctaw Roll *(Not Including Freedmen)*	CARD NO.
POST OFFICE:	Boggy Depot, I.T.				FIELD NO. **4082**

Dawes' Roll No.	NAME		Relationship to Person First Named	AGE	SEX	BLOOD	TRIBAL ENROLLMENT		
							Year	County	No.
DEAD	1 Roberts, Stephen		57	M	Full	1896	Atoka	10980
11425	2 " Georgiana	43	Wife	40	F	"	1896	"	10981
11426	3 " Emeline	7	Dau	4	"	"	1896	"	10982
11427	4 McClure, Gipson	16	S.Son	13	M	"	1896	"	9439
	5								
	6								
	7								
	8	ENROLLMENT OF NOS. 2,3 and 4 HEREON APPROVED BY THE SECRETARY OF INTERIOR Mar 10 1903							
	9								
	10								
	11	No. 1 hereon dismissed under order of							
	12	the Commission to the Five Civilized							
	13	Tribes of March 31, 1905.							
	14								
	15								
	16								
	17								

TRIBAL ENROLLMENT OF PARENTS

Name of Father	Year	County	Name of Mother	Year	County
1 Thos. Roberts	Dead	Kiamitia	Winnie Roberts	Dead	Kiamitia
2 Willis Hoyoubbee	"	Atoka	Isabelle Hoyoubbee	"	Atoka
3 No1			No2		
4 Joe McClure		Jackson	No2		
5					
6					
7					
8		No2 on 1896 roll as Sallie Ann Roberts			
9					
10					
11		No1 died July 3, 1900: proof of death filed Nov. 26, 1902			
12					
13					Date of Application for Enrollment.
14					
15					Aug 29/99
16					
17					

182

Choctaw By Blood Enrollment Cards 1898-1914

RESIDENCE: Atoka COUNTY. **Choctaw Nation** Choctaw Roll CARD NO.
POST OFFICE: Boggy Depot, I.T. *(Not Including Freedmen)* FIELD NO. 4083

Dawes' Roll No.	NAME	Relationship to Person First Named	AGE	SEX	BLOOD	TRIBAL ENROLLMENT		
						Year	County	No.
11428	1 Hoyobbee, Isabelle 63		60	F	Full	1896	Atoka	5972
11429	2 Foster, Sarah 6	G.D.	3	"	"	1896	"	4476
	3							
	4							
	5							
	6	ENROLLMENT						
	7	OF NOS. 1 and 2 HEREON APPROVED BY THE SECRETARY						
	8	OF INTERIOR MAR 10 1903						
	9							
	10							
	11							
	12							
	13							
	14							
	15							
	16							
	17							

TRIBAL ENROLLMENT OF PARENTS

	Name of Father	Year	County	Name of Mother	Year	County
1	Hak-lo-tubbee	Dead	Bok Tuklo	Harriet	Dead	Bok Tuklo
2	Abel Foster		Atoka	Julian Foster		
3						
4						
5						
6						
7						
8						
9						
10						
11						
12						
13						
14						
15				Date of Application for Enrollment.	Aug 29/99	
16						
17						

183

Choctaw By Blood Enrollment Cards 1898-1914

RESIDENCE:	Jackson	COUNTY.	Choctaw Nation	Choctaw Roll (Not Including Freedmen)	CARD NO.
POST OFFICE:	Mayhew, I.T.				FIELD NO. **4084**

Dawes' Roll No.	NAME		Relationship to Person First Named	AGE	SEX	BLOOD	TRIBAL ENROLLMENT		
							Year	County	No.
11430	1 Oshter, Lake	60	First Named	57	M	Full	1896	Jackson	9990
11431	2 " Sibbie	48	Wife	45	F	"	1896	"	9991
DEAD	3 " Sally		Dau	14	"	"	1896	"	9993
11432	4 Cravatt, Mitchell	15	Ward	12	M	"	1896	"	2793
11433	5 " Isabelle	6	"	3	F	"	1896	"	2794
	6								
	7								
	8								
	9	ENROLLMENT OF NOS. 1,2,4 and 5 HEREON APPROVED BY THE SECRETARY OF INTERIOR Mar 10 1903							
	10								
	11								
	12	No. 3 hereon dismissed under order of							
	13	the Commission to the Five Civilized							
	14	Tribes of March 31, 1905.							
	15								
	16								
	17								

TRIBAL ENROLLMENT OF PARENTS

	Name of Father	Year	County	Name of Mother	Year	County
1	Oshter	Dead	Bok Tuklo	She-ma-hoke	Dead	Bok Tuklo
2	Charliston	"	Jacks Fork		"	Jacks Fork
3	No 1			No 2		
4	Austin Cravatt	Dead	Jackson	Salen Cravatt	Dead	Jackson
5	" "	"	"	" "	"	"
6						
7						
8						
9			No1 on 1896 roll as Lake Oushtubbee			
10			No2 ' 1896 " " Sibbie "			
11			No3 ' 1896 " " Sally "			
12			Nos 4-5 on 1896 roll as Cravett			
13			No5 on 1896 roll as Isabelle Cravette.			
14			No3 died March 15, 1902, proof of death filed Nov 25, 1902			
15					Date of Application for Enrollment.	Aug 29/99
16						
17			P.O. Boswell, I.T.	11/20/02		

184

Choctaw By Blood Enrollment Cards 1898-1914

RESIDENCE: Atoka COUNTY.
POST OFFICE: Coalgate, I.T.

Choctaw Nation

Choctaw Roll (Not Including Freedmen)

CARD NO.
FIELD NO. 4085

Dawes' Roll No.	NAME	Relationship to Person First Named	AGE	SEX	BLOOD	TRIBAL ENROLLMENT Year	County	No.
11434	1 Billy, Edmund 47	First Named	44	M	Full	1896	Atoka	1740
11435	2 " Rebecca 34	Wife	31	F	"	1896	Jacks Fork	6122
DEAD.	3 " Wesley DEAD.	Son	16	M	"	1896	Atoka	1742
11436	4 " Louvisa 12	Dau	9	F	"	1896	"	1745
11437	5 " Simon 8	Son	5	M	"	1896	"	1743
11438	6 " Rhoda 4	Dau	1	F	"			
DEAD.	7 Hudson, Bessie DEAD.	S.Dau	6	"	"	1896	Jacks Fork	6140
	8							
	9							
	10							
	11	ENROLLMENT OF NOS. 1,2,4,5 and 6 HEREON APPROVED BY THE SECRETARY OF INTERIOR MAR 10 1903						
	12							
	13							
	14	No. 3 and 7 HEREON DISMISSED UNDER ORDER OF THE COMMISSION TO THE FIVE CIVILIZED TRIBES OF MARCH 31, 1905.						
	15							
	16							
	17							

TRIBAL ENROLLMENT OF PARENTS

	Name of Father	Year	County	Name of Mother	Year	County
1	Simon Billy	Dead	Cedar	Ho-ta-o-na	Dead	Cedar
2	Coleman Cole	"	"	Becky Cole	"	"
3	No1			Susan Billy	"	Atoka
4	No1			" "	"	"
5	No1			" "	"	"
6	No1			No2		
7	James Hudson	Dead	Jacks Fork	No2		
8						
9						
10						
11	No2 on 1896 roll as Rebecca Hudson					
12	No6- Affidavit of birth to be					
13	supplied:- Filed Oct 26/99					
14	No3 Died March 1901 proof of death filed Nov. 22 1902					
15	No7 Died August 31, 1899; proof of death filed Nov. 22, 1902			Date of Application for Enrollment.		Aug 29/99
16						
17						

185

Choctaw By Blood Enrollment Cards 1898-1914

RESIDENCE:	Atoka		COUNTY.	**Choctaw Nation**			**Choctaw Roll**		CARD NO.	
POST OFFICE:	Atoka, I.T.						*(Not Including Freedmen)*		FIELD NO.	4086

Dawes' Roll No.	NAME		Relationship to Person First Named	AGE	SEX	BLOOD	TRIBAL ENROLLMENT			
							Year	County		No.
11439	1 James, Sampson	33	First Named	30	M	Full	1896	Atoka		7266
11440	2 " Zona	17	Dau	14	F	"	1896	"		7268
	3									
	4									
	5									
	6	ENROLLMENT								
	7	OF NOS. 1 and 2 HEREON								
	8	APPROVED BY THE SECRETARY OF INTERIOR MAR 10 1903								
	9									
	10									
	11									
	12									
	13									
	14									
	15									
	16									
	17									

TRIBAL ENROLLMENT OF PARENTS

	Name of Father	Year	County	Name of Mother	Year	County
1	Jackson Unchahubbee	Dead	Kiamitia	Sally Unchahubbee	Dead	Kiamitia
2	No1			Betsey James	"	Atoka
3						
4						
5						
6	No2 on 1896 roll as Soney James					
7						
8						
9						
10						
11						
12						
13						
14						Date of Application for Enrollment.
15						Aug 29/99
16						
17						

Choctaw By Blood Enrollment Cards 1898-1914

RESIDENCE: Atoka COUNTY. **Choctaw Nation** Choctaw Roll CARD NO.
POST OFFICE: Coalgate, I.T. *(Not Including Freedmen)* FIELD NO. **4087**

Dawes' Roll No.	NAME	Relationship to Person First Named	AGE	SEX	BLOOD	TRIBAL ENROLLMENT		
						Year	County	No.
11441	₁ Durant, Jackson ⁵³	First Named	50	M	Full	1896	Atoka	3576
DEAD	₂ " Narcy	Wife	35	F	"	1896	"	1860
11442	₃ Byington, Julius ¹⁵	S.Son	12	M	"	1896	"	1861
11443	₄ " Robinson ¹¹	"	8	"	"	1896	"	1862
	₅							
	₆							
	₇							
	₈	ENROLLMENT OF NOS. 1,3 and 4 HEREON APPROVED BY THE SECRETARY OF INTERIOR Mar 10 1903						
	₉							
	₁₀							
	₁₁	No. 2 hereon dismissed under order of						
	₁₂	the Commission to the Five Civilized						
	₁₃	Tribes of March 31, 1905.						
	₁₄							
	₁₅							
	₁₆							
	₁₇							

TRIBAL ENROLLMENT OF PARENTS

	Name of Father	Year	County	Name of Mother	Year	County
₁	Mon-tubbee	Dead	Skullyville	Pesa-me-yo-key		Skullyville
₂	Me-hom-bey	"	Atoka		Dead	Atoka
₃	Jackson Byington	"	Tobucksy	No2		
₄	" "	"	"	No2		
₅						
₆						
₇						
₈		No2 on 1896 roll as Wisey Byington				
₉		No4 " 1896 " " Roberson "				
₁₀		No2 died – day of – 1901 Proof of death filed Nov. 22 1902				
₁₁						
₁₂						
₁₃						
₁₄					Date of Application for Enrollment	
₁₅					Aug 29/99	
₁₆						
₁₇						

187

Choctaw By Blood Enrollment Cards 1898-1914

Dawes' Roll No.	NAME		Relationship to Person	AGE	SEX	BLOOD	TRIBAL ENROLLMENT		
							Year	County	No.
11444	1 Armstrong, Nicy	46	First Named	43	F	Full	1896	Atoka	428
11445	2 " Ellis	17	Son	14	M	1/2	1896	"	429
11446	3 " Enoch	16	"	13	"	1/2	1896	"	430
11447	4 Jacob, Sina	21	Dau	18	F	1/2	1896	"	7264
11448	5 Jacob, Fulsom	1	Son of No4	1½	M	1/2			
	6								
	7								
	8								
	9	ENROLLMENT							
	10	OF NOS. 1,2,3,4 and 5 HEREON APPROVED BY THE SECRETARY							
	11	OF INTERIOR Mar 10 1903							
	12								
	13								
	14								
	15								
	16								
	17								

TRIBAL ENROLLMENT OF PARENTS

	Name of Father	Year	County	Name of Mother	Year	County
1	To-ki-ya	Dead	Atoka	Ma-ko-ha-to-na	Dead	Atoka
2	Wallace Armstrong		Chick Roll	No1		
3	" "		" "	No1		
4	" "		" "	No1		
5	Eastman Jacob		Choctaw	No4		
6						
7						
8						
9	No4 on 1896 roll as Sinie Jones					
10	No4 now the wife of Eastman Jacob Choctaw card #4081			11/17/02		
11	No5 born July 25, 1901: enrolled Nov. 25, 1902					
12	No.4 has a child named Folsom Jacob 11/17/02					
13	For child of No4 see NB (Nar 3'05) Card #283					
14	No.4 Reported by husband (Eastman Jacob) as having died Sept, 1909 #1 to 4					
15				Date of Application for Enrollment Aug 29/99		
16						
17						

188

RESIDENCE:	**Atoka**	COUNTY.	**Choctaw Nation**		**Choctaw Roll**	CARD No.		
POST OFFICE:	Atoka, I.T.				*(Not Including Freedmen)*	FIELD No.	**4089**	

Dawes' Roll No.		NAME	Relationship to Person First Named	AGE	SEX	BLOOD	TRIBAL ENROLLMENT		
							Year	County	No.
11449	1	Lewis, Noah ~~DIED PRIOR TO SEPTEMBER 25,~~ 52 1902	Named	49	M	Full	1896	Atoka	8268
11450	2	Jacob, Sarah 33	Wife	30	F	"	1896	"	8269
11451	3	Lewis, Levi 9	Son	6	M	"	1896	"	8270
11452	4	" Jesse 8	"	5	"	"	1896	"	8271
11453	5	" Atoka 3	"	2wk	"	"			
11454	6	Jacob, Elsey 1	Dau of No2	1	~~M~~ F	"			
	7								
	8								
	9								
	10	ENROLLMENT OF NOS. 1,2,3,4,5 and 6 HEREON							
	11	APPROVED BY THE SECRETARY							
	12	OF INTERIOR Mar 10 1903							
	13								
	14								
	15								
	16								
	17								

TRIBAL ENROLLMENT OF PARENTS

	Name of Father	Year	County	Name of Mother	Year	County
1	A-che-le-tubbee	Dead	Kiamitia		Dead	Kiamitia
2	Jas Harrison		Jackson	Liza A Harrison	"	Jackson
3	No1			No2		
4	No1			No2		
5	No1			No2		
6	Austin Jacob			No2		
7						
8	No5 born December 3, 1899 transferred to this card May 24, 1902					
9						
10	Atoka Lewis, born Dec 3/99, son of Nos 1-2 on Card No D-540					
11	No2 is now separated from Noah Lewis and said to be wife of Austin Jacob					
12	No6 born Oct 30, 1901: enrolled Nov. 25, 1902			on Choctaw card #4081		
13	No.1 died Oct 20,1901: Enrollment cancelled by Department July 8, 1904					
14	No5 Died prior to September 25, 1902, not entitled to land or money. See Indian Office Letter May 5 1908 (L and – 25853-1908)					
15						
16				Date of Application for Enrollment. Aug 29/99		
17						

189

Choctaw By Blood Enrollment Cards 1898-1914

RESIDENCE:	Atoka	COUNTY.						CARD No.	
POST OFFICE:	Coalgate, I.T.							FIELD No. 4090	

Choctaw Nation

Choctaw Roll (Not Including Freedmen)

Dawes' Roll No.	NAME	Relationship to Person First Named	AGE	SEX	BLOOD	TRIBAL ENROLLMENT		
						Year	County	No.
11455	1 Noah, Alfred ²⁹	First Named	26	M	Full	1896	Atoka	9842
11456	2 " Isabinda ²⁶	Wife	23	F	"	1896	"	9843
11457	3 " Esias ⁶	Son	2	M	"			
11458	4 " Jackson ²	Son	2mo	M	"			
	5							
	6							
	7							
	8	ENROLLMENT						
	9	OF NOS. 1,2,3 and 4 HEREON APPROVED BY THE SECRETARY						
	10	OF INTERIOR MAR 10 1903						
	11							
	12							
	13							
	14							
	15							
	16							
	17							

TRIBAL ENROLLMENT OF PARENTS

	Name of Father	Year	County	Name of Mother	Year	County
1	Cha-fa-tubbee		Atoka	Mary Noah		Atoka
2	Blank Wade	Dead	Tobucksy	Salotey Wade	Dead	Tobucksy
3	No1			No2		
4	No.1			No.2		
5						
6						
7						
8						
9			No2 on 1896 roll as Sebindee Nowa			
10			No1 " 1896 " " Alfred "			
11			No3 Affidavit of birth to be			
12			supplied.- Filed Nov 2/99			
13			No.4 Enrolled Atoka Jany 6, 1900.		#1 to 3	
14	No.3 also on 1896 Choctaw census roll, Tobucksy County, No 906				Date of Application for Enrollment.	
15	as Sibillie Brown		For child of Nos 1&2 see NB (March 3, 1905) #1436		Aug 29/99	
16						
17	PO Cairo, IT 2/14/03					

190

Choctaw By Blood Enrollment Cards 1898-1914

RESIDENCE: Atoka COUNTY. **Choctaw Nation** CARD

POST OFFICE: Coalgate, I.T.

Choctaw Roll
(Not Including Freedmen)

FIELD NO. 4091

Dawes' Roll No.	NAME	Relationship to Person First Named	AGE	SEX	BLOOD	TRIBAL ENROLLMENT Year	County	No.
11459	1 Noah, Mary 53	First Named	50	F	Full	1896	Atoka	9839
11460	2 " Lottie 18	Dau	15	"	"	1896	"	9840
11461	3 " Salena 15	"	12	"	"	1896	"	9841
	4							
	5							
	6							
	7	ENROLLMENT OF NOS. 1,2 and 3 HEREON						
	8	APPROVED BY THE SECRETARY						
	9	OF INTERIOR MAR 10 1903						
	10							
	11							
	12							
	13							
	14							
	15							
	16							
	17							

TRIBAL ENROLLMENT OF PARENTS

	Name of Father	Year	County	Name of Mother	Year	County
1	Ca-ta-fa-chee	Dead	Sans Bois	Polly	Dead	Atoka
2	Cha-fa-tubbee Noah		Atoka	No 1		
3	" "		"	No 1		
4						
5						
6						
7	No 1 on 1896 roll as Mary Nowa					
8	No2 " 1896 " " Salaskey Nowa					
9	No3 " 1896 " " Selina "					
10	No.1 "Died prior to September 25, 1902; not entitled to land or money." See copy of Indian Office Letter of November 7, 1907 (I.T. 82862-1907)					
11						
12						
13						
14						
15					Date of Application for Enrollment.	Aug 29/99
16						
17						

Choctaw By Blood Enrollment Cards 1898-1914

| RESIDENCE: | Atoka | COUNTY. | Choctaw Nation | Choctaw Roll | CARD NO. |
| POST OFFICE: | Coalgate, I.T. | | | (Not Including Freedmen) | FIELD NO. 4092 |

Dawes' Roll No.	NAME	Relationship to Person First Named	AGE	SEX	BLOOD	TRIBAL ENROLLMENT		
						Year	County	No.
11462	1 Anderson, Tennessee [36]	First Named	33	F	Full	1893	Atoka	784
	2							
	3							
	4	ENROLLMENT						
	5	OF NOS. 1 HEREON						
	6	APPROVED BY THE SECRETARY OF INTERIOR						
	7	Mar 10 1903						
	8							
	9							
	10							
	11							
	12							
	13							
	14							
	15							
	16							
	17							

TRIBAL ENROLLMENT OF PARENTS

	Name of Father	Year	County	Name of Mother	Year	County
1	Stephen Folsom	Dead	Atoka	Winnie Folsom	Dead	Atoka
2						
3						
4						
5						
6						
7						
8	On 1893 Pay roll, Page 75, No 784, Atoka Co,					
9	as Tennessee Mohamby					
10						
11						
12						
13						
14						
15					Date of Application for Enrollment.	Aug 29/99
16						
17						

192

Choctaw By Blood Enrollment Cards 1898-1914

RESIDENCE: Atoka COUNTY. **Choctaw Nation** Choctaw Roll CARD NO.
POST OFFICE: Atoka, I.T. (Not Including Freedmen) FIELD NO. **4093**

Dawes' Roll No.	NAME		Relationship to Person First Named	AGE	SEX	BLOOD	TRIBAL ENROLLMENT		
							Year	County	No.
11463	1 Durant, Taylor	66	First Named	63	M	Full	1896	Atoka	3578
11464	2 Moore, Annie	34	Ward	31	F	"	1896	"	8808
11465	3 Durant, Nancy	17	G.D.	14	"	"	1896	"	3579
	4								
	5								
	6								
	7	ENROLLMENT							
	8	OF NOS. 1,2 and 3 HEREON APPROVED BY THE SECRETARY							
	9	OF INTERIOR Mar 10 1903							
	10								
	11								
	12								
	13								
	14								
	15								
	16								
	17								

TRIBAL ENROLLMENT OF PARENTS

	Name of Father	Year	County	Name of Mother	Year	County
1	Chas Durant	Dead	Jackson	Ye-men-ta-huma	Dead	Atoka
2	Wesley Moore	"	Blue	Sillen Moore	"	"
3	Mikey Durant	"	Atoka	Susan Durant	"	"
4						
5						
6						
7						
8	Father of Nº3 is John Durant, dead. Mother is Maggie Durant dead. See					
9	testimony of Nº1 of July 22, 1903					
10						
11						
12						
13						
14					Date of Application for Enrollment	
15					Aug 29/99	
16						
17						

Choctaw By Blood Enrollment Cards 1898-1914

RESIDENCE:	Atoka	COUNTY.					CARD NO.	
POST OFFICE:	Atoka, I.T.	**Choctaw Nation**			Choctaw Roll (Not Including Freedmen)		FIELD NO. 4094	

Dawes' Roll No.	NAME	Relationship to Person	AGE	SEX	BLOOD	TRIBAL ENROLLMENT		
						Year	County	No.
I.W.**391**	1 Sumter, Robert O. ²⁸	First Named	26	M	IW	1896	Atoka	15068
DEAD.	2 " Louisa S	Wife	26	F	3/4	1896	Atoka	12460
	3							
	4							
	5							
	6 No. 2 HEREON DISMISSED UNDER							
	7 ORDER OF THE COMMISSION TO THE FIVE CIVILIZED TRIBES OF MARCH 31, 1905							
	8							
	9 ENROLLMENT							
	10 OF NOS. 1 HEREON APPROVED BY THE SECRETARY							
	11 OF INTERIOR SEP 12 1903							
	12							
	13							
	14							
	15							
	16							
	17							

TRIBAL ENROLLMENT OF PARENTS

Name of Father	Year	County	Name of Mother	Year	County
1 Robt E Sumter		Non Citz	Maggie Sumter		Non Citz
2 Simeon Turnbull	Dead	Blue	Eliz. Turnbull	Dead	Atoka
3					
4					
5					
6					
7 No2 on 1896 roll as Louisa Turnbull					
8 No1 " 1896 " " R. O. Sumpter					
9					
10					
11 No2 died Sept 10, 1901; Proof of death filed Nov 25, 1902					
12					
13					
14				Date of Application for Enrollment.	
15				Aug 29/99	
16					
17					

Choctaw By Blood Enrollment Cards 1898-1914

RESIDENCE: Chickasaw Nation ~~COUNTY.~~
POST OFFICE:

Choctaw Nation

Choctaw Roll
(Not Including Freedmen)

CARD No.
FIELD No. **4095**

Dawes' Roll No.	NAME		Relationship to Person First Named	AGE	SEX	BLOOD	TRIBAL ENROLLMENT		
							Year	County	No.
11466	1 Bolling, John F	27	First Named	24	M	1/8	1896	Tobucksy	951
11467	2 " Walter C.	25	Bro	22	"	1/8	1896	"	952
I.W. 1130	3 " George F.	50	Father	50	M	I.W.	1896	Tobucksy	14304
I.W. 1337	4 " Hazel Bell	18	Wife of No.2	18	F	I.W.			
	5								
	6 ENROLLMENT								
	OF NOS. 1 and 2 HEREON 7 APPROVED BY THE SECRETARY 8 OF INTERIOR Mar 10 1903								
	9								
	10 ENROLLMENT								
	11 OF NOS. ~~~ 3 HEREON APPROVED BY THE SECRETARY 12 OF INTERIOR Nov 16 1904								
	13								
	14 ENROLLMENT								
	OF NOS. 4 HEREON 15 APPROVED BY THE SECRETARY OF INTERIOR Mar 14 1905 16								
	17								

TRIBAL ENROLLMENT OF PARENTS

	Name of Father	Year	County	Name of Mother	Year	County
1	Geo. F. Bolling		Non Citz	Octavia Bolling	Dead	Tobucksy
2	" " "		" "	" "	"	"
3	T. W. Bolling		non-cit	Nancy B. Bolling		non cit
4	Theo. C. Dickson	dead	non citizen	Ora Belle Dickson		non citizen

5 No.4 was married to number two Aug. 24, 1902
6 No.4 originally listed for enrollment on Choctaw card D-775 Aug 25'02 transferred to this card Jan 28,1905
7 No1 on 1896 roll as John F. Bollin { See decision of Jan. 12,1905
  No2 " 1896 " " Walter C. "
8 Nos. 1 and 2 are the sons of George F. Bolling
9 on Choctaw card #D.458
10 Wife of No.2 on Choctaw #D 775
11 ~~No1 is now husband of Nancy I Denton on Choctaw card #2822~~
  evidence of marriage filed in Choctaw case #2822 Nov. 21, 1902
12 No.3 transferred from Choctaw card #D-458 Oct. 31,1904: See decision of Oct. 15, 1904
13 For child of No1 see NB (Mar 3-05) Card #198
14 P.O. Canadian I.T. ~~Record as to enrollment of #4 forwarded Department Mar 14,1906~~ | Date of Application for Enrollment.
15 General of March 15, 1906 in case of Omer R. Nicholson. | Aug 29/99
16 For children of Nos 2&4 see NB (Mar 3'05) Card No. 284
17 No.4 P.O. McAlester I.T. 12/29/04

No.3 P.O. South McAlester I.T. 12/24/02

Choctaw By Blood Enrollment Cards 1898-1914

RESIDENCE: Atoka   COUNTY. **Choctaw Nation**   **Choctaw Roll** *(Not Including Freedmen)*   CARD NO.

POST OFFICE: Atoka, I.T.   FIELD NO. **4096**

Dawes' Roll No.	NAME		Relationship to Person First Named	AGE	SEX	BLOOD	TRIBAL ENROLLMENT		
							Year	County	No.
DEAD	₁ Sexton, David		Named	33	M	Full	1896	Atoka	11636
11468	₂ " Eliza A	33	Wife	30	F	"	1896	"	11637
11469	₃ " Shepard	13	Son	10	M	"	1896	"	11638
11470	₄ " Susie A	11	Dau	8	F	"	1896	"	11640
11471	₅ " Elsie	9	"	6	"	"	1896	"	11639
11472	₆ " Nellie	7	"	4	"	"	1896	"	11641
DEAD	₇ " Martha		"	2	"	"			
DEAD	₈ " Sofy		"	3mo	"	"			
11473	₉ " David Jr	1	Son	3mo	M	"			
	10								
	11 No1 died Mch 10, 1902 proof of death filed Nov 22, 1902								
	12 No7 died-day of-1900 proof filed Nov 22, 1902								
	13 No8 died Feby 8, 1901 proof of death filed Nov 22, 1902								
	14 ENROLLMENT								
	15 OF NOS. 2,3,4,5,6 and 9 HEREON								
	16 APPROVED BY THE SECRETARY OF INTERIOR Mar 10 1903								
	17								

TRIBAL ENROLLMENT OF PARENTS

	Name of Father	Year	County	Name of Mother	Year	County
₁	Sim Okleubbee	Dead		Lucy Sexton		Atoka
₂	Simon Lewis	"	Atoka	Lona Lewis	Dead	"
₃	No1			No2		
₄	No1			No2		
₅	No1			No2		
₆	No1			No2		
₇	No1			No2		
₈	No1			No2		
₉	"			"		
10				No. 1,7 and 8 hereon dismissed under		
11				order of the Commission to the Five		
12	No4 on 1896 roll as Susa Ann Sexton			Civilized Tribes of March 31, 1905.		
13	No5 " 1896 " " Alsey "					
	No6 " 1896 " " Nettie "					
14	No7- Affidavit of birth to be					
15	supplied"- Filed Dec 14/99			Date of Application for Enrollment Aug 29/99		
16	No.8 Enrolled May 24, 1900					
17	Nº9 Born August 20 1902 Erolled[sic] Nov 22 1902					

RESIDENCE: Atoka	COUNTY.	Choctaw Nation	Choctaw Roll	CARD NO.
POST OFFICE: Atoka, I.T.			(Not Including Freedmen)	FIELD NO. **4097**

Dawes' Roll No.	NAME	Relationship to Person First Named	AGE	SEX	BLOOD	TRIBAL ENROLLMENT Year	County	No.
11474	1 Williams, Mucktila 33		30	F	Full	1896	Atoka	7267
11475	2 Franklin, Crosby 17	Nephew	14	M	"	1896	"	4426
11476	3 " Esau 18	"	15	"	"	1896	"	4427
11477	4 Anderson, Willie 17	"	14	"	"	1896	"	441
11478	5 " Sila 15	Niece	12	F	"	1896	"	442
	6							
	7							
	8							
	9	ENROLLMENT						
	10 OF NOS. 1,2,3,4 and 5 HEREON							
	APPROVED BY THE SECRETARY							
	11 OF INTERIOR Mar 10 1903							
	12							
	13							
	14							
	15							
	16							
	17							

TRIBAL ENROLLMENT OF PARENTS

Name of Father	Year	County	Name of Mother	Year	County
1 Lewitt Simpty	Dead	Atoka		Dead	Atoka
2 Stephen Franklin	DEAD	"	Ada Franklin	"	"
3 " "	DEAD	"	" "	"	"
4 Ilis Anderson	Dead	"	Muckala Anderson	"	"
5 " "	"	"	" "	"	"
6					
7					
8 No1 on 1896 roll as Mucktella James					
9 No4 " 1896 " " Willis Anderson					
10 No5 " 1896 " " Sillie "					
11					
12 For child of No5 see NB (Apr 26 '06) Card #1199					
13					
14					
15			Date of Application for Enrollment.	Aug 29/99	
16					
17					

197

RESIDENCE:	Jackson	COUNTY.	**Choctaw Nation**		**Choctaw Roll**	CARD NO.	
POST OFFICE:	Mayhew I.T.				*(Not Including Freedmen)*	FIELD NO. **4098**	

Dawes' Roll No.	NAME		Relationship to Person First Named	AGE	SEX	BLOOD	TRIBAL ENROLLMENT		
							Year	County	No.
11479	1 Belvin, Stephen N	54	First Named	51	M	Full	1896	Jackson	1509
11480	2 " Elsie	27	Wife	24	F	1/2	1896	"	8163
11481	3 " Annie B	7	Dau	4	F	3/4	1896	"	8164
11482	4 " Easter	4	"	1	F	3/4			
DEAD	5 ~~" Lunia~~	1	"	~~1 mo~~	~~F~~	~~3/4~~			
	6								
	7								
	8								
	9	ENROLLMENT OF NOS. 1,2,3 and 4 HEREON							
	10	APPROVED BY THE SECRETARY OF INTERIOR Mar 10 1903							
	11								
	12	No. 5 hereon dismissed under order of							
	13	the Commission to the Five Civilized							
	14	Tribes of March 31, 1905.							
	15								
	16								
	17								

TRIBAL ENROLLMENT OF PARENTS

	Name of Father	Year	County	Name of Mother	Year	County
1	Solomon Belvin	Dead	Jackson	Rhoda Belvin	Dead	Jackson
2	Chickum Lata	"	Chick Rolle	Bicey	"	Atoka
3	No1			No2		
4	No1			No2		
5	~~No1~~			~~No2~~		
6						
7						
8	No1 on 1896 roll as S. N. Belvin					
9	No2 " 1896 " " Elza Leader					
10	No3 " 1896 " " Annie Belle "					
11	~~No4 Affidavit of birth to be~~ supplied"- Filed Oct 26/99					
12	No5 Born April 20th 1902 Enrolled June 25th 1902					
13	~~No5 Died Sept 21, 1901: proof of death filed Dec 11, 1902~~					
14	~~For child of Nos 1&2 see NB (March 3,1905) #1510~~			Date of Application for Enrollment.		
15				Aug 29/99		
16						
17	PO Bennington I.T. 12/28/05					

Choctaw By Blood Enrollment Cards 1898-1914

RESIDENCE: Atoka COUNTY.
POST OFFICE: Wapanucka I.T.

Choctaw Nation

Choctaw Roll
(Not Including Freedmen)

CARD No.
FIELD No. **4099**

Dawes' Roll No.	NAME	Relationship to Person First Named	AGE	SEX	BLOOD	TRIBAL ENROLLMENT		
						Year	County	No.
11483	1 Bond, Eastman S 43	First Named	40	M	Full	1896	Atoka	1737
11484	2 " Susie A 58	Wife	55	F	"	1896	"	1738
	3							
	4							
	5							
	6	ENROLLMENT						
	7	OF NOS. 1 and 2 HEREON						
		APPROVED BY THE SECRETARY						
	8	OF INTERIOR Mar 10 1903						
	9							
	10							
	11							
	12							
	13							
	14							
	15							
	16							
	17							

TRIBAL ENROLLMENT OF PARENTS

	Name of Father	Year	County	Name of Mother	Year	County
1	Sam Bond	Dead	Nashoba	Adeline Bond	Dead	Atoka
2	Joe Williams	"	Atoka	Untelema	"	"
3						
4						
5						
6						
7	No1 on 1896 roll as E. S. Bond					
8	No2 " 1896 " " Susan "					
9						
10						
11						
12						
13						
14						
15				Date of Application for Enrollment.	Aug 29/99	
16						
17						

[Application 4100 was not given]

Choctaw By Blood Enrollment Cards 1898-1914

RESIDENCE:	Blue	COUNTY.						
POST OFFICE:	Jackson, I.T.							

Choctaw Nation

Choctaw Roll (Not Including Freedmen)

CARD NO. FIELD NO. **4101**

Dawes' Roll No.	NAME	Relationship to Person First Named	AGE	SEX	BLOOD	TRIBAL ENROLLMENT		
						Year	County	No.
11488	1 Cochnauer, Turner 38	First Named	35	M	Full	1896	Blue	2885
11489	2 " Rena 18	Dau	15	F	"	1896	"	2887
11490	3 " Sophia 6	"	3	"	"	1896	"	2888
11491	4 " Nicholas 9	Son	6	M	"	1896	"	2889
15585	5 Frye, Betsy 1	Dau of No2	19mo	F	"			
	6							
	7							
	8	ENROLLMENT OF NOS. 1,2,3 and 4 HEREON APPROVED BY THE SECRETARY OF INTERIOR Mar 10, 19033						
	9							
	10							
	11	ENROLLMENT OF NOS. 5 HEREON APPROVED BY THE SECRETARY OF INTERIOR SEP 22, 1904						
	12							
	13							
	14							
	15							
	16							
	17							

TRIBAL ENROLLMENT OF PARENTS

	Name of Father	Year	County	Name of Mother	Year	County
1	Nicholas Cochnauer	Dead	Blue	Jane Cochnauer	Dead	Blue
2	No. 1			Wicey Cochnauer	"	Jackson
3	No 1			Louisa Cochnauer	"	Blue
4	No 1			" "	"	"
5	William Fry[sic]	1896	Jackson	No 2		
6						
7						
8						
9	Surnames of all on 1896 roll as Cochnor					
10	No5 Born Jany 17, 1902. Application received Dec 5, 1902 and returned					
11	for idenfication[sic] of the mother and affidavit of midwife. No5 enrolled Aug 19, 1903 No5 affidavits of Rena Frye and Emily Nicholas as to birth filed May 18, 1904					
12	For child of No.2 see NB (Apr 26'06) Card #252					
13						
14					#1 to 4	
15					Date of Application for Enrollment.	
16					Aug 29/99	
17	P.O. No2 Bennington Ok 1/8/12					

Choctaw By Blood Enrollment Cards 1898-1914

RESIDENCE:	Atoka	COUNTY.	**Choctaw Nation**	**Choctaw Roll** (Not Including Freedmen)	CARD NO. FIELD NO. **4102**

POST OFFICE: Kiowa, I.T.

Dawes' Roll No.	NAME	Relationship to Person	AGE	SEX	BLOOD	TRIBAL ENROLLMENT Year	County	No.
11492	1 Benjamin, Simeon 36	First Named	33	M	Full	1896	Atoka	1830
11493	2 " , Katie 36	Wife	33	F	"	1896	"	1831
11494	3 " , Betsy 15	Dau	12	F	"	1896	"	1864
11495	4 " , Sampson 7	Son	4	M	"	1896	"	1832
~~DEAD~~	5 ~~" , Sarlin~~	~~Dau~~	~~1~~	~~F~~	~~"~~			
	6							
	7							
	8							
	9	ENROLLMENT						
	10	OF NOS. 1,2,3 and 4 HEREON APPROVED BY THE SECRETARY						
	11	OF INTERIOR Mar. 10, 1903.						
	12							
	13	No.5 hereon dismissed under order of the Commission to the Five Civilized						
	14	Tribes of March 31, 1905.						
	15							
	16							
	17							

TRIBAL ENROLLMENT OF PARENTS

Name of Father	Year	County	Name of Mother	Year	County
1 Chas Benjamin		Atoka	Empsie Benjamin	Dead	Atoka
2 James Myer	Dead	Blue		"	Blue
3 No1			No2		
4 No1			No2		
5 ~~No1~~			~~No2~~		
6					
7					
8					
9					
10	No5 Affidavit of birth to be supplied:- Filed Nov 2/99				
11					
12					
13	No5 died Aug. 1, 1901: Proof of death filed Nov. 25, 1902				
14	For child of Nos 1&2 see NB (Mar 3, 1905) #611			Date of Application for Enrollment.	
15				Aug 29/99	
16					
17	PO Herbert, I.T. 11/20/02				

Choctaw By Blood Enrollment Cards 1898-1914

RESIDENCE: Jackson	COUNTY.						

RESIDENCE: Jackson **COUNTY.**
POST OFFICE: Mayhew, IT

Choctaw Nation

Choctaw Roll (Not Including Freedmen)

CARD NO.
FIELD NO. 4103

Dawes' Roll No.	NAME	Relationship to Person First Named	AGE	SEX	BLOOD	TRIBAL ENROLLMENT		
						Year	County	No.
11496	1 Oshter, Byington 36		33	M	Full	1896	Jackson	9994
	2							
	3							
	4							
	5							
	6							
	7							
ERTIFICATE 8								
1903 9								
	10							
	11							
	12							
	13	ENROLLMENT OF NOS. 1 HEREON						
	14	APPROVED BY THE SECRETARY OF INTERIOR MAR 10 1903						
	15							
	16							
	17							

TRIBAL ENROLLMENT OF PARENTS

Name of Father	Year	County	Name of Mother	Year	County
1 Lake Oshter		Jackson	Sarah Oshter	Dead	Jackson
2					
3					
4					
5					
6					
7	On 1896 roll as Byington Oushtubbee				
8					
9					
10					
11					
12					
13					
14					
15				Aug 29/99	
16					
17					

Choctaw By Blood Enrollment Cards 1898-1914

RESIDENCE: Atoka COUNTY. **Choctaw Nation** **Choctaw Roll** CARD NO.
POST OFFICE: Atoka, I.T. *(Not Including Freedmen)* FIELD NO. 4104

Dawes' Roll No.	NAME	Relationship to Person First Named	AGE	SEX	BLOOD	TRIBAL ENROLLMENT		
						Year	County	No.
11497	1 Smallwood, Annie 70	First Named	67	F	1/2	1896	Atoka	11642
11498	2 " Ada 21	G.Dau	18	"	1/8	1896	"	11643
	3							
	4							
	5							
	6	ENROLLMENT						
	7	OF NOS. 1 and 2 HEREON APPROVED BY THE SECRETARY						
	8	OF INTERIOR MAR 10 1903						
	9							
	10							
	11							
	12							
	13							
	14							
	15							
	16							
	17							

TRIBAL ENROLLMENT OF PARENTS

	Name of Father	Year	County	Name of Mother	Year	County
1	John Moore	Dead	Non Citz	Betsy Moore	Dead	in Mississippi
2	Ben Smallwood	"	Atoka	Agnes Smallwood	"	Non Citz
3						
4						
5						
6			No2 As to marriage of parents, see			
7			testimony of No1			
8						
9						
10						
11						
12						
13						
14						
15				Date of Application for Enrollment		Aug 29/99
16						
17						

RESIDENCE: Atoka COUNTY. **Choctaw Nation** Choctaw Roll CARD No.

POST OFFICE: Atoka, I.T. *(Not Including Freedmen)* FIELD No. 4105

Dawes' Roll No.	NAME	Relationship to Person First Named	AGE	SEX	BLOOD	TRIBAL ENROLLMENT		
						Year	County	No.
11499	1 Ellis, Mary 25	First Named	22	F	1/8	1896	Atoka	11003
11500	2 Ray, Benton 10	Son	7	M	1/16	1896	"	11004
11501	3 Ray, Theresa 8	Dau	5	F	1/16			
11502	4 Ray, Ralph 6	Son	2	M	1/16			
11503	5 Ray, Alta 4	Dau	6mo	F	1/16			
	6							
	7							
	8							
	9	ENROLLMENT						
	10	OF NOS. 1,2,3,4 and 5 HEREON APPROVED BY THE SECRETARY						
	11	OF INTERIOR MAR 10 1903						
	12							
	13							
	14							
	15							
	16							
	17							

TRIBAL ENROLLMENT OF PARENTS

	Name of Father	Year	County	Name of Mother	Year	County
1	John Dillon	Dead	Non Citz	Susan Dillon		Atoka
2	W. B. Ray	"	" "	No1		
3	" " "	"	" "	No1		
4	" " "	"	" "	No1		
5	" " "	"	" "	No1		
6						
7						
8						
9	Nos 3-4 Affidavits of birth to be					
10	supplied:- Filed Oct 26/99					
11						
12	Nos 2 and 3 were admitted as citizens by blood by Dawes Commission					
13	Choctaw Case #678: No appeal a non-citizen					
14	No1 is now wife of Chas. W. Ellis ^ See affidavits filed December 17, 1902 11/20/02					
15					Date of Application for Enrollment.	Aug 29/99
16						
17	P.O. Denison Texas 12/17/02					

Choctaw By Blood Enrollment Cards 1898-1914

RESIDENCE:	Atoka	COUNTY.	**Choctaw Nation**				**Choctaw Roll** *(Not Including Freedmen)*	CARD NO.
POST OFFICE:	Atoka, I.T.							FIELD NO. 4106

Dawes' Roll No.	NAME		Relationship to Person	AGE	SEX	BLOOD	TRIBAL ENROLLMENT		
							Year	County	No.
11504	1 Dillon, Susan	42	First Named	39	F	1/2	1893	Atoka	197
11505	2 " Thomas	17	Son	14	M	1/4	1896	"	3606
11506	3 " Richard	12	"	9	"	1/4	1896	"	3604
11507	4 " Angie	10	Dau	7	F	1/4	1896	"	3606
	5								
	6								
	7	ENROLLMENT OF NOS. 1,2,3 and 4 HEREON							
	8	APPROVED BY THE SECRETARY OF INTERIOR MAR 10 1903							
	9								
	10								
	11								
	12								
	13								
	14								
	15								
	16								
	17								

TRIBAL ENROLLMENT OF PARENTS

	Name of Father	Year	County	Name of Mother	Year	County
1	John Smallwood	Dead	Kiamitia	Annie Smallwood		Atoka
2	John Dillon	"	Non Citz	No1		
3	" "	"	" "	No1		
4	" "	"	" "	No1		
5						
6						
7						
8			No3 on 1896 roll as Pick Dillon			
9			No1 on 1893 Pay Roll, Page 19, No 197,			
10			Atoka Co.			
11						
12						
13						
14						
15				Date of Application for Enrollment.		Aug 29/99
16						
17						

RESIDENCE:	Atoka	COUNTY.	**Choctaw Nation**	**Choctaw Roll**	CARD NO.
POST OFFICE:	Atoka, I.T.			*(Not Including Freedmen)*	FIELD NO. 4107

Dawes' Roll No.	NAME	Relationship to Person First Named	AGE	SEX	BLOOD	TRIBAL ENROLLMENT Year	County	No.
I.W. 392	1 Standley, Bertha M 28		26	F	IW			
11508	2 " Marie S 7	Dau	4	"	1/32	1896	Atoka	11635
	3							
	4							
	5							
	6	ENROLLMENT						
	7	OF NOS. 2 HEREON						
	8	APPROVED BY THE SECRETARY OF INTERIOR MAR 10 1903						
	9	ENROLLMENT						
	10	OF NOS. 1 HEREON APPROVED BY THE SECRETARY						
	11	OF INTERIOR SEP 12 1903						
	12							
	13							
	14							
	15							
	16							
	17							

TRIBAL ENROLLMENT OF PARENTS

Name of Father	Year	County	Name of Mother	Year	County
1 J. B. Salmon		Non Citz	Emiline Salmon		Non Citz
2 J. S. Standley Jr	Dead	Atoka	No1		
3					
4					
5					
6					
7		No1 was admitted by Dawes Com.			
8		Case No 816			
9		No2 on 1896 roll as M. S. Standley			
10					
11		No1 was wife of J S Standley Jr who was admitted by act of Choctaw			
12		Council of Oct 1874. No2 is his child			
13					
14					
15			Date of Application for Enrollment.		Aug 29/99
16					
17					

Choctaw By Blood Enrollment Cards 1898-1914

RESIDENCE:	Atoka	COUNTY.	**Choctaw Nation**			**Choctaw Roll** *(Not Including Freedmen)*		CARD NO.
POST OFFICE:	Atoka, I.T.							FIELD NO. 41

Dawes' Roll No.	NAME		Relationship to Person First Named	AGE	SEX	BLOOD	TRIBAL ENROLLMENT		
							Year	County	No.
I.W.393	1 Smiser, Butler S	40	First Named	37	M	IW			
11509	2 " Norma E	37	Wife	34	F	1/16	1896	Atoka	11626
11510	3 " Norma E Jr	15	Dau	12	"	1/32	1896	"	11631
11511	4 " Butler S Jr	12	Son	9	M	1/32	1896	"	11627
11512	5 " Ira M	8	"	5	"	1/32	1896	"	11628
11513	6 " Garnett S	7	"	4	"	1/32	1896	"	11624
11514	7 " Posey B	6	"	3	"	1/32	1896	"	11630
	8								
	9								
	10								
	11	ENROLLMENT OF NOS. 2,3,4,5,6 and 7 HEREON APPROVED BY THE SECRETARY OF INTERIOR MAR 10 1903							
	12								
	13								
	14	ENROLLMENT OF NOS. 1 HEREON APPROVED BY THE SECRETARY OF INTERIOR SEP 12 1903							
	15								
	16								
	17								

TRIBAL ENROLLMENT OF PARENTS

	Name of Father	Year	County	Name of Mother	Year	County
1	J. L. Smiser		Non Citz	Eliza J Smiser	Dead	Non Citz
2	J. S. Standley		Atoka	Alice Standley	"	" "
3	No1			No2		
4	No1			No2		
5	No1			No2		
6	No1			No2		
7	No1			No2		
8	No2 was admitted by act of Choctaw Council of Oct, 1874					
9	No1 Was admitted by Dawes Com, Case					
10	No 1065 as B. S. Smisir No2 on 1896 roll as N. E. Smiser					
11	No3 " 1896 " " Earl "					
12	No4 " 1896 " " B. S. " No6 " 1896 " " G. S. "					
13	No2- Evidence as to marriage of parents					Date of Application for Enrollment.
14	to be supplied:- See Card of J. G. Ralls, No 4364					
15						Aug 29/99
16						
17						

Choctaw By Blood Enrollment Cards 1898-1914

RESIDENCE: Atoka COUNTY.								
POST OFFICE: Coalgate, I.T.	**Choctaw Nation**				Choctaw Roll (Not Including Freedmen)	CARD NO. FIELD NO. 4109		

Dawes' Roll No.	NAME	Relationship to Person First Named	AGE	SEX	BLOOD	TRIBAL ENROLLMENT		
						Year	County	No.
11515	1 Palmer, Lubbin 53	First Named	50	M	Full	1896	Atoka	10551
11516	2 " Lina 43	Wife	40	F	"	1896	"	14071
11517	3 " Watson 8	Son	5	M	"	1896	"	1867
11518	4 " Hicks 4	"	1	"	"			
11519	5 " Castin 18	Ward	15	"	"	1896	Atoka	10553
11520	6 Byington, Amos 17	S Son	14	"	"	1896	"	1866
	7							
	8							
	9	ENROLLMENT						
	10	OF NOS. 1,2,3,4,5 and 6 HEREON APPROVED BY THE SECRETARY						
	11	OF INTERIOR MAR 10 1903						
	12							
	13							
	14							
	15							
	16							
	17							

TRIBAL ENROLLMENT OF PARENTS

	Name of Father	Year	County	Name of Mother	Year	County
1		Dead	Bok Tuklo	I-te-a-ho-na	Dead	Atoka
2	John Forester	"	Atoka	Nellie Forester	"	"
3	No1			No2		
4	No1			No2		
5	Colson Palmer	Dead	Atoka	Siley Wesley		Tobucksy
6	Dixon Byington	"	"	No2		
7						
8						
9						
10		No1 on 1896 roll as Lubbin Pruner				
11		No2 " 1896 " " Limie Williams				
12		No5 " 1896 " " Carton Pruner				
13		No3 " 1896 " " Watson Byington				
		No4 Affidavit of birth to be				
14		supplied:- Filed Dec 16/99			Date of Application for Enrollment.	
15					Aug 29/99	
16						
17						

Choctaw By Blood Enrollment Cards 1898-1914

RESIDENCE:	Atoka	COUNTY.				
POST OFFICE:	Lehigh, I.T.					

Choctaw Nation

Choctaw Roll *(Not Including Freedmen)*

CARD NO. FIELD NO. 4110

Dawes' Roll No.	NAME		Relationship to Person First Named	AGE	SEX	BLOOD	TRIBAL ENROLLMENT		
							Year	County	No.
DEAD.	1 Harris, David		Named	69	M	Full	1896	Atoka	6010
11521	2 "	Eastman 21	Son	18	"	"	1896	"	6012
11522	3 "	Allen 19	"	16	"	"	1896	"	6013
11523	4 "	Solomon 15	"	12	"	"	1896	"	6014
11524	5 "	Minnie 11	Dau	10	F	"	1896	"	6015
	6								
	7								
	8								
	9	ENROLLMENT							
	10	OF NOS. 2,3,4 and 5 HEREON APPROVED BY THE SECRETARY							
	11	OF INTERIOR MAR 10 1903							
	12	No. 1 HEREON DISMISSED UNDER							
	13	ORDER OF THE COMMISSION TO THE FIVE CIVILIZED TRIBES OF MARCH 31, 1905.							
	14								
	15								
	16								
	17								

TRIBAL ENROLLMENT OF PARENTS

	Name of Father	Year	County	Name of Mother	Year	County
1	To-tubbee	Dead	Towson	Oka-ho-thla	Dead	Towson
2	No1			Liley Harris	"	Atoka
3	No1			" "	"	"
4	No1			" "	"	"
5	No1			" "	"	"
6						
7						
8	No1 on 1896 roll as Davis Harris					
9	No5 " 1896 " " Minnie "					
10	No1 died Feby – 1901, proof filed Nov 22, 1902					
11						
12						
13						
14						
15					Date of Application for Enrollment	Aug 29/99
16						
17						

Choctaw By Blood Enrollment Cards 1898-1914

RESIDENCE: Chickasaw Nation ~~COUNTY~~.
POST OFFICE: Viola, I.T.

Choctaw Nation

Choctaw Roll
(Not Including Freedmen)

CARD NO.
FIELD NO. **4111**

Dawes' Roll No.	NAME		Relationship to Person First Named	AGE	SEX	BLOOD	TRIBAL ENROLLMENT		
							Year	County	No.
14392	₁ Luttrel, Ida	22	First Named	19	F	1/16	1896	Atoka	6059
14393	₂ " Dexter	2	Dau	2m	F	1/32			
14394	₃ " Jessie	1	~~Dau~~ Son	2mo	~~F~~M	1/32			
	4								
	5								
	6								
	7	ENROLLMENT OF NOS. 1 2 and 3 HEREON APPROVED BY THE SECRETARY OF INTERIOR Apr 11 1903							
	8								
	9								
	10								
	11								
	12								
	13								
	14								
	15								
	16								
	17								

TRIBAL ENROLLMENT OF PARENTS

	Name of Father	Year	County	Name of Mother	Year	County
1	Jasper Hendrix		Intermarried	Belle Hendrix		Atoka
2	Elzy Luttrel		Non Citizen	No1		
3	" "		" "	No1		
4						
5	On 1896 roll as Ida Hendrix					
6	Admitted by Dawes Com					
7	Case No 1130 as Ida Hendrix No appeal					
8	As to residence, see testimony of mother Belle Hendrix					
9	No.2 Enrolled June 11, 1900					
10	No3 Born Jany 4, 1902: Enrolled March 8, 1902					
11	No3 is a male, see testimony of No1 taken May 23, 1903					
12	No1 admitted by U.S Indian Agent Feb 8, 1896					
13	12/3/23 For child of No.1 see NB (March 3,1905) #1302					
14	* No.3 Sex changed from "F" to "M" by authority of Dept. letter of Nov 23 1923 -7318				Date of Application for Enrollment.	
15					Aug 30/99	
16						
17	P.O. Atoka I.T. 4/27/05					

Choctaw By Blood Enrollment Cards 1898-1914

RESIDENCE: Atoka	COUNTY. **Choctaw Nation**	**Choctaw Roll** (Not Including Freedmen)	CARD NO.
POST OFFICE: Atoka, I.T.			FIELD NO. **4112**

Dawes' Roll No.	NAME	Relationship to Person First Named	AGE	SEX	BLOOD	TRIBAL ENROLLMENT Year	County	No.
11525	1 Harrison, William H 51		48	M	1/2	1896	Tobucksy	5353
I.W. 792	2 " Serilda J *(41)	Wife	38	F	IW	1896	"	14616
11526	3 Camden, Ida B 21	Dau	18	"	1/4	1896	"	5354
11527	4 Harrison, Etta 15	"	12	"	1/4	1896	"	5355
11528	5 " Ada 13	"	10	"	1/4	1896	"	5356
11529	6 " Mabel 9	"	6	"	1/4	1896	"	5357
11530	7 " William H Jr 7	Son	4	M	1/4	1896	"	5358
11531	8 " Guy 1	Son	3mo	M	1/4			
11532	9 " Victor V 3	Son	1mo	M	1/4			
	10 Victor V Harrison							
	11 born Dec 19/99. On Card							
	12 No D-551							
	13 No9 born December 19, 1899							
	14 transferred to this card							
	May 24, 1902							
	15 No8 born Oct. 15, 1901; Enrolled Dec. 31, 1901							
	16 For child of Nos 1&2 see NB (Apr 26'06) Card #181							
	17 " " " No3 " " (Mar 3'05) " #1096							

TRIBAL ENROLLMENT OF PARENTS

	Name of Father	Year	County	Name of Mother	Year	County
1	Zadoe Harrison	Dead	Kiamitia	Eliz. Harrison		Atoka
2	J. W. McCaslin		Non Citz	Mary McCaslin	Dead	Non Citz
3	No1			No2		
4	No1			No2		
5	No1			No2		
6	No1			No2		
7	No1			No2		
8	No1			No2		
9	No1			No2		

ENROLLMENT OF NOS. 2 HEREON APPROVED BY THE SECRETARY OF INTERIOR May 9 1904

10 No2 denied in 96 Case #1410
11 No3 is now the wife of A.B. Camden on Choctaw card #D802 Sept. 23 1902 5904
12 No1 on 1896 roll as Wm H. Harrison
13 No3 " 1896 " " Ida "
14 No7 " 1896 " " Wm H "
15 No2 admitted by U.S. Court, Central Dist, June 22/97 Case No 112 as an
16 Intermarried Citizen *Decision of U.S. Court Cent Dist June 22, 1896 vacated and
set aside by Decree of Choctaw Chickasaw Citizenship Court Decr 17 1902: admitted
17 as an intermarried Choctaw by citizenship court

ENROLLMENT OF NOS. 1,3,4,5,6,7,8 and 9 HEREON APPROVED BY THE SECRETARY OF INTERIOR Mar 10 1903

Date of Application for Enrollment Aug 30/99

P.O. Robbers Roost I.T. 1/16/03   April 30, 1903, Case No. 14

212

Choctaw By Blood Enrollment Cards 1898-1914

Dawes' Roll No.	NAME	Relationship to Person First Named	AGE	SEX	BLOOD	TRIBAL ENROLLMENT		
						Year	County	No.
11533	1 Plummer, Walter G. 47	First Named	44	M	1/8	1896	Atoka	10566
D.P.	2 " Mary	Wife	29	F	I.W.			
11534	3 Morgan, Stella 19	Dau	16	"	1/16	1896	Atoka	10569
11535	4 Payte, Nettie W 16	"	13	"	1/16	1896	"	10570
11536	5 Plummer, Archie F 14	Son	11	M	1/16	1896	"	10567
DEAD	6 " Thomas A	"	9	"	1/16	1896	"	10568
11537	7 " Walter George 1	"	3mo	M	1/16			
11538	8 Morgan, Reginal M 1	Grand Son	1mo	M	1/32			
	9							
	10					ENROLLMENT		
	11 No1 is divorced from his					OF NOS. HEREON		
	12 wife Mary and is now the					APPROVED BY THE SECRETARY OF INTERIOR		
	13 husband of Minnie Plummer on Choctaw Card #5940 Dec 11, 1900.					No. hereon dismissed under order of		
	14 No.2 Refused Feb. 14, 1907					the Commission to the Five Civilized		
	15 No.7 Born August 29, 1901					Tribes of March 31, 1905.		
	16 N°4 is now the wife of A. J. Payte, a non-citizen. Evidence of marriage filed 10/2/02.							
	17							

TRIBAL ENROLLMENT OF PARENTS

	Name of Father	Year	County	Name of Mother	Year	County
1	J. R. Plummer		Atoka	Mary S. Plummer		Non Citz
2	John Skeggs	Dead	Non Citz	Mary Skeggs	Dead	" "
3	No1			Octavia Plummer	"	" " "
4	No1			"	"	" " "
5	No1			"	"	" " "
6	No1			"	"	" " "
7	No1			Minnie Plummer		
8	Wm K. Morgan		non citz	No.3		
9	All but No2 were admitted by Act of Choctaw Council No 39, approved Nov 8/95			No8 born Oct 25, 1901 and enrolled Nov 26,1901		
10	As to residence, see testimony of No1			No3 is now the wife of Wm K Morgan a non		
11	No4 on 1896 roll as Nettie Plummer			citizen Nov 26, 1901. Evidence of marriage		
12	No5 " 1896 " " Archer "			filed Dec 2, 1901		
13	No6 " 1896 " " Tommy "			No.6 hereon dismissed under order		
14	No2 – Evidence of marriage to be supplied:- Filed Oct 26/99			of the Commission to the Five Civilized Tribes of March 31, 1905.		
15	No2 is now divorced from No.1 Plummer having alleged					Date of Application for Enrollment.
16	his wife abandoned him. See testimony of Dec. 11, 1900					Aug 29/99
17						

No.6 died March 16,1901. Proof of death filed Nov. 25, 1902. For child of No1 see NB (Apr 26'06) Card #244

No.2 see other side [no info. given]

Choctaw By Blood Enrollment Cards 1898-1914

RESIDENCE:	Atoka		COUNTY. **Choctaw Nation**				**Choctaw Roll** *(Not Including Freedmen)*		CARD NO.	
POST OFFICE:	Kiowa, I.T.								FIELD NO. 4114	

Dawes' Roll No.	NAME		Relationship to Person	AGE	SEX	BLOOD	TRIBAL ENROLLMENT		
							Year	County	No.
11539	1 Willis, Simpson	56	First Named	53	M	Full	1896	Atoka	13944
11540	2 " Phoebe	56	Wife	53	F	"	1896	"	13945
11541	3 " Josiah	16	Son	13	M	"	1896	"	13946
	4								
	5								
	6								
	7	ENROLLMENT							
	8	OF NOS. 1,2 and 3 HEREON APPROVED BY THE SECRETARY							
	9	OF INTERIOR MAR 10 1903							
	10								
	11								
	12								
	13								
	14								
	15								
	16								
	17								

TRIBAL ENROLLMENT OF PARENTS

	Name of Father	Year	County	Name of Mother	Year	County
1	Lo-ha	Dead	Jacks Fork	On-na	Dead	Jacks Fork
2	E-la-he-nubbee	"	Cedar	Ah-cha-ba	"	Cedar
3	No1			No2		
4						
5						
6						
7						
8		No1 on 1896 roll as Sim Willis				
9		Nº3 is 22 years old. See copy of testimony of July 11, 1903				
10						
11						
12						
13						
14						
15				Date of Application for Enrollment.	Aug 29/99	
16						
17						

Choctaw By Blood Enrollment Cards 1898-1914

RESIDENCE: Atoka   COUNTY. **Choctaw Nation**   **Choctaw Roll**   CARD No.

POST OFFICE: Atoka, I.T.   *(Not Including Freedmen)*   FIELD No. 4115

Dawes' Roll No.	NAME	Relationship to Person First Named	AGE	SEX	BLOOD	TRIBAL ENROLLMENT		
						Year	County	No.
11542	₁ Wilson, Kitsy ⁴³		40	F	Full	1896	Atoka	14052
11543	₂ Peter, Thompson ²⁶	Son	23	M	"	1893	"	1056
11544	₃ " William ⁴	G.S.	1	"	"			
	₄							
	₅							
	₆							
	₇	ENROLLMENT						
	₈	OF NOS. 1,2 and 3 HEREON APPROVED BY THE SECRETARY						
	₉	OF INTERIOR MAR 10 1903						
	10							
	11							
	12							
	13							
	14							
	15							
	16							
	17							

TRIBAL ENROLLMENT OF PARENTS

	Name of Father	Year	County	Name of Mother	Year	County
₁	E-all	Dead	Bok Tuklo	Lucy Wilson		Atoka
₂	Simon Peter	"	Atoka	No1		
₃	No2			Anne Peter		Atoka
₄						
₅						
₆						

₇ No2 on 1893 Pay Roll, Page 111, No 1056, Atoka Co

₈ No1 on 1896 roll as Tillsey Wilson

₉ No2 " 1896 " " Peter Thompson, No 325,

No 12474, Atoka Co.

10 No2 is now the husband of Sarah Sunny on

11 Choctaw Card #4034, March 25, 1901

12 Evidence of birth of No.3 received and filed Feby 27, 1902

13 For child of No.2 see NB (March 3,1905) #1369.

Date of Application for Enrollment.

Aug 29/99

215

Choctaw By Blood Enrollment Cards 1898-1914

RESIDENCE: Atoka	COUNTY. **Choctaw Nation**	**Choctaw Roll**	CARD NO.
POST OFFICE: Coalgate, I.T.		(Not Including Freedmen)	FIELD NO. 4116

Dawes' Roll No.	NAME		Relationship to Person First Named	AGE	SEX	BLOOD	TRIBAL ENROLLMENT		
							Year	County	No.
11545	1 Noah, Irvin	27	First Named	24	M	Full	1896	Atoka	9844
11546	2 " Libbey	26	Wife	24	F	"	1896	Tobucksy	5379
11547	3 " Aurora	2	Dau	1mo	F	"			
15848	4 " Mulsey		"	1	F	"			
	5								
	6								
	7	ENROLLMENT							
	8	OF NOS. 1,2 and 3 HEREON APPROVED BY THE SECRETARY							
	9	OF INTERIOR MAR 10 1903							
	10	ENROLLMENT							
	11	OF NOS. ~~~ 4 ~~~ HEREON APPROVED BY THE SECRETARY							
	12	OF INTERIOR JUN 12 1905							
	16								
	17								

TRIBAL ENROLLMENT OF PARENTS

	Name of Father	Year	County	Name of Mother	Year	County
1	Chafatubbee Noah		Atoka	Mary Noah		Atoka
2	Adam LeFlore	Dead	Choctaw	Molsey Seeley		Choctaw
3	No.1			No.2		
4	No1			No2		
5						
6			On 1896 roll as Ervin Nowa			
7			~~No2 on 1896 roll as Sibbey Hachubbi~~			
8						
9						
10			Nos 2 and 3 Enrolled at Atoka, June 6, 1900			
11			No2 on 1896 roll as Sibbey Hachubbi			
12			No4 born Jan 4, 1902; application received and No4 placed on			
13			this card April 10, 1905, under Act of Congress approved March 3, 1905			
14						
15				Date of Application for Enrollment. Aug 29/99		
16						
17						

Choctaw By Blood Enrollment Cards 1898-1914

RESIDENCE: Jacks Fork COUNTY.	Choctaw Nation	Choctaw Roll	4117 CARD No.
POST OFFICE: Stringtown, I.T.		(Not Including Freedmen) #417	FIELD No. 41

Dawes' Roll No.	NAME		Relationship to Person First Named	AGE	SEX	BLOOD	TRIBAL ENROLLMENT		
							Year	County	No.
11548	1 Pain, James	48		45	M	Full	1896	Jacks Fork	10585
DEAD.	2 " Sibbie		Wife	18	F	"	1896	" "	4507
	3								
	4								
	5								
	6	ENROLLMENT							
	7	OF NOS. 1 HEREON APPROVED BY THE SECRETARY							
	8	OF INTERIOR MAR 10 1903							
	9	No. 2 HEREON DISMISSED UNDER							
	10	ORDER OF THE COMMISSION TO THE FIVE CIVILIZED TRIBES OF MARCH 31, 1905.							
	11								
	12								
	13								
	14								
	15								
	16								
	17								

TRIBAL ENROLLMENT OF PARENTS

	Name of Father	Year	County	Name of Mother	Year	County
1	Thos. Pain	Dead	Gaines	Hokey Pain	Dead	Jacks Fork
2	Daniel Frazier	"	Jacks Fork	Lottie Frazier	"	" "
3						
4						
5						
6	No 2 on 1896 roll as Sibby Frazier					
7	N°2 Died Oct. 22, 1899, proof of death filed			May 16, 1903		
8						
9						
10						
11						
12						
13						
14						
15				DATE OF APPLICATION FOR ENROLLMENT.	Aug 29/99	
16						
17						

217

Choctaw By Blood Enrollment Cards 1898-1914

RESIDENCE:	Atoka	COUNTY.	Choctaw		Choctaw Roll	CARD NO.	
POST OFFICE:	Atoka, I.T.				*(Not Including Freedmen)*	FIELD NO. 4118	

Dawes' Roll No.		NAME	Relationship to Person First Named	AGE	SEX	BLOOD	TRIBAL ENROLLMENT		
							Year	County	No.
DEAD.	1	Mullin, Silas	Named	55	M	Full	1896	Atoka	8811
11549	2	" Sallie ⁴⁸	Wife	45	F	"	1896	"	8812
	3								
	4								
	5								
	6	ENROLLMENT							
	7	OF NOS. 2 HEREON APPROVED BY THE SECRETARY							
	8	OF INTERIOR MAR 10 1903							
	9	No. 2 HEREON DISMISSED UNDER							
	10	ORDER OF THE COMMISSION TO THE FIVE							
	11	CIVILIZED TRIBES OF MARCH 31, 1905.							
	12								
	13								
	14								
	15								
	16								
	17								

TRIBAL ENROLLMENT OF PARENTS

	Name of Father	Year	County	Name of Mother	Year	County
1	O-wa-tubbee	Dead	Atoka	I-yo-kia	Dead	Atoka
2	Pe-sa-mak-kin-tubbee	"	"	Beckey	"	"
3						
4		N°2 is wife of Isaac Folsom, Choctaw card #4249.				
5						
6						
7						
8						
9		No 1 died January 15, 1901; proof of death filed Nov 26, 1902.				
10						
11						
12						
13						
14				Date of Application for Enrollment.		
15					Aug 29/99	
16						
17						

Choctaw By Blood Enrollment Cards 1898-1914

RESIDENCE: **Atoka** COUNTY. **Choctaw Nation**   **Choctaw Roll**   CARD No.

POST OFFICE: **Lehigh, I.T.**   (Not Including Freedmen)   FIELD No. **4119**

Dawes' Roll No.	NAME	Relationship to Person First Named	AGE	SEX	BLOOD	TRIBAL ENROLLMENT Year	County	No.
11550	1 Young, Nancy 43		40	F	Full	1896	Atoka	14243
	2							
	3							
	4							
	5	ENROLLMENT OF NOS. 1 HEREON						
	6	APPROVED BY THE SECRETARY OF INTERIOR Mar 10, 1903						
	7							
	8							
	9							
	10							
	11							
	12							
	13							
	14							
	15							
	16							
	17							

TRIBAL ENROLLMENT OF PARENTS

	Name of Father	Year	County	Name of Mother	Year	County
1	James Collins	Dead	Atoka	Eliz Collins	Dead	Atoka
2						
3						
4						
5						
6						
7						
8						
9						
10						
11						
12						
13						
14					Date of Application for Enrollment.	
15					Aug 29/99	
16						
17						

Choctaw By Blood Enrollment Cards 1898-1914

RESIDENCE: Atoka
POST OFFICE: Kiowa, I.T.

COUNTY. **Choctaw Nation**

Choctaw Roll *(Not Including Freedmen)*

CARD NO.
FIELD NO. **4120**

Dawes' Roll No.	NAME		Relationship to Person First Named	AGE	SEX	BLOOD	TRIBAL ENROLLMENT		
							Year	County	No.
11551	1 Ward, Henry P	46	First Named	43	M	1/32	1896	Atoka	14009
I.W.394	2 " Mary D	48	Wife	44	F	I.W.			
11552	3 Crisp, Ella M	25	Dau	22	"	1/64	1896	Atoka	14012
11553	4 Ward, Bessie E	19	"	16	"	1/64	1896	"	14013
11554	5 " William D	13	Son	10	M	1/64	1896	"	14010
11555	6 " Naomi P	11	Dau	8	F	1/64	1896	"	14014
11556	7 " Herbert S	8	Son	5	M	1/64	1896	"	14011
I.W.1338	8 Crisp, Moses E	32	Husband of No.3	32	M	I.W.			
	9								
	10	ENROLLMENT							
	11	OF NOS. 1,3,4,5,6 and 7 HEREON APPROVED BY THE SECRETARY							
	12	OF INTERIOR Mar. 10, 1903							
	13	No3 is now the wife of Moses E. Crisp on							
	14	Choctaw Card #D810, Sept. 25, 1902							
	15	No.4 on 1896 roll as Bessie E. Ward							
	16								
	17	No.3 and 8 were married Sept 23, 1902							

NB see Card #158 For child of Nos 3&8 (Apr 26'06) Card #158

TRIBAL ENROLLMENT OF PARENTS

	Name of Father	Year	County	Name of Mother	Year	County
1	Joseph Ward	Dead	Non Citz	Eliz Ward	Dead	Atoka
2	James Depart	"	" "	Lou Depart	"	Non Citz
3	No1			No2		
4	No1			No2		
5	No1	ENROLLMENT OF NOS. 8 HEREON APPROVED BY THE SECRETARY OF INTERIOR Mar. 14, 1905		No2	ENROLLMENT OF NOS. 2 HEREON	
6	No1			No2	APPROVED BY THE SECRETARY OF INTERIOR Sep 12, 1903	
7	No1			No2		
8	Wm M Crisp		Non Citz	Mary Crisp	Dead	Non Citz
9	Record as to enrolment of No8 forwarded Department March 14, 1906					
10	Record returned see opinion of Assistant Attorney General of March 15, 1906, in case of					
11	Omer R Nicholson } No1 on 1896 roll as H.P. Ward			Marriage certificate of Henry P Ward		
	No5 " 1896 " " Wm D "			to Mary J Depart July 11-15 in due		
12	No6 " 1896 " " Neomi "			form exhibited and satisfactory, but		
13	No3 " 1896 " " Minerva "			not in condition to be files 9/5/99		
14	No2 Evidence of marriage					#1 to 7
15	to be supplied:- No2 admitted as an intermarried citizen by				Date of Application for Enrollment.	
16	Dawes Commission: Choctaw case #503, No appeal				Aug 29/99	
17	No8 originally listed for enrollment on Choctaw card D-810, Sept 25, 1902; transferred to this card					

Feb 1, 1905: See decision of Jan 16, 1905

220

Choctaw By Blood Enrollment Cards 1898-1914

RESIDENCE: Atoka   COUNTY. **Choctaw Nation**   **Choctaw Roll**   CARD No.
POST OFFICE: Atoka, I.T.   *(Not Including Freedmen)*   FIELD No. **4121**

Dawes' Roll No.	NAME		Relationship to Person First Named	AGE	SEX	BLOOD	TRIBAL ENROLLMENT		
							Year	County	No.
I.W. 395	1 Selsor, John	46		42	M	I.W.	1896	Atoka	15065
11557	2 " Agnes	32	Wife	29	F	1/2	1893	Chick Dist	502
11558	3 " Joe A	15	Dau	12	"	1/4	1893	" "	503
11559	4 " Ela R	13	"	10	"	1/4	1893	" "	504
11560	5 " Ida S	11	"	8	"	1/4	1893	" "	505
11561	6 " Arthur A	9	Son	6	M	1/4	1893	" "	506
11562	7 " Leona G	7	Dau	3	F	1/4			
11563	8 " Lee Nora	4	"	1	"	1/4			
11564	9 " Bernice	2	Dau	2mo	F	1/4			
	10								
	11 No 7, 8 Affidavits of birth to								
	12 be supplied:- Filed Nov 2/99								
	No2 on 1896 roll No 12476 Agnes Turnbull								
	13 No3 " 1896 roll " 12477 Joe A "								
	14 No4 " 1896 roll " 12478 Rebecca E "								
	15 No5 " 1896 roll " 12479 Stella I "								
	No6 " 1896 roll " 12480 Alex A "								
	16 No7 " 1896 roll " 12481 Grace L "								
	17 All but Nos 1-8 are on Page 325, 1896 roll Atoka Co.								

TRIBAL ENROLLMENT OF PARENTS

	Name of Father	Year	County	Name of Mother	Year	County
1	Alex Selsor	Dead	Non Citz	Jane Selsor	Dead	Non Citz
2	Daniel Turnbull	"	Blue	Rebecca Turnbull	"	Blue
3	No1			No2		
4	No1			No2		
5	No1			No2		
6	No1			No2		
7	No1			No2		
8	No1			No2		
9	No1			No2		

ENROLLMENT OF NOS. 2,3,4,5,6,7,8 and 9 HEREON APPROVED BY THE SECRETARY OF INTERIOR Mar 10 1903

ENROLLMENT OF NOS 1 HEREON APPROVED BY THE SECRETARY OF INTERIOR Sep 12 1903

10   No1 on 1896 roll as John Sulser. Evidence of
11 marriage to be supplied: Filed Nov 2/99
12 No2 on 1893 Pay Roll, Page 53, No 502, Chick Dist
13 No3 " " " " " " 503 " " as J.A. Selsor
14 No4 " " " " " " 504 " " as E.R "
15 No5 " " " " " " 505 " " as I.S. "
16 No6 " " " " " " 506 " " as A.A "

Date of Application for Enrollment.
Aug 29/99

No.9 Enrolled December 16, 1900 } No1 was admitted as an intermarried
citizen by Dawes Commission: Choctaw Case #793: No appeal

17 For children of Nos 1&2 see NB (Mar 3-05) Card #292

P.O. Glove, I.T. 11/19/02

221

Choctaw By Blood Enrollment Cards 1898-1914

(COPY)

RESIDENCE: Atoka COUNTY. **Choctaw Nation** Choctaw Roll CARD NO.
POST OFFICE: Atoka, Indian Territory *(Not Including Freedmen)* FIELD NO. 4122

Dawes' Roll No.	NAME		Relationship to Person First Named	AGE	SEX	BLOOD	TRIBAL ENROLLMENT		
							Year	County	No.
11565	1 Jones, Edmond	52	First Named	49	M	full	1896	Atoka	7252
11566	2 " Alice	24	wife	21	F	full	1896	"	7253
11567	3 " Joseph	7	son	4	M	full	1896	"	7254
11568	4 " Emma Dead	4	dau	1	F	full			
11569	5 " Peter	22	son	19	M	full	1896	Atoka	7255
11579(sic)	6 " Amanda	2	dau	5mo	F	full			
	7								
	8								
	9								
	10	ENROLLMENT OF NOS. 1,2,3,4,5, & 6 HEREON APPROVED BY THE SECRETARY							
	11	OF INTERIOR Mar 10 1903							
	12								
	13	Citiz'p Certif. No. 3,4 & 6 May 6, 1903 Issued for							
	14								
	15	Citiz'p Certif. No. 1 April 25, 1903 Issued for							
	16								
	17	Citiz'p Certif. No. 5 April 21, 1903 Issued for							

TRIBAL ENROLLMENT OF PARENTS

	Name of Father	Year	County	Name of Mother	Year	County
1	Soloman Jones	dead	Jackson		dead	Bok Tuklo
2	Horne	"		Phalisa Horne		Jacks Fork
3	No. 1			Alice Jones No.2		Atoka
4	No. 1			" " " "		"
5	No. 1			No. 2		"
6	No. 1			No. 2		
7						
8						
9	No. 4 – Affidavit of birth to be supplied; Filed Oct. 26, '99					
10	No. 6 Enrolled June 15, 1901.					
11						
12						
13						
14						
15				Date of Application for Enrollment.		
16						
17				Aug. 29, 1899		

Choctaw By Blood Enrollment Cards 1898-1914

RESIDENCE: Atoka   COUNTY. **Choctaw Nation**   **Choctaw Roll**   CARD No.
POST OFFICE: Owl, I.T.   *(Not Including Freedmen)*   FIELD No. **4123**

Dawes' Roll No.	NAME	Relationship to Person First Named	AGE	SEX	BLOOD	TRIBAL ENROLLMENT Year	County	No.
11571	1 Josey, John	First Named	35	M	Full	1893	Atoka	575
11572	2 " Malinda 29	Wife	26	F	"	1893	Jacks Fork	356
11573	3 " Susan 15	Dau	12	"	"	1896	" "	7259
11574	4 " Isabelle 11	"	8	"	"	1896	" "	7260
11575	5 Holmes, Johnson 13	S.Son	10	M	"	1896	" "	6090
11576	6 " Joseph 10	"	7	"	"	1896	" "	6091
11577	7 " Allen 8	"	5	"	"	1896	" "	6092
11578	8 " Sampson 21	Ward	18	"	"	1896	" "	6089
11579	9 Hampton, Sealy A 21	S.Dau	18	F	"	1896	" "	6093

(DIED PRIOR TO SEPTEMBER 25 1902 — struck through on line 1)

10 No.1 died prior to September 25, 1902: not entitled to land or money
11 (See Indian Office letter Aug 24-1910, D.C. # 196-1910)
No.9 on 1896 roll a Salam Hampton
12 No.1 died July - 1901: Enrolment
13 cancelled by Department July 8, 1904
14
15   ENROLLMENT
16 OF NOS.1,2,3,4,5,6,7,8 and 9 HEREON
APPROVED BY THE SECRETARY
17 OF INTERIOR   Mar 10 1903

TRIBAL ENROLLMENT OF PARENTS

	Name of Father	Year	County	Name of Mother	Year	County
1	Josey Chitto	Dead	Atoka	Pe-sa-te-ma	Dead	Atoka
2	Sanimta[sic] Frazier	"	Jacks Fork	Wa-le-lue-na	"	Jacks Fork
3	No1			Mollie Josey	"	Atoka
4	No1			" "	"	"
5	Alexander Homes[sic]	Dead	Jacks Fork	No2		
6	" "	"	" "	No2		
7	" "	"	" "	No2		
8	" "	"	" "	Jennie Holmes	Dead	Jacks Fork
9	Simon Hampton	"	Atoka	No2		
10						
11	No1 on 1893 Pay Roll, Page 55, No 575, Atoka Co					
12	No2 " 1893 " " " 39, " 356 Jacks					
	Fork Co., Melinda Homes					
13	No5 on 1896 roll as Johnson Home				Date of Application for Enrollment.	
14	No6 " 1896 " " Joseph "					
15	No7 " 1896 " " Allen "				Aug 29/99	
16	No8 " 1896 " " Sampson "					
17						

223

Choctaw By Blood Enrollment Cards 1898-1914

RESIDENCE: Chickasaw Nation ~~COUNTY~~. **Choctaw Nation** **Choctaw Roll** CARD NO.
POST OFFICE: Byrds Mill, I.T. *(Not Including Freedmen)* FIELD NO. 4124

Dawes' Roll No.	NAME	Relationship to Person First Named	AGE	SEX	BLOOD	TRIBAL ENROLLMENT		
						Year	County	No.
1	Gott, Rhoda	Named	57	F	1/4			
2	" Ross	Son	20	M	1/8			
3								
4								
5								
6								
7								
8								
9								
10								
11								
12								
13								
14								
15								
16								
17								

DISMISSED
SEP 22 1904

TRIBAL ENROLLMENT OF PARENTS

	Name of Father	Year	County	Name of Mother	Year	County
1	Thos. Farmer	Dead	Choctaw	Tempy Farmer	Dead	Non Citz
2	Richard Gott		Non Citz	No1		
3						
4						
5						
6	No1&2 denied in 96 Case #1156					
7	Admitted by U.S. Court, Central Dist Aug 24/97, Case No 31					
8	No1 was admitted as Rhoda Gant No2 " " " " Ross "					
9	As to residence, see testimony of No1					
10	Judgment of U.S. Crt admitting Nos 1 and 2 vacated and set aside by Decree of Choctaw Chickasaw Citizenship Court Dec' 17'02					
11	No appeal to C.C.C.C.					
12						
13						
14						
15					Date of Application for Enrollment.	Aug 30/99
16						
17						

Choctaw By Blood Enrollment Cards 1898-1914

Choctaw Nation

Choctaw Roll (Not Including Freedmen)

CARD NO.

FIELD NO. 4125

Dawes' Roll No.	NAME	Relationship to Person First Named	AGE	SEX	BLOOD	TRIBAL ENROLLMENT		
						Year	County	No.
1	Gott, John	Named	23	M	1/8			
2								
3								
4								
5								
6								
7								
8								
9								
10								
11								
12								
13								
14								
15								
16								
17								

DISMISSED

SEP 22 1904

TRIBAL ENROLLMENT OF PARENTS

	Name of Father	Year	County	Name of Mother	Year	County
1	Richard Gott		Non-Citz	Rhoda Gott		Choctaw
2						
3						
4						
5						
6						
7						
8						
9						
10						
11						
12						
13						
14						
15						
16						
17						

No1 denied in 96 Case #1156
Admitted by U.S. Court, Central
Dist., Aug 24/97, Case No 31 as
John Gant
As to residence, see his testimony
Judgment of U.S. Court vacating Not vacated and set aside by Decree of Choctaw Chickasaw Citizenship Court Dec 17/02
No appeal to C.C.C.C.

Date of Application for Enrollment. Aug 30/99

RESIDENCE: Chickasaw Nation ~~COUNTY.~~ **Choctaw Nation** **Choctaw Roll** CARD No.

POST OFFICE: Franks, I.T. *(Not Including Freedmen)* FIELD No. 4126

Dawes' Roll No.	NAME	Relationship to Person First Named	AGE	SEX	BLOOD	TRIBAL ENROLLMENT		
						Year	County	No.
1	~~Gott, George~~		24	M	1/8			
2								
3								
4								
5								
6								
7								
8								
9								
10								
11								
12								
13								
14								
15								
16								
17								

DISMISSED

SEP 22 1904

TRIBAL ENROLLMENT OF PARENTS

	Name of Father	Year	County	Name of Mother	Year	County
1	Richard Gott		Non Citz	Rhoda Gott		Choctaw
2						
3						
4						
5				No		
6						
7						
8						
9						
10						
11						
12						
13						
14						
15						
16						
17						

No1 denied in 96 Case #1156
Admitted by U.S. Court, Central
Dist., Aug 24/97, Case No 31 as
George Gant. As to residence, see
his testimony

No appeal to C.C.C.

Date of Application for Enrollment. Aug 30/99

Choctaw By Blood Enrollment Cards 1898-1914

RESIDENCE: Chickasaw Nation COUNTY.
POST OFFICE: Franks, I.T.

Choctaw Nation

Choctaw Roll (Not Including Freedmen)

CARD NO.
FIELD NO. 4127

Dawes' Roll No.	NAME	Relationship to Person First Named	AGE	SEX	BLOOD	TRIBAL ENROLLMENT		
						Year	County	No.
1	Parker, Cynthia	Named	38	F	1/8			
2	" Willie	Son	1½	M	1/16			
3	" Alma	Dau	6 wk	F	1/16			
4								
5								
6								
7								
8								
9								
10								
11								
12								
13								
14								
15								
16								
17								

DISMISSED

SEP 22 1904

TRIBAL ENROLLMENT OF PARENTS

	Name of Father	Year	County	Name of Mother	Year	County
1	Richard Gott		Non Citz	Rhoda Gott		Choctaw
2	W. A. Parker		" "	No1		
3	"		" "	No1		

4
No1 appeal to C.C.C.C.
5 Judgements of U.S. C. admitting No1 vacated and set aside by Decree of Choctaw Chickasaw Citizenship Court Decr 1702
6 No1 Denied in 96 Case #1156
7 No3 born November 7, 1899; transferred to this card May 24, 1902
8 No1 admitted by U.S. Court, Central
9 Dist., Aug 24/97, Case No 31
As to residence and birth of No2, which
10 occurred April 18/98, see testimony of
11 W.A. Parker
No2- "Affidavit of birth to be
12 supplied" Recd Dec 18/99. Irregular
13 and returned for correction. Returned corrected and filed Feby 20, 1900.
14
15 Alma Parker daughter of No1, born

Date of Application for Enrollment. Aug 30/99

16 Nov 7/99 on card D-543.
17

227

Choctaw By Blood Enrollment Cards 1898-1914

RESIDENCE: Jacks Fork	COUNTY.	Choctaw Nation	Choctaw Roll	CARD NO.
POST OFFICE: Kosoma, I.T.			(Not Including Freedmen)	FIELD NO. **4128**

Dawes' Roll No.	NAME		Relationship to Person First Named	AGE	SEX	BLOOD	TRIBAL ENROLLMENT		
							Year	County	No.
11580	1 Loman, Charles	53	First Named	50	M	Full	1896	Jacks Fork	8354
11581	2 " Kitsie	53	Wife	50	F	"	1896	" "	8355
11582	3 " Stephen	12	Ward	9	M		1896	" "	8356
	4								
	5								
	6								
	7	ENROLLMENT							
	8	OF NOS. 1,2 and 3 HEREON APPROVED BY THE SECRETARY							
	9	OF INTERIOR Mar. 10, 1903							
	10								
	11								
	12								
	13								
	14								
	15								
	16								
	17								

TRIBAL ENROLLMENT OF PARENTS

	Name of Father	Year	County	Name of Mother	Year	County
1	Henson Loman	Dead	Skullyville	Phoebe Loman	Dead	Jacks Fork
2	William Jenks	"	Atoka	Me-ha-ta-che	"	Kiamitia
3	Solomon Morris	"	Jacks Fork	Easter Morris	"	Jacks Fork
4						
5						
6						
7						
8						
9						
10						
11						
12						
13						
14					Date of Application for Enrollment.	
15					Aug 30/99	
16						
17						

228

Choctaw By Blood Enrollment Cards 1898-1914

RESIDENCE: Jacks Fork   COUNTY.   **Choctaw Nation**   **Choctaw Roll** *(Not Including Freedmen)*   CARD NO.

POST OFFICE: Stringtown, I.T.   FIELD NO. **4129**

Dawes' Roll No.	NAME	Relationship to Person First Named	AGE	SEX	BLOOD	TRIBAL ENROLLMENT		
						Year	County	No.
11583	1 Cole, Jimson 48	First Named	45	M	Full	1896	Jacks Fork	2991
11584	2 " Lucy 46	Wife	43	F	"	1896	" "	2992
11585	3 Peter, Salena 20	S.D.	17	"	"	1896	" "	2993
11586	4 Colbert, Charlie 18	Ward	15	M	1/2	1896	" "	2994
	5							
	6							
	7							
	8	ENROLLMENT						
	9	OF NOS. 1,2,3 and 4 HEREON APPROVED BY THE SECRETARY						
	10	OF INTERIOR Mar 10 1903						
	11							
	12							
	13							
	14							
	15							
	16							
	17							

TRIBAL ENROLLMENT OF PARENTS

Name of Father	Year	County	Name of Mother	Year	County
1 Colbert Cole	Dead	Cedar		Dead	Cedar
2 Tok-lun-tubbee	"	Jacks Fork	Ho-tey	"	Jacks Fork
3 James Peter	"	Atoka	No2		
4 Jackson Colbert	"	Chickasaw	Siley Colbert	"	Jacks Fork
5					
6					
7					
8					
9	No1 on 1896 roll as Sim Cole				
10	No2 " 1896 " " Ruthie "				
11	No3 " 1896 " " Seline "				
12	No4 " 1896 " " Charlie "				
13	Nos 1 and 2 have separated and No.1 is now the husband of				
14	Elizabeth Peter, Choctaw Card #4019 11/17/02			Date of Application for Enrollment.	
15	No.2 is now wife of Solomon Dwight on Choctaw Card #4040			Aug 30/99	
16	Correct age of No.4 is 23 years. See his sworn statement taken May 11, 1903				
17	No3 Cairo Okla in 1903				

Choctaw By Blood Enrollment Cards 1898-1914

RESIDENCE: Atoka	COUNTY.							
POST OFFICE: Lehigh, I.T.		**Choctaw Nation** *(Not Including Freedmen)*			**Choctaw Roll**		CARD NO. FIELD NO. **4130**	

Dawes' Roll No.	NAME	Relationship to Person	AGE	SEX	BLOOD	TRIBAL ENROLLMENT		
						Year	County	No.
11587	1 Hall, Allington 32	First Named	29	M	Full	1893	Atoka	450
11588	2 " Melissa 23	Wife	20	F	"	1896	"	1744
11589	3 " Dickerson 1	Son	14mo	F M	"			
	4							
	5							
	6							
	7							
	8 ENROLLMENT							
	9 OF NOS. 1, 2 and 3 HEREON APPROVED BY THE SECRETARY							
	10 OF INTERIOR Mar 10 1903							
	11							
	12							
	13							
	14							
	15							
	16							
	17							

TRIBAL ENROLLMENT OF PARENTS

	Name of Father	Year	County	Name of Mother	Year	County
1	Roberson Hall	Dead	Blue	Wacey Hall	Dead	Jacks Fork
2	Edmond Billy		Atoka	Susan Billy	"	Atoka
3	No1			No2		
4						
5						
6						
7						
8						
9	No1 on 1893 Pay Roll, Page 43, No 450					
10	Atoka Co					
11	No2 on 1896 roll as Malessa Billy					
12	No3 Born Oct 10,1901. Proof of birth received and filed Dec 24,1902					
	For child of No2 see NB (March 3,1905) #1485					
13						
14						
15						Date of Application for Enrollment.
16						
17			P.O. Coalgate I T			Aug 30/99

230

Choctaw By Blood Enrollment Cards 1898-1914

| RESIDENCE: | Atoka | COUNTY. | **Choctaw Nation** | | **Choctaw Roll** | CARD NO. |
| POST OFFICE: | Coalgate, I.T. | | | | *(Not Including Freedmen)* | FIELD NO. 4131 |

Dawes' Roll No.	NAME		Relationship to Person First Named	AGE	SEX	BLOOD	TRIBAL ENROLLMENT		
							Year	County	No.
11590	1 Billy, Nicholas	21	First Named	18	M	Full	1896	Atoka	1741
11591	2 " Elizabeth	18	Wife	15	F	"	1893	Jacks Fork	393
	3								
	4								
	5								
	6	ENROLLMENT							
	7	OF NOS. 1 and 2 HEREON APPROVED BY THE SECRETARY							
	8	OF INTERIOR MAR 10 1903							
	9								
	10								
	11								
	12								
	13								
	14								
	15								
	16								
	17								

TRIBAL ENROLLMENT OF PARENTS

	Name of Father	Year	County	Name of Mother	Year	County
1	Edmond Billy		Atoka	Susan Billy	Dead	Atoka
2	James Hudson	Dead	"	Rebecca Billy		"
3						
4						
5						
6						
7						
8	No2 on 1893 Pay Roll, Page 42, No 393					
9	Jacks Fork Co as Elizabeth Hudson					
10	For child of No2 see NB (March 3 1905) #1117					
11						
12						
13						5/31/16 ECF
14						Date of Application for Enrollment.
15						Aug 30 1899
16						
17						

Choctaw By Blood Enrollment Cards 1898-1914

RESIDENCE: Atoka   COUNTY. **Choctaw Nation**   **Choctaw Roll**   CARD NO.
POST OFFICE: Lehigh, I.T.   *(Not Including Freedmen)*   FIELD NO. **4132**

Dawes' Roll No.	NAME		Relationship to Person	AGE	SEX	BLOOD	TRIBAL ENROLLMENT		
							Year	County	No.
11592	1 Wade, Allington	22	First Named	19	M	Full	1896	Atoka	13926
11593	2 " Piley	57	Wife	54	F	"	1896	"	13975
	3								
	4								
	5								
	6	ENROLLMENT OF NOS. 1 and 2 HEREON							
	7	APPROVED BY THE SECRETARY							
	8	OF INTERIOR Mar 10 1903							
	9								
	10								
	11								
	12								
	13								
	14								
	15								
	16								
	17								

TRIBAL ENROLLMENT OF PARENTS

	Name of Father	Year	County	Name of Mother	Year	County
1	Bible Wade		Tobucksy	Lizzie Wade	Dead	Atoka
2	E-ma-le-tubbee	Dead	Cedar	O-co-na-tema	"	Cedar
3						
4						
5						
6	No1 on 1896 roll as Alington Wade					
7	No2 " 1896 " " Piley Washington					
8						
9	No1 and 2 have separated					
10						
11						
12						
13				Date of Application for Enrollment.		
14						
15				Aug 30/99		
16						
17						

RESIDENCE:	Atoka	COUNTY.						
POST OFFICE:	Coalgate, I.T.							

Choctaw Nation

Choctaw Roll (Not Including Freedmen)

CARD No. FIELD No. **4133**

Dawes' Roll No.	NAME		Relationship to Person First Named	AGE	SEX	BLOOD	TRIBAL ENROLLMENT		
							Year	County	No.
11594	1 Ott, Johnson	48	First Named	45	M	Full	1896	Atoka	10022
11595	2 " Bicy	51	Wife	48	F	"	1896	"	10023
	3								
	4								
	5								
	6 ENROLLMENT OF NOS. 1 and 2 HEREON								
	7 APPROVED BY THE SECRETARY								
	8 OF INTERIOR Mar 10 1903								
	9								
	10								
	11								
	12								
	13								
	14								
	15								
	16								
	17								

TRIBAL ENROLLMENT OF PARENTS

	Name of Father	Year	County	Name of Mother	Year	County
1	Sam Ott	Dead	Gaines	Caliste Ott	Dead	Gaines
2	Jefferson Sexton	"	Atoka	Lizzie Sexton	"	Atoka
3						
4						
5						
6						
7	No.2 on 1896 roll as Bicey Ott					
8						
9						
10						
11						
12						
13						
14				Date of Application for Enrollment.		
15				Aug 30/99		
16						
17						

Choctaw By Blood Enrollment Cards 1898-1914

RESIDENCE: Chickasaw Nation ~~COUNTY.~~ **Choctaw Nation**   **Choctaw Roll** CARD NO.
POST OFFICE: Hewitt, I.T.   9/14/04   *(Not Including Freedmen)* FIELD NO. **4134**

Dawes' Roll No.	NAME		Relationship to Person First Named	AGE	SEX	BLOOD	TRIBAL ENROLLMENT		
							Year	County	No.
11596	1 Ward, Charles	53	First Named	50	M	1/16	1896	Tobucksy	13017
11597	2 " Benjamin F	24	Son	21	"	1/32	1896	"	13997
11598	3 " William A	20	"	17	"	1/32	1896	"	13019
11599	4 " Aaron	13	"	10	"	1/32	1896	"	13020
11600	5 " Ira	10	"	7	"	1/32	1896	"	13021
I.W.1010	6 " Sallie P	38	Wife	36	F	I.W.			15161
I.W.1131	7 " Lockey	17	Wife of No 2	17	F	I.W.			
	8								
	9	ENROLLMENT							
	10	OF NOS. 1,2,3,4 and 5 APPROVED BY THE SECRETARY	HEREON						
	11	OF INTERIOR Mar 10 1903							
	12	ENROLLMENT OF NOS. ~~7~~	HEREON						
	13	APPROVED BY THE SECRETARY							
	14	OF INTERIOR Nov. 16 1904							
	15	ENROLLMENT OF NOS. ~~6~~	HEREON						
	16	APPROVED BY THE SECRETARY OF INTERIOR Oct 21 1904							
	17								

TRIBAL ENROLLMENT OF PARENTS

Name of Father	Year	County	Name of Mother	Year	County
1 Joseph Ward	Dead	Non Citz	Elizabeth Ward	Dead	Atoka
2 No1			Mary E Ward	"	Non Citz
3 No1			" " "	"	" "
4 No1			" " "	"	" "
5 No1			" " "	"	" "
6 L.F.J. Amos		non-citizen	Mary W. Amos	"	" "
7 Jim Todd		" "	Mollie Todd	"	" "
8					
9	For child of Nos 2&7 see NB (Act Mar 3-05) Card #293				
10	No2 on 1896 roll as Ben F. Ward				
	No3 " 1896 " " Wm G "				
11	No 7 transferred from Choctaw card #D-712 Oct 31,1904: See decision of Oct 15, 1904				
12	As to marriage of parents of above				
13	parties, see testimony of Charles LeFlore				
14	No6 Admitted by Dawes Commission as an intermarried citizen in case No.501. No appeal.				
15	Contested by Choctaw Commission #1 to 5			Date of Application for Enrollment.	
16	No.6 transferred from Choctaw D.290 to this card June 13,1900			Aug 30/99	
	No2 is the husband of Lockey Ward on Choctaw card #D.712: April 25, 1902				
17					

P.O. Kiowa I.T. 1/24/03

234

RESIDENCE:	Tobucksy	COUNTY.							

Choctaw Nation **Choctaw Roll** (Not Including Freedmen)

POST OFFICE: Kiowa, I.T.

CARD NO. FIELD NO. **4135**

Dawes' Roll No.	NAME	Relationship to Person First Named	AGE	SEX	BLOOD	TRIBAL ENROLLMENT		
						Year	County	No.
11601 1	Ward, Charles O 27	First Named	24	M	1/32	1896	Atoka	13996
I.W. 396 2	" Lucy D 24	Wife	21	F	I.W.			
11602 3	" Henry Lee 2	Son	2mo	M	1/64			
15849 4	" Mary Margaret	Dau	1	F	1/64			
5								
6	CITIZENSHIP CERTIFICATE							
7	ISSUED FOR NO 1 & 3							
8	APR 23 1903							
9	ENROLLMENT							
10	OF NOS. ~~~4~~~ HEREON APPROVED BY THE SECRETARY							
11	OF INTERIOR JUN 12 1905							
12	ENROLLMENT							
13	OF NOS. 1 – 3 HEREON APPROVED BY THE SECRETARY							
14	OF INTERIOR MAR 10 1903							
15	ENROLLMENT							
16	OF NOS. ~~~~2~~~~ HEREON APPROVED BY THE SECRETARY							
17	OF INTERIOR SEP 12 1903							

TRIBAL ENROLLMENT OF PARENTS

	Name of Father	Year	County	Name of Mother	Year	County
1	Chas. Ward		Tobucksy	Mary E Ward	Dead	Non Citz
2	Robt L Patrick	Dead	Non Citz	Lucy M Patrick	"	" "
3	No.1			No.2		
4	No.1			No.2		
5						
6						
7						
8						
9						
10	No.1 on 1896 roll as Oliver C. Ward – as to marriage of parents, see enrollment of father Chas. Ward					
11	No3 Enrolled Aug. 22, 1900					
12						
13	Affidavit of No.2 as to residence of No.1 at time of his marriage to her					
14	filed May 13, 1903.					
15	No.4 was born Jan 19, 1902; application received and No.4 placed hereon					
16	March 24, 1905 under Act of Congress approved March 3, 1905.					Aug 30/99
17						

235

Choctaw By Blood Enrollment Cards 1898-1914

RESIDENCE:	Atoka	COUNTY.								

Choctaw Nation

Choctaw Roll (Not Including Freedmen)

POST OFFICE:	Atoka, I.T.					CARD NO. FIELD NO. **4136**		

Dawes' Roll No.	NAME	Relationship to Person First Named	AGE	SEX	BLOOD	TRIBAL ENROLLMENT		
						Year	County	No.
I.W. 753	1 Wheeler, Robert J (31)	Named	29	M	I.W.	1896	Tobucksy	15169
	2							
	3							
	4							
	5							
	6							
	7	ENROLLMENT						
	8	OF NOS. ~~~ 1 ~~~ HEREON APPROVED BY THE SECRETARY						
	9	OF INTERIOR May 7 1904						
	10							
	11							
	12							
	13							
	14							
	15							
	16							
	17							

TRIBAL ENROLLMENT OF PARENTS

	Name of Father	Year	County	Name of Mother	Year	County
1	Jesse Wheeler		Non Citz	Susanna Wheeler		Non Citz
2						
3						
4						
5						
6						
7	No1 see decision of Mar. 2 '04					
8	Admitted by Dawes Com. Case No					
9	509 as R. J. Wheeler No Appeal					
10	As to marriage, separation and divorce, see his testimony					
11	On 1896 roll as R. Judson Wheeler					
12	No.1 is now the husband of Erna Tucker on Choctaw Card #4304, May 7, 1901 #12035					
13	Evidence of marriage filed with papers in Choctaw Case #4304 May 7, 1901					
14	See additional testimony of Nº1 taken October 20, 1901					
15	See petition and oath of Robert J Wheeler and other papers filed herein Oct. 23, 1902			Date of Application for Enrollment	Aug 30/99	
16						
17	P.O. Wynnewood, I.T.					

1/23/03

Choctaw By Blood Enrollment Cards 1898-1914

RESIDENCE: Chickasaw Nation ~~COUNTY~~. **Choctaw Nation** Choctaw Roll   CARD NO.
POST OFFICE: Wynnewood, I.T.   (Not Including Freedmen)   FIELD NO. 4137

Dawes' Roll No.	NAME	Relationship to Person First Named	AGE	SEX	BLOOD	TRIBAL ENROLLMENT		
						Year	County	No.
I.W. 397 ₁	Wheeler, Walter R ²⁹	First Named	26	M	I.W.			
11603 ₂	" Eva L ²⁴	Wife	21	F	1/4	1896	Jacks Fork	12490
11604 ₃	" Jessie ²	Dau	3wks	F	1/8			
₄								
₅								
₆								
₇	ENROLLMENT							
₈	OF NOS. 2 and 3 HEREON APPROVED BY THE SECRETARY							
₉	OF INTERIOR Mar 10 1903							
₁₀	ENROLLMENT							
₁₁	OF NOS. 1 HEREON APPROVED BY THE SECRETARY							
₁₂	OF INTERIOR SEP 12 1903							
₁₃								
₁₄								
₁₅								
₁₆								
₁₇								

TRIBAL ENROLLMENT OF PARENTS

	Name of Father	Year	County	Name of Mother	Year	County
₁	Jesse Wheeler		Non Citz	Susanna Wheeler		Non Citz
₂	Eaton Tucker		Jacks Fork	Susan Tucker		Jacks Fork
₃	No1			No2		
₄						
₅						
₆						
₇	No2 on 1896 roll as Eva Tucker					
₈	No.3 Enrolled March 12 1901					
₉	Certificate of marriage between Nᵒˢ 1 and 2 received and filed Oct. 23, 1902					
₁₀						
₁₁						
₁₂	See additional testimony of Nᵒ 1 taken October 20, 1902.					
₁₃						
₁₄						
₁₅				Date of Application for Enrollment	Aug 30/99	
₁₆						
₁₇						

Choctaw By Blood Enrollment Cards 1898-1914

Dawes' Roll No.	NAME	Relationship to Person First Named	AGE	SEX	BLOOD	TRIBAL ENROLLMENT		
						Year	County	No.
11605	1 Brown, Melvina 43	First Named	40	F	Full	1896	Atoka	1750
DEAD.	2 " Louisa DEAD	Dau	17	"	1/2	1896	"	1751
11606	3 " Rosa E 14	"	11	"	1/2	1896	"	1752
DEAD	4 " Thompson	Son	9	M	1/2	1896	"	1753
	5							
	6							
	7							
No2 Died March 15, 1900: proof of death								
filed Nov, 25, 1902	9							
No4 died Nov. 28, 1901: proof of								
death filed Nov. 25, 1902								
	11							
	12							
	13							
	14	ENROLLMENT						
	15	OF NOS. 1 and 3 HEREON APPROVED BY THE SECRETARY			No. 2 and 4 HEREON DISMISSED UNDER			
	16	OF INTERIOR MAR 10 1903			ORDER OF THE COMMISSION TO THE FIVE CIVILIZED TRIBES OF MARCH 31, 1905.			
	17							

TRIBAL ENROLLMENT OF PARENTS

	Name of Father	Year	County	Name of Mother	Year	County
1	Ellis Franklin	Dead	Atoka	Betsy Franklin	Dead	Atoka
2	George Brown	"	Non Citz	No1		
3	" "	"	" "	No1		
4	" "	"	" "	No1		
5						
6						
7						
8			No3 on 1896 roll as Roseola Brown			
9				Father of No.1 is Harris Franklin		
10						
11						
12			6/4/1900: Husband of #1 on Choctaw card #5331			
13						
14						Date of Application for Enrollment.
15						Aug 30/99
16						
17						

Choctaw By Blood Enrollment Cards 1898-1914

RESIDENCE: Atoka COUNTY. **Choctaw Nation** (Not Including Freedmen) Choctaw Roll CARD NO.
POST OFFICE: Atoka, I.T. FIELD NO. **4139**

Dawes' Roll No.	NAME		Relationship to Person First Named	AGE	SEX	BLOOD	TRIBAL ENROLLMENT		
							Year	County	No.
11607	1 Willis, Eastman	33	First Named	30	M	Full	1896	Atoka	14058
11608	2 " Bicy	24	Wife	21	F	"	1896	"	13939
11609	3 Webster, Rena	7	S.D.	4	"	"	1896	"	13941
11610	4 " Summie	6	S.S.	3	M	"	1896	"	13940
11611	5 Leader, Louis	11	Ward	8	"	"	1896	"	8324
11612	6 Willis, Isaac	2	Son	3W	M	"			
	7								
	8								
	9								
	10								
	11								
	12								
	13								
	14								
	15								
	16								
	17								

ENROLLMENT
OF NOS 1,2,3,4,5 and 6 HEREON
APPROVED BY THE SECRETARY
OF INTERIOR Mar 10 1903

TRIBAL ENROLLMENT OF PARENTS

	Name of Father	Year	County	Name of Mother	Year	County
1	John Willis	Dead	Atoka	Susie Wade	Dead	Atoka
2	David Sexton		"	Liza A. Sexton		"
3	Allen Webster	"	"	No2		
4	" "	"	"	No2		
5	Sim Leader	"	"	Sallie Collins	Dead	Atoka
6	No1			No2		
7						
8	No2 on 1896 roll as Bisey Webster					
9	No4 " 1896 " " Sonney "					
10	No.6 Enrolled January 30, 1901					
	For child of Nos 1&2 see NB Mar 3'05 Card #294					
11						
12						
13					#1 to 5 inc.	
14					Date of Application for Enrollment	
15					Aug 30/99	
16						
17						

Choctaw By Blood Enrollment Cards 1898-1914

RESIDENCE: Atoka COUNTY. **Choctaw Nation** Choctaw Roll CARD NO.
POST OFFICE: Atoka, I.T. *(Not Including Freedmen)* FIELD NO. **4140**

Dawes' Roll No.	NAME	Relationship to Person First Named	AGE	SEX	BLOOD	TRIBAL ENROLLMENT Year	County	No.
11613	1 Frazier, Smallwood 33	First Named	30	M	Full	1896	Atoka	4485
11614	2 " Louisa 53	Wife	50	F	"	1896	"	4486
	3							
	4							
	5							
	6 ENROLLMENT							
	7 OF NOS. 1 and 2 HEREON APPROVED BY THE SECRETARY							
	8 OF INTERIOR Mar 10 1903							
	9							
	10							
	11							
	12							
	13							
	14							
	15							
	16							
	17							

TRIBAL ENROLLMENT OF PARENTS

Name of Father	Year	County	Name of Mother	Year	County
1 Summy Frazier	Dead	Kiamitia	Phoebe Frazier	Dead	Atoka
2 Jacob Anderson	"	Atoka	Abe-hu-na	"	"
3					
4					
5					
6 No2 on 1896 roll as Lewisa Frazier					
7					
8					
9					
10					
11					
12					
13					
14				Date of Application for Enrollment.	
15				Aug 30/99	
16					
17					

RESIDENCE:	Atoka	COUNTY.							

RESIDENCE: Atoka **COUNTY.** **Choctaw Nation**

POST OFFICE: Wapanucka, I.T.

Choctaw Roll *(Not Including Freedmen)*

CARD NO.

FIELD NO. 4141

Dawes' Roll No.	NAME		Relationship to Person	AGE	SEX	BLOOD	TRIBAL ENROLLMENT		
							Year	County	No.
11615	1 Wallace, Mary	40	First Named	37	F	1/2	1896	Atoka	13935
*11616	2 " Jean	13	Son Dau	10	M F	1/4	1896	"	13936
11617	3 " Robert A	10	Son	7	M	1/4	1896	"	13937
11618	4 " Nellie	7	Dau	4	F	1/4	1896	"	13938
11619	5 " Anna	5	"	2	"	1/4			
11620	6 " David	1	Son	1wk	M	1/4			
	7								
	8								
	9 No1 also on 1896 roll No 14033								
	10 No2 " " 1896 " " 14036								
	11 No3 " " 1896 " " 14034								
	No4 " " 1896 " " 14035								
	12 No2 on roll as Jennie Wallace								
	13 No3 " " " Robert "								
	14 No4 " " " Nellie D "								
	All on Page No 368								
	15								
	16								
	17								

TRIBAL ENROLLMENT OF PARENTS

	Name of Father	Year	County	Name of Mother	Year	County
1	Allen Wright	Dead	Atoka	Harriet Wright	Dead	Non Citz
2	Thos Wallace		Non Citz	No1		
3	" "		" "	No1		
4	" "		" "	No1		
5	" "		" "	No1		
6	" "		" "	No1		
7						
8						
9						
10	No2 on 1896 roll as Jeane[sic] Wallace					
11	No3 " 1896 " " Robert "			ENROLLMENT		
12	No1 - As to marriage of parents			OF NOS. 1,2,3,4,5 and 6 HEREON		
	see enrollment of Anna B. Ludlow			APPROVED BY THE SECRETARY		
13	her sister.			OF INTERIOR Mar 10 1903		
14	No.5 – Affidavit of birth to be			Date of Application for Enrollment.		
15	supplied :- Filed Oct 26/99					
	No6 Born July 31, 1902: enrolled Aug 9, 1902			Aug 30/99		
16	* Changing of the sex from "M" to "F". See Departmental letter of Nov. 21, 1908					
17	(Land 76225-1908) D.C. No. 1713-1908					

Choctaw By Blood Enrollment Cards 1898-1914

RESIDENCE: Jackson   COUNTY. **Choctaw Nation**   **Choctaw Roll**   CARD No.

POST OFFICE: Mayhew, I.T.   (Not Including Freedmen)   FIELD No. 4142

Dawes' Roll No.	NAME		Relationship to Person First Named	AGE	SEX	BLOOD	TRIBAL ENROLLMENT		
							Year	County	No.
11621	1 Samuel, Louie	28	First Named	25	M	Full	1896	Jackson	11568
11622	2 " Annie	31	Wife	28	F	"	1896	"	11569
	3								
	4								
	5								
	6	ENROLLMENT							
	7	OF NOS. 1 and 2 HEREON APPROVED BY THE SECRETARY							
	8	OF INTERIOR MAR 10 1903							
	9								
	10								
	11								
	12								
	13								
	14								
	15								
	16								
	17								

TRIBAL ENROLLMENT OF PARENTS

	Name of Father	Year	County	Name of Mother	Year	County
1	Ne-tak-en-lubbee	Dead	Kiamitia		Dead	Kiamitia
2	Benson Cravatt	"	Jackson	Sophie Cravatt	"	Jackson
3						
4						
5						
6	No.2 is now the wife of Sammie Durant, Choctaw card #4195 12/1/02					
7						
8	No.1 "Died prior to September 25, 1902; not entitled to land or money."					
9	(See Indian Office letter Nov. 2, 1910)					
10						
11						
12						
13					Date of Application for Enrollment.	
14						
15					Aug 30/99	
16						
17	P.O. Boswell, Okla 3/23/09					

242

Choctaw By Blood Enrollment Cards 1898-1914

RESIDENCE: Atoka   **COUNTY.**   **Choctaw Nation**   **Choctaw Roll**   **CARD NO.**
POST OFFICE: Owl, I.T.   *(Not Including Freedmen)*   **FIELD NO.** **4143**

Dawes' Roll No.		NAME		Relationship to Person First Named	AGE	SEX	BLOOD	TRIBAL ENROLLMENT		
								Year	County	No.
11623	1	Monds, Richard	31	First Named	28	M	1/8	1896	Atoka	8833
IW398	2	" Mollie	31	Wife	28	F	I.W.			
11624	3	" Minda L	7	Dau	4	"	1/16	1896	Atoka	8834
11625	4	" Farris	5	Son	2	M	1/16			
DEAD	5	" Frank		"	5mo	"	1/16			
DEAD	6	" Nevada		Dau	2wk	F	1/16			
11626	7	" Josie Lee	1	Dau	1mo	F	1/16			
	8	No. 5 and 6 hereon dismissed under								
	9	order of the Commission to the Five								
		Civilized Tribes of March 31, 1905.								
	10									
	11	ENROLLMENT OF NOS. 1,3,4 and 7 HEREON								
	12	APPROVED BY THE SECRETARY OF INTERIOR Mar 10, 1903								
	13	ENROLLMENT								
	14	OF NOS. 2 HEREON APPROVED BY THE SECRETARY								
		OF INTERIOR Sep. 12, 1903								
	16									
	17									

TRIBAL ENROLLMENT OF PARENTS

	Name of Father	Year	County	Name of Mother	Year	County
1	Sam Monds		Non Citz	Jane Monds	Dead	Jacks Fork
2	Jack Tudor	Dead	" "	Julie Tudor		non citz
3	No1			No2		
4	No1			No2		
5	No1			No2		
6	No1			No2		
7	No1			No2		
8						
9	No3 on 1896 roll as Mary L Monds					
10						
11	Nos 4-5 Affidavits of birth to be supplied Filed Oct 26/99			For child of Nos 1&2 see NB (Mar 3'05) #469		
12	No.6 Enrolled Nov 2d 1900					
13	No7 Born March 20, 1902: enrolled April 16, 1902					#1 to 5 inc
14	No5 died January 22, 1900: proof of death filed Nov. 26, 1902					Date of Application for Enrollment
15	No6 " October 20, 1901 " " " " " "					
	For child of No1&2 see N.B. (Apr. 26, 1906) Card No. 18					Aug 30/99
16						
17						

Choctaw By Blood Enrollment Cards 1898-1914

RESIDENCE:	Atoka	COUNTY.					
POST OFFICE:	Lehigh, I.T.						

Choctaw Nation

Choctaw Roll (Not Including Freedmen)

CARD NO. FIELD NO. **4144**

Dawes' Roll No.	NAME		Relationship to Person First Named	AGE	SEX	BLOOD	TRIBAL ENROLLMENT		
							Year	County	No.
DEAD	1	Harris, Reason		24	M	Full	1896	Atoka	5935
11627	2	" Blannie	27 Wife	24	F	"	1896	"	5936
DEAD	3	" Aben	Son	5	M	"	1896	"	5937
11628	4	" Osborne	4 "	2	"	"			
11629	5	" Agnes	2 Dau	2mo	F	"			
	6								
	7								
	8								
	9	No1 died February 9, 1901; proof of							
	10	death filed Nov 25, 1902.							
	11	No3 died November 12, 1900, proof of death filed Nov. 25, 1902.							
	12								
	13	ENROLLMENT OF NOS. 2, 4 and 5 HEREON							
	14	APPROVED BY THE SECRETARY OF INTERIOR Mar. 10, 1903							
	15	No. 1 and 3 Hereon dismissed under							
	16	order of the Commission to the Five							
	17	Civilized Tribes of March 31, 1905.							

TRIBAL ENROLLMENT OF PARENTS

	Name of Father	Year	County	Name of Mother	Year	County
1	David Harris		Atoka	Betsy Harris	Dead	Atoka
2	Sam Willis	Dead	Tobucksy	Lucy Willis	"	"
3	No1			No2		
4	No1			No2		
5	No1			No2		
6	Name of No.1 is probably Rason, June 7, 1900					
7						
8	No.2 on 1896 roll as Delina Harrison					
9	All above surnames appear on 1896 roll as Harrison					
10	No4 affidavit of birth to be					
11	supplied; Filed Oct. 26/99 No5 Enrolled June 7, 1900					
12						
13						
14					#1 to 4	
15				Date of Application for Enrollment.	Aug 30/99	
16						
17						

Choctaw By Blood Enrollment Cards 1898-1914

RESIDENCE: Atoka COUNTY.
POST OFFICE: Atoka, I.T. P.O. Lone Grove I.T. 10/20/02

Choctaw Nation

Choctaw Roll
(Not Including Freedmen)

CARD NO.
FIELD NO. **4145**

Dawes' Roll No.	NAME	Relationship to Person First Named	AGE	SEX	BLOOD	TRIBAL ENROLLMENT Year	County	No.
I.W.399	1 Ridgeway, George W.	First Named	47	M	I.W.	1896	Atoka	14993
11630	2 " Sarah E	Wife	25	F	1/8	1896	"	10976
11631	3 " Annie	Dau	9	"	1/16	1896	"	10978
11632	4 " Mary L	"	7	"	1/16	1896	"	10979
11633	5 " William L	Son	1½	M	1/16			
DEAD.	6 Brooks, Lucy DEAD.	S in L	18	F	1/8	1896	Atoka	1765
11634	7 " Susie	"	16	"	1/8	1896	Atoka	1766
DEAD.	8 " Belle	"	14	"	1/8	1896	Atoka	1767
11635	9 Ridgeway, Henry E	Son	1mo	M	1/16			
	10							
	CITIZENSHIP CERTIFICATE ISSUED FOR NO. 2-3-4-5-9 MAY 9 1903							
	12							
	13							
	SHIP CERTIFICATE OR NO. 7							
Oct 6 1903	15							
CERTIFICATE 1 1903	16 17							

ENROLLMENT
OF NOS. 2 3 4 5 7-9 HEREON
APPROVED BY THE SECRETARY
OF INTERIOR MAR 10 1903

ENROLLMENT
OF NOS. One HEREON
APPROVED BY THE SECRETARY
OF INTERIOR SEP 12 1903

TRIBAL ENROLLMENT OF PARENTS

	Name of Father	Year	County	Name of Mother	Year	County
1	John Ridgeway	Dead	Non Citz	Louisa Ridgeway	Dead	Non Citz
2	Jack Campbell	" "		Mary J Campbell	"	Atoka
3	No.1			No.2		
4	No.1			No.2		
5	No.1			No.2		
6	Chas. Brooks		Non Citz	Mary J Campbell	Dead	Atoka
7	" "		" "	" " "	"	"
8	" "		" "	" " "	"	"
9	No.1			No.2		
10						
11						

12 No.1 on 1896 roll as G.W. Ridgeway – admitted by Dawes Com, Case No 652 as G.W. Ridgeway
13 No.2 on 1896 roll as Mrs. G.W. Ridgeway – was admitted as Emeline Brooks by Act of Council
approved October 22, 1880. Mother of Nos 6-7-8, Mary J Brooks, or Mary J Campbell
14 admitted as Mary Jane Lowery by act of Choctaw Council, approved October[sic] 22, 1880
15 No.5 Affidavit of birth to be supplied: Rec'd Dec. 18/99, but irregular and returned for correction
Received and Filed Jan'y 17, 1900.
16 No.6 Died January 1901:- Proof of death filed Nov. 21, 1902.
17 No.9 Enrolled Aug. 18, 1900.
No8-Died Sept 7 1902: Proof of Death filed Dec 23/1902

Aug 30/99

245

Choctaw By Blood Enrollment Cards 1898-1914

RESIDENCE:	Atoka		COUNTY.				
POST OFFICE:	Atoka, I.T.						

Choctaw Nation

Choctaw Roll *(Not Including Freedmen)*

CARD NO.

FIELD NO. **4146**

Dawes' Roll No.		NAME		Relationship to Person First Named	AGE	SEX	BLOOD	TRIBAL ENROLLMENT		
								Year	County	No.
DEAD	1	Peter, Abner	DEAD	First Named	27	M	Full	1893	Atoka	851
DEAD	2	" Winnie	DEAD	Wife	28	F	"	1893	"	952
11636	3	" Esias	8	Son	5	M	"			
DEAD	4	" John[sic]	DEAD	Dau	2	F	"			
	5									
	6									
	7	ENROLLMENT OF NOS. ~ 3 ~ HEREON								
	8	APPROVED BY THE SECRETARY OF INTERIOR Mar 10, 1903								
	9									
	10	No. 1,2 and 4 hereon dismissed under								
	11	order of the Commission to the Five Civilized Tribes of March 31, 1905.								
	12									
	13									
	14									
	15									
	16									
	17									

TRIBAL ENROLLMENT OF PARENTS

	Name of Father	Year	County	Name of Mother	Year	County
1	William Peter		Atoka	Ish-te-a-ho-yo	Dead	Atoka
2	Jack Caneomontubbee	Dead	"	Sophie Caneomontubbee	"	"
3	No.1			No.2		
4	No.1			No.2		
5						
6						
7						
8						
9	No.1 on 1893 Pay Roll, Page 86, No 851, Atoka Co					
10	No.2 " 1893 " " " 86 " 852, " "					
11	Nos 3-4 Affidavits of birth to be supplied:					
12	No.1 died Nov. 1901 proof of death filed Nov. 26, 1902					
13	No.2 " Nov. 1901 " " " " " " "					
14	No.3 " Aug. 1902 " " " " " " "				Date of Application for Enrollment.	
15					Aug 30/99	
16						
17						

Choctaw By Blood Enrollment Cards 1898-1914

RESIDENCE: Jackson COUNTY. **Choctaw Nation** Choctaw Roll 4147 CARD No.
POST OFFICE: Mayhew, I.T. (Not Including Freedmen) FIELD No. 414,

Dawes' Roll No.	NAME		Relationship to Person	AGE	SEX	BLOOD	TRIBAL ENROLLMENT		
							Year	County	No.
11637	1 Jones, Davis	23	First Named	20	M	Full	1896	Jackson	7126
	2								
	3								
	4								
	5	ENROLLMENT							
	6	OF NOS. 1 HEREON APPROVED BY THE SECRETARY							
	7	OF INTERIOR MAR 10 1903							
	8								
	9								
	10								
	11								
	12								
	13								
	14								
	15								
	16								
	17								

TRIBAL ENROLLMENT OF PARENTS

	Name of Father	Year	County	Name of Mother	Year	County
1	Davis Jones	Dead	Jacks Fork	Mary Jones	Dead	Jackson
2						
3						
4						
5						
6						
7						
8						
9						
10						
11						
12						
13						
14						
15				Date of Application for Enrollment.	Aug 30/99	
16						
17						

"Died prior to September 25, 1902, not entitled to land or money." (See Indian Office Letter November 21, 1910)

Choctaw By Blood Enrollment Cards 1898-1914

RESIDENCE: Atoka   COUNTY. **Choctaw Nation**   **Choctaw Roll**   CARD NO.
POST OFFICE: Coalgate, I.T.   *(Not Including Freedmen)*   FIELD NO. 4148

Dawes' Roll No.	NAME		Relationship to Person First Named	AGE	SEX	BLOOD	TRIBAL ENROLLMENT		
							Year	County	No.
11638	1 Wilson, Joseph	27		24	M	Full	1896	Atoka	14062
	2								
	3								
	4								
	5	ENROLLMENT							
	6	OF NOS. 1 HEREON APPROVED BY THE SECRETARY							
	7	OF INTERIOR MAR 10 1903							
	8								
	9								
	10								
	11								
	12								
	13								
	14								
	15								
	16								
	17								

TRIBAL ENROLLMENT OF PARENTS

	Name of Father	Year	County	Name of Mother	Year	County
1	Rabon Wilson	Dead	Atoka	Sophie Wilson	Dead	Atoka
2						
3						
4						
5						
6	On 1896 roll as Josephus Wilson					
7						
8						
9						
10						
11						
12						
13						
14						
15				Date of Application for Enrollment.		Aug 30/99
16						
17						

248

Choctaw By Blood Enrollment Cards 1898-1914

RESIDENCE: **Atoka**   COUNTY.   **Choctaw Nation**   **Choctaw Roll**   CARD No.
POST OFFICE: Atoka, I.T.   *(Not Including Freedmen)*   FIELD No. **4149**

Dawes' Roll No.		NAME		Relationship to Person	AGE	SEX	BLOOD	TRIBAL ENROLLMENT		
								Year	County	No.
11639	1	Katiotubbi, Milton	22	First Named	19	M	Full	1896	Atoka	7658
	2									
	3									
	4									
	5	ENROLLMENT OF NOS. 1 HEREON								
	6	APPROVED BY THE SECRETARY								
	7	OF INTERIOR MAR 10 1903								
	8									
	9									
	10									
	11									
	12									
	13									
	14									
	15									
	16									
	17									

TRIBAL ENROLLMENT OF PARENTS

	Name of Father	Year	County	Name of Mother	Year	County
1	Katiotubbi	Dead	Jacks Fork	Alice Katiotubbi	Dead	Jacks Fork
2						
3						
4						
5						
6	On 1896 roll as Ilton Katiotubbi					
7						
8						
9						
10						
11						
12						
13						
14					Date of Application for Enrollment.	
15					Aug 30/99	
16						
17						

Choctaw By Blood Enrollment Cards 1898-1914

RESIDENCE: Atoka COUNTY. **Choctaw Nation** **Choctaw Roll** CARD NO.
POST OFFICE: Coalgate, I.T. *(Not Including Freedmen)* FIELD NO. 4150

Dawes' Roll No.	NAME		Relationship to Person	AGE	SEX	BLOOD	TRIBAL ENROLLMENT		
							Year	County	No.
11640	1 Byington, Lefus	39	First Named	36	M	Full	1896	Atoka	1771
11641	2 " Annie	25	Wife	22	F	"	1896	"	14059
11642	3 " Agnes	2	Dau	22mo	F	"			
	4								
	5								
	6								
	7	ENROLLMENT OF NOS. 1,2 and 3 HEREON							
	8	APPROVED BY THE SECRETARY OF INTERIOR MAR 10 1903							
	9								
	10								
	11								
	12								
	13								
	14								
	15								
	16								
	17								

TRIBAL ENROLLMENT OF PARENTS

	Name of Father	Year	County	Name of Mother	Year	County
1	Chas Byington	Dead	Atoka	Le-ma-hu-na	Dead	Atoka
2	Dixon Byington	"	"	Liza	"	"
3	No1			No2		
4						
5						
6						
7			No2 on 1896 roll as Annie Willis			
8			No3 Born Feb 26, 1901: enrolled Dec 10, 1902			
9						
10	For children of No1 see NB (Apr 26-06) Card #308					
11						
12						
13						
14					#1&2	
15					Aug 30/99	
16						
17						

250

Choctaw By Blood Enrollment Cards 1898-1914

RESIDENCE: Jacks Fork COUNTY. **Choctaw Nation** Choctaw Roll CARD NO.
POST OFFICE: Antlers, I.T. *(Not Including Freedmen)* FIELD NO. 4151

Dawes' Roll No.	NAME	Relationship to Person First Named	AGE	SEX	BLOOD	TRIBAL ENROLLMENT		
						Year	County	No.
DEAD. 1	Simpiy, Ellen DEAD.	Named	28	F	1/2	1896	Jacks Fork	11701
DEAD. 2	Wesley, Josephine DEAD.	Dau	3mo	"	1/4			
3								
4								
5								
6								
7								
8								
9								
10								
11								
12								
13								
14								
15								
16								
17								

No. 1 and 2 HEREON DISMISSED UNDER ORDER OF THE COMMISSION TO THE FIVE CIVILIZED TRIBES OF MARCH 31, 1905.

TRIBAL ENROLLMENT OF PARENTS

	Name of Father	Year	County	Name of Mother	Year	County
1	Ona-ha-tubbee	Dead	Chick Roll	Jennie	Dead	Tobucksy
2	Simeon Wesley		Jacks Fork	No 1		
3						
4						
5						
6						
7	No1 died Dec. 1900; proof of death filed Dec. 5, 1902					
8	No2 " July, 1901; " " " " " " "					
9						
10						
11						
12						
13						
14						
15					Date of Application for Enrollment.	Aug 30/99
16						
17						

Choctaw By Blood Enrollment Cards 1898-1914

RESIDENCE:	Jacks Fork	COUNTY.	**Choctaw Nation**				**Choctaw Roll** *(Not Including Freedmen)*		CARD No.
POST OFFICE:	Stringtown, I.T.								FIELD No. **4152**

Dawes' Roll No.	NAME		Relationship to Person	AGE	SEX	BLOOD	TRIBAL ENROLLMENT		
							Year	County	No.
11643	1 Bond, Reason	27	First Named	24	M	Full	1896	Jacks Fork	1920
DEAD	2 " Sis		Wife	21	F	"	1893	Kiamitia	724
11644	3 " Edna	14	Ward	11	"	"	1896	Jacks Fork	1922
	4								
	5								
	6								
	7	ENROLLMENT							
	8	OF NOS. 1 and 3 HEREON APPROVED BY THE SECRETARY							
	9	OF INTERIOR Mar 10 1903							
	10								
	11	No.2 hereon dismissed under order of							
	12	the Commission to the Five Civilized							
	13	Tribes of March 31, 1905.							
	14								
	15								
	16								
	17								

TRIBAL ENROLLMENT OF PARENTS

	Name of Father	Year	County	Name of Mother	Year	County
1	Moses Bond		Jacks Fork	Narcie Bond	Dead	Jacks Fork
2	Sebal Harrison	Dead	Kiamitia	Jincy Harrison	"	Kiamitia
3	Anderson William	"	Jacks Fork	Liza William	"	Atoka
4						
5						
6						
7						
8	No2 on 1893 Pay Roll, Page 87, No. 724, Kiamitia					
9	Co, as Sis Smith					
	No3 on 1896 roll as Edney Bond					
10						
11						
12	No2 died July 8, 1902, proof of death filed Nov. 25, 1902					
13	No1 is now husband of Salema Peter on Choctaw card #4157; evidence of					
14	marriage filed Nov. 28, 1902					
15	For child of No3 see NB (Apr 26'06) #1265			Date of Application for Enrollment.	Aug 30/99	
16						
17						

Choctaw By Blood Enrollment Cards 1898-1914

RESIDENCE: **Atoka** COUNTY.   Choctaw Nation   Choctaw Roll   CARD NO.
POST OFFICE: **Atoka, I.T.**   FIELD NO. **4153**

Dawes' Roll No.	NAME	Relationship to Person First Named	AGE	SEX	BLOOD	TRIBAL ENROLLMENT		
						Year	County	No.
11845	1 Franklin, Stephen DIED PRIOR TO SEPTEMBER 25, 1902		44	M	Full	1896	Atoka	4425
	2							
	3							
	4							
	5							
	6	ENROLLMENT OF NOS. 1 HEREON APPROVED BY THE SECRETARY OF INTERIOR MAR 10 1903						
	7							
	8							
	9							
	10							
	11							
	12							
	13							
	14							
	15							
	16							
	17							

TRIBAL ENROLLMENT OF PARENTS

	Name of Father	Year	County	Name of Mother	Year	County
1	Harris Franklin	Dead	Atoka	Betsey Franklin	Dead	Atoka
2						
3						
4						
5						
6	No. 1 died March 11, 1901 Enrollment cancelled by Department July 8, 1905					
7						
8						
9						
10						
11						
12						
13						
14						
15					Date of Application for Enrollment.	Aug 30/99
16						
17						

Choctaw By Blood Enrollment Cards 1898-1914

		RESIDENCE:	Jacks Fork	COUNTY.	**Choctaw Nation**		**Choctaw Roll**	CARD NO.

RESIDENCE: Jacks Fork COUNTY. **Choctaw Nation** **Choctaw Roll** CARD NO.
POST OFFICE: Kosoma, I.T. *(Not Including Freedmen)* FIELD NO. 4154

Dawes' Roll No.	NAME		Relationship to Person First Named	AGE	SEX	BLOOD	TRIBAL ENROLLMENT		
							Year	County	No.
11646	1 Nowabbi, Liston	58	First Named	55	M	Full	1896	Jacks Fork	9853
11647	2 " Mary	55	Wife	52	F	"	1896	" "	9854
11648	3 " James	24	Son	21	M	"	1896	" "	9855
11649	4 " Alfred	21	"	18	"	"	1896	" "	9857
11650	5 " Jincy	20	Dau	17	F	"	1896	" "	9856
11651	6 " Amy	16	"	13	"	"	1896	" "	9858
	7								
	8								
	9								
	10	ENROLLMENT OF NOS. 1,2,3,4,5 and 6 HEREON							
	11	APPROVED BY THE SECRETARY							
	12	OF INTERIOR MAR 10 1903							
	13								
	14								
	15								
	16								
	17								

TRIBAL ENROLLMENT OF PARENTS

	Name of Father	Year	County	Name of Mother	Year	County
1	No-wabbi	Dead	Skullyville	Poth-key	Dead	Skullyville
2	James Lewis	"	Kiamitia	Sibel Lewis	"	Kiamitia
3	No1			No2		
4	No1			No2		
5	No1			No2		
6	No1			No2		
7						
8						
9						
10	No5 on 1896 roll as Quincy Nowabbi					
11	No6 " 1896 " " Annie "					
12				Nowabbi		
13	No.3 is now husband of Hannah ~~Austin~~ Choctaw card #4231					
14	For child of No.3 see NB (Mar. 3,1905) card #320					
15				Date of Application for Enrollment	Aug 30/99	
16						
17						

Choctaw By Blood Enrollment Cards 1898-1914

RESIDENCE: Jacks Fork COUNTY. **Choctaw Nation** **Choctaw Roll** CARD NO.
POST OFFICE: Kosoma, I.T. *(Not Including Freedmen)* FIELD NO. 4155

Dawes' Roll No.	NAME	Relationship to Person First Named	AGE	SEX	BLOOD	TRIBAL ENROLLMENT		
						Year	County	No.
11652	1 McCann, Loli 77		74	F	Full	1896	Jacks Fork	9460
	2							
	3							
	4							
	5	ENROLLMENT						
	6	OF NOS. 1 HEREON						
	7	APPROVED BY THE SECRETARY						
	8	OF INTERIOR MAR 10 1903						
	9							
	10							
	11							
	12							
	13							
	14							
	15							
	16							
	17							

TRIBAL ENROLLMENT OF PARENTS

	Name of Father	Year	County	Name of Mother	Year	County
1		Dead			Dead	
2						
3						
4						
5						
6						
7	No.1 on 1896 roll as Lolie McCann					
8	Deaf and dumb – parents unknown					
9						
10						
11						
12						
13						
14						
15				Date of Application for Enrollment.		Aug 30/99
16						
17						

Choctaw By Blood Enrollment Cards 1898-1914

POST: Stringtown, I.T.   **Choctaw Nation**   Choctaw Roll *(Not Including Freedmen)*   FIELD NO. **4156**

RESIDENCE: Jacks Fork   COUNTY

Dawes Roll		NAME		Relationship to Person First Named	AGE	SEX	BLOOD	TRIBAL ENROLLMENT		
								Year	County	No.
		Allington	42	First Named	39	M	Full	1896	Jacks Fork	8866
		Emma	43	Wife	40	F	"	1896	" "	8867
11	"	Temelius	20	Dau	17	"	"	1896	" "	8868
11656	4 "	Forbis	11	Son	8	M	"	1896	" "	8871
11657	5 "	Malinda	7	Dau	4	F	"	1896	" "	8872
11658	6 "	William	14	S.S.	11	M	"	1896	" "	8870
11659	7 "	Peter	2	Son	2mo	M	"			
	8									
	9									
	10									
	11									
	12									
	13									
	14									
	15									
	16									
	17									

ENROLLMENT
OF NOS. 1,2,3,4,5,6 and 7 HEREON
APPROVED BY THE SECRETARY
OF INTERIOR   MAR 10 1903

TRIBAL ENROLLMENT OF PARENTS

	Name of Father	Year	County	Name of Mother	Year	County
1	Jim Morris	Dead	Jacks Fork	E-ya-ho-ma	Dead	Jackson
2	Thos. Homma	"	Towson	Delila Homma	"	Towson
3	No 1			Eliz. Morris	"	Jacks Fork
4	No 1			No 2		
5	No 1			No 2		
6	Elias Tarby	Dead	Skullyville	No 2		
7	No. 1			No. 2		
8						
9			No 2 on 1896 roll as Melinda Morrison			
10			No 3 on 1896 roll as Dammeris Morrison			
11			All surnames on 1896 roll as Morrison			
12			No.7 Enrolled June 28th, 1900			
13			No.3 is now wife of Ellis Colbert Choctaw card #1968			#1 to 6 inc
14			For child of Nos 1&2 see NB (Mar 3-05) Card #1153			Date of Application for Enrollment.
15			" " " No 3 " " " " " # 833f			Aug 30/99
16						
17						

Choctaw By Blood Enrollment Cards 1898-1914

RESIDENCE: Jacks Fork   COUNTY.   **Choctaw Nation**   **Choctaw Roll**   CARD NO.

POST OFFICE: Stringtown, I.T.   *(Not Including Freedmen)*   FIELD NO. **4157**

Dawes' Roll No.	NAME		Relationship to Person First Named	AGE	SEX	BLOOD	TRIBAL ENROLLMENT		
							Year	County	No.
11660	1 Bond, Salema	22		19	F	Full	1896	Jacks Fork	8869
15474	2 Peter, Levicy	5	Dau	2	"	"			
11661	3 Bond, Ida	1	Dau	10mo	F	"			
	4								
	5								
	6								
	7	ENROLLMENT OF NOS. 1 and 3 HEREON APPROVED BY THE SECRETARY OF INTERIOR Mar 10 1903							
	8								
	9								
	10								
	11	ENROLLMENT OF NOS. 2 HEREON APPROVED BY THE SECRETARY OF INTERIOR May 9 1904							
	12								
	13								
	14								
	15								
	16								
	17								

TRIBAL ENROLLMENT OF PARENTS

	Name of Father	Year	County	Name of Mother	Year	County
1	Jefferson Peter	Dead	Jacks Fork	Mollie Peter	Dead	Jacks Fork
2	Bertie Anderson	"	Jackson	No1		
3	Reason Bond		Jacks Fork	No1		
4						
5						
6						
7						
8	No2 – Affidavit of birth to be supplied:- Recd Dec 18/99. Irregular & returned for correction					
9	No.1 on 1896 roll as Selina Morrison					
10	No1 is now wife of Reason Bond on Choctaw card #4152: evidence of marriage filed Nov. 28, 1902					
11	No3 born Jan. 22, 1902: Enrolled Nov. 28, 1902					
12	Nº2 Born in Oct 1897. Affidavits as to birth filed Feby 26th, 1904					
13						#1&2
14						Date of Application for Enrollment.
15						Aug 30/99
16						
17						

Choctaw By Blood Enrollment Cards 1898-1914

RESIDENCE: Atoka   COUNTY. **Choctaw Nation**   **Choctaw Roll**   CARD NO.
POST OFFICE: Lehigh, I.T.   *(Not Including Freedmen)*   FIELD NO. **4158**

Dawes' Roll No.	NAME	Relationship to Person First Named	AGE	SEX	BLOOD	TRIBAL ENROLLMENT Year	County	No.
11662	1 Wade, Kingsberry ²⁴	Named	21	M	Full	1896	Atoka	14055
11663	2 " Jennie ²¹	Wife	18	F	"	1896	"	14056
DEAD	3 " Mary	Dau	2mo	"	"			
11664	4 " James ⁷	S.S.	4	M	"	1896	Atoka	14057
11665	5 " Sarlin ¹	Son	11mo	M	"			
	6							
	7							
	8							
	9	ENROLLMENT						
	10	OF NOS. 1,2,4 and 5 HEREON APPROVED BY THE SECRETARY						
	11	OF INTERIOR Mar 10 1903						
	12							
	13							
	14	No.3 hereon dismissed under order						
	15	of the Commissioner to the Five						
	16	Civilized Tribes of July 18, 1905.						
	17							

TRIBAL ENROLLMENT OF PARENTS

	Name of Father	Year	County	Name of Mother	Year	County
1	Joel Wade	Dead	Atoka	Phebis Wade	Dead	Atoka
2	William Peter		"	Siley Peter	"	"
3	No1			No2		
4	Silas Lata		Atoka	No2		
5	N⁰1			N⁰2		
6						
7				No.4 hereon roll No 11664 is a duplicate		
8				of James Leader No.3 on Choctaw card		
9	No2 on 1896 roll as Jinnie Wade			#4274: Choctaw roll by blood No 11971.		
10	No3 Affidavit of birth to be			Enrollment of James Wade Choctaw roll by blood cancelled by Secretary of		
11	supplied.- Filed Oct 26/99			Interior, Aug 21. 1905 (I.T.D. 10264-1905)		
12	No1 on 1896 roll as Kingsbury Wade					
13	N⁰5 Born June 23, 1901: enrolled May 12, 1902					
14	No3 died in September, 1900: proof of death filed Nov. 25, 1902					
15	Nos 1 and 2 separated			Date of Application for Enrollment		Aug 30/99
16	For child of No.2 see NB (Mar 3, 1905) #625			⟩ 1 to 4		
17						

RESIDENCE:	Chickasaw Nation ~~COUNTY~~.	**Choctaw Nation**				Choctaw Roll		CARD NO.	
POST OFFICE:	Dibble I.T.					*(Not Including Freedmen)*		FIELD NO. **4159**	

Dawes' Roll No.	NAME	Relationship to Person First Named	AGE	SEX	BLOOD	TRIBAL ENROLLMENT		
						Year	County	No.
11666	₁ Barnett, Elizabeth J ⁴⁸		45	F	1/8	1896	Atoka	1781
11667	₂ Weeden Agnes ²¹	Dau	18	"	1/16	1896	"	1786
11668	₃ Weeden Maggie ¹⁹	"	16	"	1/16	1896	"	1787
11669	₄ Barnett Levi ¹⁷	Son	14	M	1/16	1896	"	1783
11670	₅ " James ¹⁵	"	12	"	1/16	1896	"	1784
11671	₆ " Jesse ¹⁴	"	11	"	1/16	1896	"	1785
11672	₇ " Viola ¹⁰	Dau	7	F	1/16	1896	"	1788
11673	₈ " Liddie E ⁸	"	5	"	1/16	1896	"	1789
11674	₉ " Bessie ³	"	4wks	"	1/16			
11675	₁₀ Vice Robert ²¹	Nephew	18	M	1/16	1896	Atoka	12616
11676	₁₁ Weeden, Buddy Lee ¹	GrandSon	1mo	M	1/32			
I.W. 754	₁₂ Barnett Archibald J S⁽⁵³⁾	Husb	53	M	I.W.	1896	Atoka	14346
	₁₃ No.3 is now the wife of Lee Weeden							
	See Choctaw card #R707 Jany 25,1902							
	₁₄ ~~For child of No4 see NB (Apr 26-06) Card #359~~							
	₁₅ " " " "3 " " " " "467							
	₁₆ No.11 born Dec 28 1901 and enrolled hereon							
	Jan 25,1902							
	₁₇ ~~No12 transferred from Choctaw card #386 See decision of Feby 27,1904~~							

TRIBAL ENROLLMENT OF PARENTS

	Name of Father	Year	County	Name of Mother	Year	County
₁	Druery Airington	Dead	Non Citz	Eliz Airington	Dead	Blue
₂	A.J.S. Barnett		white man	No1		
₃	" " " "		" "	No1		
₄	" " " "		" "	No1		
₅	" " " "		" "	No1		
₆	" " " "		" "	No1		
₇	" " " "		" "	No1		
₈	" " " "		" "	No1		
₉	" " " "		" "	No1		
₁₀	Robert Vice	Dead	Non Citz	Mary A Vice	Dead	Blue
₁₁	Lee Weeden		non citizen	No.3		
₁₂	A.J.S. Barnett	Dead	" "	Eliz. Barnett	Dead	Non Citz
₁₃	No8 on 1896 roll as Liddie Barnett					
₁₄	Husband A.J.S. Barnett on					
	Card No D386 No12 admitted in 96 Case #925					
₁₅	No.9 Affidavit of birth to be					
₁₆	supplied:- Filed Oct 26/99					
	~~No2 is now the wife of Hugh Weeden Aug 2, 1900~~					
₁₇	~~For child of No10 see NB (March 3 1905) #1151~~					

ENROLLMENT
OF NOS. ~~~~ 12 ~~~~ HEREON
APPROVED BY THE SECRETARY
OF INTERIOR May 7 1904

ENROLLMENT
OF NOS.1,2,3,4,5,6,7,8,9,10and11 HEREON
APPROVED BY THE SECRETARY
OF INTERIOR Mar 10 1903

Date of Application for Enrollment.

Aug 30/99

P.O. Folsom I.T. 4/8/05

Choctaw By Blood Enrollment Cards 1898-1914

RESIDENCE: Chickasaw Nation ~~COUNTY~~. **Choctaw Nation** — Choctaw Roll — CARD NO.
POST OFFICE: Allen I.T. *(Not Including Freedmen)* FIELD NO. **4160**

Dawes' Roll No.	NAME		Relationship to Person First Named	AGE	SEX	BLOOD	TRIBAL ENROLLMENT		
							Year	County	No.
11677	1 Grant, Mary E	30	First Named	27	F	1/16	1896	Atoka	7304
11678	2 Jones, Arthur L	13	Son	10	M	1/32	1896	"	7305
11679	3 " William F	11	"	8	"	1/32	1896	"	7306
11680	4 " Maggie B	10	Dau	7	F	1/32	1896	"	7309
11681	5 " Wyatt M	8	Son	5	M	1/32	1896	"	7308
11682	6 " Jesse E	6	"	3	"	1/32	1896	"	7307
11683	7 " Ida K	5	Dau	1	F	1/32			
DEAD	8 " ~~Nora Agnes~~ DEAD		~~Dau~~	~~2mo~~	~~F~~	~~1/32~~			
11684	9 " Frank Pierce	1	Son	1mo	M	1/32			
	10		No.8 Hereon Dismissed under order of the						
	11		Commission to the Five Civilized Tribes of March 31, 1905.						
	12		No.8 Died January 6, 1900: Proof of death						
	13		filed Dec. 23, 1902						
	14		No.1 is now the wife of T.W. Grant, a						
	15		non-citizen. Evidence of marriage filed Dec. 24, 1902.						
	16		For child of No1 see N.B. (Apr 26-06) Card No 522						
	17		" " " " " " (Mar 3-05) " ' 847.						

TRIBAL ENROLLMENT OF PARENTS

	Name of Father	Year	County	Name of Mother	Year	County
1	A.J.S. Barnett		White man	Eliz Barnett		Atoka
2	Frank P. Jones		" "	No1		
3	" " "		" "	No1		
4	" " "		" "	No1		
5	" " "		" "	No1		
6	" " "		" "	No1		
7	" " "		" "	No1		
8	" " "		" "	~~No1~~		
9	" " "		" "	No1		
10						
11	No1 on 1896 roll as Mary Jones					
12	No2 " 1896 " " Arthur "			No.9 Enrolled Sept. 17, 1901		
13	No3 " 1896 " " Wm A "			#1 to 7 inc		
14	Husband, Frank P. Jones, on Card No D 387					
15	No7 Affidavit of birth to be supplied Filed Oct 26/99					
16	No4 on 1896 roll as Margaret E. Jones					
17	No8 Enrolled June 11, 1900					

ENROLLMENT
OF NOS. 1,2,3,4,5,6,7 and 9 HEREON
APPROVED BY THE SECRETARY
OF INTERIOR Mar. 10, 1903

Date of Application for Enrollment.
Aug 30/99

Choctaw By Blood Enrollment Cards 1898-1914

RESIDENCE: **Atoka**
POST OFFICE: **Atoka, I.T.**

COUNTY. **Choctaw Nation**

Choctaw Roll
(Not Including Freedmen)

CARD NO.
FIELD NO. **4161**

Dawes' Roll No.	NAME	Relationship to Person First Named	AGE	SEX	BLOOD	TRIBAL ENROLLMENT		
						Year	County	No.
11685	₁ Wesley, Betsy ⁶⁶	First Named	63	F	Full	1896	Atoka	14037
DEAD	₂ " Sam	Nephew	19	M	"	1896	"	14038
	3							
	4							
	5	ENROLLMENT						
	6	OF NOS. 1 HEREON APPROVED BY THE SECRETARY						
	7	OF INTERIOR Mar 10, 1903						
	8							
	9	No. 2 hereon dismissed under order of						
	10	the Commission to the Five Civilized						
	11	Tribes of March 31, 1905.						
	12							
	13							
	14							
	15							
	16							
	17							

TRIBAL ENROLLMENT OF PARENTS

	Name of Father	Year	County	Name of Mother	Year	County
1	Pe-sa-hubbee	Dead	Cedar	A-mok-le-huna	Dead	Cedar
2	Tolbert Paine	"	Atoka	Lotie[sic] Paine	"	Atoka
3						
4						
5	No1 on 1896 roll as Wetsy Wesley					
6						
7	No2 is marked "dead" on 1896					
8	roll, also on index to roll Sept. 26/99					
9						
10	No2 died in August, 1899· proof of death filed Nov. 25, 1902					
11						
12						
13						
14						
15				Date of Application for Enrollment.	Aug 30/99	
16						
17						

Choctaw By Blood Enrollment Cards 1898-1914

RESIDENCE: Atoka   COUNTY. **Choctaw Nation**   **Choctaw Roll** *(Not Including Freedmen)*   CARD NO.

POST OFFICE: Atoka, I.T.   FIELD NO. 4162

Dawes' Roll No.	NAME	Relationship to Person First Named	AGE	SEX	BLOOD	TRIBAL ENROLLMENT		
						Year	County	No.
11686	1 Paine, Annie 23		20	F	Full	1893	Jacks Fork	626
11687	2 Jones, Simon DIED PRIOR TO SEPTEMBER 25, 1902	Son	6mo	M	"			
	3							
	4							
	5							
	6 ENROLLMENT							
	7 OF NOS. 1 and 2 HEREON APPROVED BY THE SECRETARY							
	8 OF INTERIOR MAR 10 1903							
	9							
	10							
	11							
	12							
	13							
	14							
	15							
	16							
	17							

TRIBAL ENROLLMENT OF PARENTS

	Name of Father	Year	County	Name of Mother	Year	County
1	Tolbert Paine	Dead	Atoka	Rhoda Paine	Dead	Jacks Fork
2	Israel Jones		"	No1		
3						
4						
5						
6	No1 on 1893 Pay Roll, Page 70, No 626, Jacks					
7	Fork Co., as Annie P[illegible]					
8	No.2 died Aug 1901. Enrollment cancelled by Department July 8, 1904					
9						
10						
11						
12						
13						
14						
15				Date of Application for Enrollment.	Aug 30/99	
16						
17						

Choctaw By Blood Enrollment Cards 1898-1914

RESIDENCE: Chickasaw Nation ~~COUNTY.~~
POST OFFICE: Purcell, I.T.

Choctaw Nation

Choctaw Roll CARD NO.
(Not Including Freedmen) FIELD NO. **4163**

Dawes' Roll No.	NAME	Relationship to Person First Named	AGE	SEX	BLOOD	TRIBAL ENROLLMENT Year	County	No.
11688	₁ Ward, Adah ²³		20	F	1/16	1896	Atoka	6039
11689	₂ Hail, Nettie V ⁵	Dau	2	"	1/32			
11690	₃ " Rachael ³	Dau	6mo	F	1/32			
	₄							
	₅							
	₆	~~ENROLLMENT~~						
	₇	OF NOS. 1,2 and 3 HEREON						
	₈	~~APPROVED BY THE SECRETARY OF INTERIOR~~ Mar 10 1903						
	₉							
	10							
	11							
	12							
	13	Nº1 is now the wife of Lon Ward						
	14							
	15							
	16							
	17							

TRIBAL ENROLLMENT OF PARENTS

Name of Father	Year	County	Name of Mother	Year	County
₁ A.J.S. Barnett		white man	Eliz. Barnett		Atoka
₂ John T. Hail		" "	No1		
₃ " " "		" "	No.1		
₄					
₅					
₆	No1 on 1896 roll as Ida Hail				
₇	Husband John T. Hail, on				
₈	Card No D388				
₉	~~No2 Affidavit of birth to be~~ supplied:- Filed Oct 26/99				
10	Evidence of marriage between Nº1 and Lon Ward filed Oct. 21, 1902				
11	For children of No1 see (Act Mar 3'05) Card #291				
12					
13			No.3 Enrolled May 24, 1900		
14					
15			Date of Application for Enrollment.		Aug 30/99
16					
17	P.O. Dibble I.T. 4/6/05				

263

Choctaw By Blood Enrollment Cards 1898-1914

RESIDENCE: Atoka COUNTY. **Choctaw Nation** Choctaw Roll CARD NO.
POST OFFICE: Atoka, I.T. *(Not Including Freedmen)* FIELD NO. **4164**

Dawes' Roll No.	NAME		Relationship to Person	AGE	SEX	BLOOD	TRIBAL ENROLLMENT		
							Year	County	No.
11691	1 John, Sim	48	First Named	45	M	Full	1896	Atoka	7261
11692	2 " Malissa	33	Wife	30	F	"	1896	"	7262
11693	3 " Edward	4	Son	3	M	"			
11694	4 " Jimmie	4	"	3	"	"			
11695	5 Anderson, Eden	15	Ward	12	"	"	1896	Atoka	597
11696	6 John, Susin[sic]	2	Dau	16mo	F	"			
	7								
	8								
	9								
	10 ENROLLMENT								
	11 OF NOS. 1,2,3,4,5 and 6 HEREON APPROVED BY THE SECRETARY								
	12 OF INTERIOR Mar 10 1903								
	13								
	14								
	15								
	16								
	17								

TRIBAL ENROLLMENT OF PARENTS

	Name of Father	Year	County	Name of Mother	Year	County
1	John Willis	Dead	Towson	Liza Willis	Dead	Chick Dist
2	Sam Gibson	"	Atoka	Phebe Gibson	"	Atoka
3	No1			No2		
4	No1			No2		
5	Henry Anderson	Dead	Atoka	Liney Anderson	Dead	Atoka
6	No1			No2		
7						
8			No1 on 1896 roll as Sin John			
9			No5[sic] on 1893 Pay Roll, Page 57 No			
10			597, Atoka Co			
11			Nos 3-4 Affidavits of birth to be			
12			supplied:-			
13			No.6 Enrolled Sept. 4, 1901		#1 to 5 inc	
14					Date of Application	
15					for Enrollment. Aug 30/99	
16						
17						

Choctaw By Blood Enrollment Cards 1898-1914

RESIDENCE:	Atoka	COUNTY.	Choctaw Nation		Choctaw Roll	CARD No.	
POST OFFICE:	Lehigh, I.T.				(Not Including Freedmen)	FIELD No. 4165	

Dawes' Roll No.	NAME	Relationship to Person First Named	AGE	SEX	BLOOD	TRIBAL ENROLLMENT		
						Year	County	No.
11697	1 Kampelubbi, Rhoda 51		48	F	Full	1896	Tobucksy	7507
	2							
	3							
	4							
	5	ENROLLMENT						
	6	OF NOS. 1 HEREON APPROVED BY THE SECRETARY						
	7	OF INTERIOR MAR 10 1903						
	8							
	9							
	10							
	11							
	12							
	13							
	14							
	15							
	16							
	17							

TRIBAL ENROLLMENT OF PARENTS

	Name of Father	Year	County	Name of Mother	Year	County
1	Adam Folsom	Dead	Atoka	Betsy Collins	Dead	Atoka
2						
3						
4						
5						
6						
7						
8						
9						
10						
11						
12						
13						
14						
15				Date of Application for Enrollment.	Aug 30/99	
16						
17						

265

Choctaw By Blood Enrollment Cards 1898-1914

RESIDENCE:	Atoka	COUNTY.	**Choctaw Nation**		**Choctaw Roll** *(Not Including Freedmen)*	CARD NO.
POST OFFICE:	Atoka, I.T.					FIELD NO. **4166**

Dawes' Roll No.	NAME	Relationship to Person First Named	AGE	SEX	BLOOD	TRIBAL ENROLLMENT Year	County	No.
11698	1 Katiotubbi, Phoebe ³⁶	First Named	33	F	Full	1896	Atoka	7269
11699	2 Felma, Molsey ¹¹	Dau	8	"	"	1896	"	7270
11700	3 " Miey ⁹	"	6	"	"	1896	"	7271
	4							
	5							
	6							
	7							
	8							
	9	ENROLLMENT						
	10	OF NOS. 1, 2 and 3 HEREON APPROVED BY THE SECRETARY						
	11	OF INTERIOR Mar. 10, 1903						
	12							
	13							
	14							
	15							
	16							
	17							

TRIBAL ENROLLMENT OF PARENTS

	Name of Father	Year	County	Name of Mother	Year	County
1	Hicks	Dead	Atoka	Seliney	Dead	Atoka
2	John Felma	"	"	No1		
3	" "	"	"	No1		
4						
5						
6	No1 on 1896 roll as Tiby James					
7	No2 " 1896 " " Malsey "					
8	No3 " 1896 " " Micy "					
9	No1 is now the wife of Johnson Katiotubbi, Choctaw card #4237					
10						
11						
12						
13						
14						
15				Date of Application for Enrollment.	Aug 30/99	
16						
17						

266

Choctaw By Blood Enrollment Cards 1898-1914

RESIDENCE:	Atoka	COUNTY.	**Choctaw Nation**			**Choctaw Roll**	CARD NO.	
POST OFFICE:	Atoka, I.T.					*(Not Including Freedmen)*	FIELD NO. 4167	

Dawes' Roll No.	NAME	Relationship to Person First Named	AGE	SEX	BLOOD	TRIBAL ENROLLMENT		
						Year	County	No.
11701	₁ Wilson, Elizabeth ¹⁷	First Named	14	F	1/2	1896	Atoka	9838
11702	₂ Wilson Wauneta ¹	Dau	3mo	F	1/4			
	₃							
	₄							
	₅							
	₆	ENROLLMENT						
	₇	OF NOS. 1 and 2 HEREON APPROVED BY THE SECRETARY						
	₈	OF INTERIOR MAR 10 1903						
	₉							
	₁₀							
	₁₁							
	₁₂							
	₁₃							
	₁₄							
	₁₅							
	₁₆							
	₁₇							

TRIBAL ENROLLMENT OF PARENTS

	Name of Father	Year	County	Name of Mother	Year	County
₁	Morris Nelson	Dead	Atoka	Mira Hendricks		Non Citz
₂	Lark A Wilson		non-citizen	Nº1		
₃						
₄						
₅						
₆						
₇	As to marriage of parents, see					
₈	testimony of Sallie Mullin					
₉	Nº1 is now the wife of Lark Wilson a non-citizen. Evidence of marriage					
₁₀	filed April 30, 1902.					
	Nº2 Born Jany 28, 1902· enrolled April 30, 1902					
₁₁	For child of No1 see NB (Apr 26/06) Card #381					
₁₂	" " " " " (Mar 3/05) " #818					
₁₃						
₁₄					#1	
₁₅				Date of Application for Enrollment	Aug 30/99	
₁₆						
₁₇						

Choctaw By Blood Enrollment Cards 1898-1914

RESIDENCE: Jacks Fork COUNTY. **Choctaw Nation** **Choctaw Roll** CARD NO.
POST OFFICE: Standley, I.T. *(Not Including Freedmen)* FIELD NO. 4168

Dawes' Roll No.	NAME	Relationship to Person First Named	AGE	SEX	BLOOD	TRIBAL ENROLLMENT		
						Year	County	No.
11703	1 Johns, Henry A ³¹	First Named	28	M	Full	1893	Jacks Fork	444
I.W. 1261	2 " Margaret ²³	Wife	19	F	I.W.			
11704	3 " Eva ³	Dau	1mo	"	1/2 9/16			
	4							
	5							
	6							
	7	ENROLLMENT OF NOS. 1 and 3 HEREON						
	8	APPROVED BY THE SECRETARY						
	9	OF INTERIOR MAR 10 1903						
	10							
	11							
	12							
	13							
	14	ENROLLMENT OF NOS. 2 HEREON						
	15	APPROVED BY THE SECRETARY						
	16	OF INTERIOR DEC 30 1904						
	17							

TRIBAL ENROLLMENT OF PARENTS

	Name of Father	Year	County	Name of Mother	Year	County
1	Amos Johns	Dead	Jacks Fork	Lizzie Johns	Dead	Jacks Fork
2	Jas. Underwood		Non Citz	Epsy Underwood		Choctaw
3	No1			No2		
4						
5	No2 denied in 96 Case #427 as a citizen by blood					
6	No2 no appeal to C.C.C.					
7	No1 on 1893 Pay Roll, Page 50, No 444, Jacks Fork Co as Henry A John					
8	No2 was admitted by U.S. Court			Judgment of U.S. Ct admitting No2 vacated and set aside		
9	Central Dist, Aug 24/97 as Margaret			by Decree of C.C.C.C. Dec 17 '02		
10	Underwood, Case No 32. As to residence, see testimony of No1					
11	No3 Affidavit of birth to be					
12	supplied: Recd Aug 30/99					
13						
14				Date of application for enrollment Aug 30/99		
15						
16	No 2 P.O. Wapanucka I.T. 7/19/04					
17	No2 PO Lehigh IT 2/24/04					

268

Choctaw By Blood Enrollment Cards 1898-1914

RESIDENCE: Atoka   COUNTY. **Choctaw Nation**   **Choctaw Roll**   CARD NO.
POST OFFICE: Atoka, I.T.   *(Not Including Freedmen)*   FIELD NO. 4169

Dawes' Roll No.	NAME		Relationship to Person First Named	AGE	SEX	BLOOD	TRIBAL ENROLLMENT		
							Year	County	No.
DEAD	1	Greer, Henry	39	36	M	Full	1896	Atoka	4983
14899	2	Apala, Isabelle	35	Wife	32	F	"	1896	"	4984
11705	3	Greer, Robinson	8	Son	5	M	"	1896	"	4985
11706	4	" Lowena	7	Dau	4	F	"	1896	"	4986
15059	5	" Eleas	1	Son	1	M	"			
	6	No 1 HEREON DISMISSED UNDER							
	7	ORDER OF THE COMMISSION TO THE FIVE							
	8	CIVILIZED TRIBES OF MARCH 31, 1905.							
	9	ENROLLMENT							
	10	OF NOS. 3 and 4 HEREON APPROVED BY THE SECRETARY							
	11	OF INTERIOR MAR 10 1903							
	12	ENROLLMENT							
	13	OF NOS. 2 HEREON APPROVED BY THE SECRETARY							
	14	OF INTERIOR MAY 21 1903							
	15	ENROLLMENT							
	16	OF NOS. ~~5~~ HEREON APPROVED BY THE SECRETARY							
	17	OF INTERIOR FEB 16 1904							

TRIBAL ENROLLMENT OF PARENTS

	Name of Father	Year	County	Name of Mother	Year	County
1	Enoch Greer	Dead	Atoka	Betsy Greer	Dead	Atoka
2	Amos Yahombey	"	"	Lurlis	"	"
3	No 1			No 2		
4	No 1			No 2		
5	No 1			No 2		
6						
7	Surnames of all appear on 1896 roll as					
8	Grear					
9	No 5 - Affidavit of birth to be supplied:- Recd Oct 26/99 See affidavit of Nº2 as to correct date of birth of Nº5 filed					
10	Nº2 is now the wife of Nicholas Apala on Chickasaw card #1048. Certificate of July 28,1903					
11	marriage filed Nov. 8, 1902					
12	Nº1 Died Feby 15, 1902, proof of death filed Feby 3, 1903					
13						
14					Date of Application for Enrollment	
15				Date of Application for Enrollment.	Aug 30/99	
16						
17						

Choctaw By Blood Enrollment Cards 1898-1914

RESIDENCE: Atoka	COUNTY.	**Choctaw Nation**	Choctaw Roll	CARD NO.	
POST OFFICE: Wapanucka I.T.			(Not Including Freedmen)	FIELD NO. 4170	

Dawes' Roll No.		NAME	Relationship to Person First Named	AGE	SEX	BLOOD	TRIBAL ENROLLMENT		
							Year	County	No.
✓	*	1 Underwood, Epsie	Named	48	F	1/4			
✓	*	2 " Elizabeth	Dau	17	"	1/8			
✓	*	3 " Angeline	"	14	"	1/8			
✓	*	4 " Nellie	"	12	"	1/8			
✓	*	5 " Leopold	Son	10	M	1/8			
✓	*	6 " Wilheimena	Dau	8	F	1/8			
		7							
		8							
		9							
		10							
		11							
		12							
		13							
		14							
		15							
		16							
		17							

TRIBAL ENROLLMENT OF PARENTS

	Name of Father	Year	County	Name of Mother	Year	County
1	Reuben Marlow	Dead	Non Citz	Margaret Marlow		Choctaw
2	Jas Underwood	"	"	No1		
3	" "	"	"	No1		
4	" "	"	"	No1		
5	" "	"	"	No1		
6	" "	"	"	No1		
7						
8	Nos 1 to 6 incl Denied in 96 Case #427					
9	All admitted by U.S. Court, Central					
10	Dist, Aug 24/97, Case No 32. As to					
11	residence, see testimony of No1					
	No6 was admitted as Mena Underwood					
12	Judgements of U.S. Ct admitting No 1 to 6 inc. vacated and set aside by Decree of Choctaw Chickasaw Citizenship Court Dec 17 02					
13	Nos 1 to 6 in C.C.C.C. #78					
14						
15	Nos 1 to 6 incl. denied by C.C.C.C. March 28th 04			Date of Application for Enrollment.		Aug 30/99
16						
17						

Choctaw By Blood Enrollment Cards 1898-1914

RESIDENCE:	Atoka	COUNTY.							
POST OFFICE:	Atoka, I.T.		**Choctaw Nation**				**Choctaw Roll** *(Not Including Freedmen)*	CARD No.	
								FIELD No.	4171

Dawes' Roll No.	NAME	Relationship to Person First Named	AGE	SEX	BLOOD	TRIBAL ENROLLMENT		
						Year	County	No.
11707	1 James, Logan ⁴⁵	First Named	42	M	Full	1896	Atoka	7256
	2							
	3							
	4							
	5	ENROLLMENT						
	6	OF NOS. 1 HEREON APPROVED BY THE SECRETARY						
	7	OF INTERIOR MAR 10 1903						
	8							
	9							
	10							
	11							
	12							
	13							
	14							
	15							
	16							
	17							

TRIBAL ENROLLMENT OF PARENTS

	Name of Father	Year	County	Name of Mother	Year	County
1	Wallen James	Dead	Jacks Fork	Ok-a-ste-ma	Dead	Blue
2						
3						
4						
5						
6						
7						
8						
9						
10						
11						
12						
13						
14						
15				DATE OF APPLICATION FOR ENROLLMENT	Aug 30/99	
16						
17						

Choctaw By Blood Enrollment Cards 1898-1914

RESIDENCE: **Atoka** COUNTY. **Choctaw Nation** **Choctaw Roll** CARD NO.
POST OFFICE: **Wapanucka, I.T.** (Not Including Freedmen) FIELD NO. **4172**

Dawes' Roll No.	NAME	Relationship to Person First Named	AGE	SEX	BLOOD	TRIBAL ENROLLMENT		
						Year	County	No.
✓ *	1 Underwood, John		21	M	1/8			
	2							
	3							
	4							
	5							
	6							
	7							
	8							
	9							
	10							
	11							
	12							
	13							
	14							
	15							
	16							
	17							

TRIBAL ENROLLMENT OF PARENTS

	Name of Father	Year	County	Name of Mother	Year	County
1	Jas. Underwood		Non Citz	Epsie Underwood		Choctaw
2						
3						
4	No1 Denied in 96 Case #427					
5	Admitted by U.S. Court Central Dist.,					
6	Aug 24/97, Case No 32. As to residence, see his testimony					
7	No.1 is now the husband of Mary Underwood on Choctaw card #D.697					
8	Judgment of U.S. Ct admitting No1 vacated and set aside by Decree of C.C.C.C Decr 17 '02 Jany 28, 1902					
9	No1 now in C.C.C.C. Case #78					
10						
11	No1 Denied by C.C.C.C. March 28th '04					
12						
13						
14						
15						Date of Application for Enrollment.
16						Aug 30/99
17						

Choctaw By Blood Enrollment Cards 1898-1914

RESIDENCE: Atoka   COUNTY. **Choctaw Nation**   **Choctaw Roll**   CARD No.

POST OFFICE: Lehigh, I.T.   (Not Including Freedmen)   FIELD No. 4173

Dawes' Roll No.		NAME	Relationship to Person First Named	AGE	SEX	BLOOD	TRIBAL ENROLLMENT		
							Year	County	No.
*	1	Underwood, William		23	M	1/8			
DEAD.	2	" Anna	Wife	22	F	Full	1896	Atoka	13973
11708	3	" Ruth Cleo ²	Dau	2mo	F	9/16			
	4								
	5								
	6								
	7	ENROLLMENT							
	8	OF NOS. 3 HEREON APPROVED BY THE SECRETARY							
	9	OF INTERIOR MAR 10 1903							
	10	No. 2 HEREON DISMISSED UNDER							
	11	ORDER OF THE COMMISSION TO THE FIVE CIVILIZED TRIBES OF MARCH 31, 1905.							
	12								
	13								
	14								
	15								
	16								
	17								

TRIBAL ENROLLMENT OF PARENTS

	Name of Father	Year	County	Name of Mother	Year	County
1	Jas. Underwood		Non Citz	Epsie Underwood		Choctaw
2	Henry Wilson	Dead	Atoka	Lucy Wilson		Atoka
3	No.1			No.2		
4						
5	No1 Denied in 96 Case #427					
6	No2 on 1896 roll as Annie Wilson					
7	No1- Admitted by U.S. Court,					
8	Central Dist., Aug 24/97, Case No32 As to residence see his testimony					
9	No3 Enrolled November 7th 1900					
10	No2 died August 9, 1901; proof of death filed Nov 26, 1902					
11						
12						
13	No1 Denied by C.C.C. March 29th 04					
14					Date of Application for Enrollment.	
15					Aug 30/99	
16						
17						

Choctaw By Blood Enrollment Cards 1898-1914

RESIDENCE: Jackson   COUNTY. **Choctaw Nation**   **Choctaw Roll**   CARD NO.
POST OFFICE: Jackson, I.T.   *(Not Including Freedmen)*   FIELD NO. **4174**

Dawes' Roll No.	NAME		Relationship to Person First Named	AGE	SEX	BLOOD	TRIBAL ENROLLMENT		
							Year	County	No.
11709	1 Wilson, Lane	41	First Named	38	M	Full	1896	Jackson	13785
11710	2 " Bicy	42	Wife	39	F	"	1896	"	13786
11711	3 " Peter	18	Son	15	M	"	1896	"	13787
11712	4 " Levi	13	Ward	10	"	"	1896	"	13791
11713	5 " Agnes	16	"	13	F	"	1896	"	13790
11714	6 LeFlore, Joshua	23	S.Son	20	M	"	1896	"	8162
11715	7 " Louis	18	"	15	"	"	1893	"	687
11716	8 Jones, Amanda	16	S.Dau	13	F	"	1893	"	690
11717	9 Jackson, Davis	8	Ward	5	M	"	1896	"	7107
	10								
	11								
	12								
	13	ENROLLMENT OF NOS 1 2 3 4 5 6 7 8 and 9 HEREON							
	14	APPROVED BY THE SECRETARY OF INTERIOR Mar 10 1903							
	15								
	16	For child of No.8 see NB (Mar 3'05) #575							
	17								

TRIBAL ENROLLMENT OF PARENTS

	Name of Father	Year	County	Name of Mother	Year	County
1	John Wilson	Dead	Jackson	Na-ne-ma	Dead	Jackson
2	Thos. Jones	"	"	Lo-shu-ma	"	Red River
3	No1			Silme Wilson	"	Jackson
4	Eastlum Wilson	Dead	Jackson	Nellie Wilson	"	"
5	" "	"	"	Frances "	"	"
6	Newton LeFlore	"	"	No2		
7	" "	"	"	No2		
8	Alfred Bacon	"		No2		
9	Davis Jackson	Dead	"	Lizzie Jackson	Dead	Jackson
10						
11	For child of No6 see NB (Act Mar 3-05) Card #262					
12	No2 on 1896 roll as Eliza Wilson					
13	No7 on 1893 Pay Roll, Page 79, No 687 Jackson Co					
	No8 " " " " 79 " 690 " "					
14	No8 also on 1896 roll, Page 37, No 1474 " " as				Date of Application for Enrollment.
15	Amanda Bacon					Aug 30/99
16	No.6 is now husband of Lita Anderson Choctaw card #3751					
17	No.7 is husband of Georgian Homma Choctaw card #5337					
	P.O. Boswell City I.T					

RESIDENCE:	Atoka		COUNTY.	**Choctaw Nation**				**Choctaw Roll**	CARD NO.	
POST OFFICE:	Atoka, I.T.							*(Not Including Freedmen)*	FIELD NO. **4175**	

Dawes' Roll No.	NAME		Relationship to Person First Named	AGE	SEX	BLOOD	TRIBAL ENROLLMENT		
							Year	County	No.
11718	1 Payton, William	14	First Named	11	M	1/2	1896	Atoka	10575
11719	2 " Laura	12	Sister	9	F	1/2	1896	"	10577
DEAD	3 " ~~Sarah~~		"	~~5~~	"	~~1/2~~	~~1896~~	"	~~10578~~
I.W. 1422	4 Murphy, Annie		Mother	40	"	I.W.			
	5								
	6								
	7	ENROLLMENT							
	8	OF NOS. 1 and 2 HEREON APPROVED BY THE SECRETARY							
	9	OF INTERIOR Mar 10 1903							
	10	ENROLLMENT							
	11	OF NOS.~~~~ 4 ~~~~ HEREON APPROVED BY THE SECRETARY							
	12	OF INTERIOR Jun 12 1905							
	13								
	14	No.~3~ hereon dismissed under order							
	15	of the Commission to the Five Civilized							
	16	Tribes of March 31, 1905.							
	17								

TRIBAL ENROLLMENT OF PARENTS

Name of Father	Year	County	Name of Mother	Year	County
1 Joe Payton	Dead	Blue	Annie Murphy		white woman
2 " "	"	"	" "		" "
3 " "	"	"	" "		" "
4 Joe Cooper	dead	Non Citz	Martha Cooper		Non Citz
5					
6					
7					
8					
9					
10		Mother, Annie Murphy, on Card No D.389			
11					

No.3 died in 1901: Affidavit of mother, Annie Murphy, as to death filed Nov 25, 1902
~~No.4 formerly the wife of Joe Payton, a recognized and enrolled citizen by blood of the~~
~~Choctaw Nation whose name appears on 1893 Choc. Leased Dist. Payment Roll Atoka Co,~~
~~page 87, Number 861, and who died in 1893~~
~~No.4 originally listed for enrollment on Choc. card #D-389 Aug. 30/99;~~
~~transferred to this card May 15, 1905. See decision of Feb. 7, 1905~~

	Date of Application for Enrollment
	Aug 30/99

P.O. Farris I.T. 2/7/05   P.O. Durant I.T. 11/19/02

Choctaw By Blood Enrollment Cards 1898-1914

RESIDENCE: Atoka COUNTY. **Choctaw Nation** Choctaw Roll CARD NO.
POST OFFICE: Atoka, I.T. (Not Including Freedmen) FIELD NO. 4176

Dawes' Roll No.	NAME		Relationship to Person First Named	AGE	SEX	BLOOD	TRIBAL ENROLLMENT		
							Year	County	No.
11720	1 MᶜAfee, Jackson	28	First Named	25	M	Full	1893	Jackson	512
11721	2 " Molsey	38	Wife	35	F	"	1896	Atoka	4441
11722	3 Thompson, Lucy	19	S.Dau	16	"	"	1896	"	4445
11723	4 Folsom, Charley	13	S.Son	10	M	"	1896	"	4443
11724	5 " Jincy	11	S.Dau	8	F	"	1896	"	4446
DEAD.	6 " John		S.Son	4	M	"	1896	"	4444
	7								
	8								
	9								
	10	ENROLLMENT							
	11	OF NOS. 1,2,3,4 and 5 HEREON APPROVED BY THE SECRETARY							
	12	OF INTERIOR MAR 10 1903							
	13	No. 6 HEREON DISMISSED UNDER							
	14	ORDER OF THE COMMISSION TO THE FIVE							
	15	CIVILIZED TRIBES OF MARCH 31, 1905.							
	16								
	17								

TRIBAL ENROLLMENT OF PARENTS

Name of Father	Year	County	Name of Mother	Year	County
1 Wilburn MᶜAfee	Dead	Red River	Annie Jones	Dead	Jackson
2	"	Atoka	Silen Charlison	"	Atoka
3 Aaron Folsom	"	"	No2		
4 " "	"	"	No2		
5 " "	"	"	No2		
6 " "	"	"	No2		
7					
8					
9					
10	No1 on 1893 Pay Roll, Page 57, No 512				
11	Jackson Co, as Jackson Mackafy				
12	No2 on 1896 roll as ~~ Folsom				
	No4 " 1896 " " Charles Folsom				
13	No.5 on 1896 roll as Jincey Folsom				
14	No6 died Sept. 10, 1901; proof of death filed Nov 25, 1902			Date of Application for Enrollment
15	No.3 is the wife of Elias Thompson on Choctaw card #4200 11/22/02			Aug 30/99
16	For child of No3 see NB (Apr 26'06) Card # 176			
17	" " " " " " (Mar 3,1905) " #318			

RESIDENCE: Gaines COUNTY.

POST OFFICE: Eufaula, I.T.

Choctaw Nation

Choctaw Roll
(Not Including Freedmen)

CARD No.

FIELD No. 4177

Dawes' Roll No.	NAME	Relationship to Person First Named	AGE	SEX	BLOOD	TRIBAL ENROLLMENT		
						Year	County	No.
DEAD 1	Standley, Ephraim		15	M	1/4			
2								
3								
4								
5								
6								
7								
8	No. 1 HEREON DISMISSED UNDER ORDER OF THE COMMISSION TO THE FIVE							
9	CIVILIZED TRIBES OF MARCH 31, 1905.							
10								
11								
12								
13								
14								
15								
16								
17								

TRIBAL ENROLLMENT OF PARENTS

	Name of Father	Year	County	Name of Mother	Year	County
1	Frank Standley	Dead	Choctaw	Silvey Standley		Non Citz
2						
3						
4						
5						
6	Admitted by Dawes Com, Case No 822					
7						
8	No1 Died Jan 27, 1900; Proof of death filed Nov. 10, 1902					
9						
10						
11						
12						
13						
14					Date of Application for Enrollment.	
15					Aug 30/99	
16						
17						

Choctaw By Blood Enrollment Cards 1898-1914

RESIDENCE:	Atoka	COUNTY.		CARD NO.	
POST OFFICE:	Guertie, I.T.	Choctaw Nation	Choctaw Roll (Not Including Freedmen)	FIELD NO.	4178

Dawes' Roll No.	NAME		Relationship to Person First Named	AGE	SEX	BLOOD	TRIBAL ENROLLMENT			
							Year	County		No.
11725	1 Homer, Enoch	25	First Named	22	M	Full	1896	Blue		5929
	2									
	3									
	4									
	5	ENROLLMENT								
	6	OF NOS. 1 HEREON APPROVED BY THE SECRETARY								
	7	OF INTERIOR MAR 10 1903								
	8									
	9									
	10									
	11									
	12									
	13									
	14									
	15									
	16									
	17									

TRIBAL ENROLLMENT OF PARENTS

	Name of Father	Year	County	Name of Mother	Year	County
1	Thomas Homer		Atoka	Jency Homer	Dead	Atoka
2						
3						
4						
5						
6	Nº1 is husband of Ellen Homer Choctaw card #5502					
7	For child of No.1 see NB (Mar 3'05) #539					
8						
9						
10						
11						
12						
13						
14					Date of Application for Enrollment.	
15					Aug 30/99	
16						
17						

Choctaw By Blood Enrollment Cards 1898-1914

RESIDENCE: Atoka   COUNTY. **Choctaw Nation**   **Choctaw Roll**   CARD NO.

POST OFFICE: Lehigh, I.T.   *(Not Including Freedmen)*   FIELD NO. **4179**

Dawes' Roll No.		NAME		Relationship to Person First Named	AGE	SEX	BLOOD	TRIBAL ENROLLMENT		
								Year	County	No.
I.W. 400	1	Owens, Beacham B	32		29	M	I.W.	1896	Atoka	14909
14395	2	" Mary L	25	Wife	22	F	1/8	1896	Gaines	9908
14396	3	" Cordelia B	6	Dau	3	"	1/16	1896	"	9909
14397	4	" Patti	4	"	1	"	1/16			
14398	5	" Robert Erskine	1	Son	1mo	M	1/16			
	6									
	7									
	8	ENROLLMENT OF NOS. 2,3,4 and 5 HEREON								
	9	APPROVED BY THE SECRETARY								
	10	OF INTERIOR Apr 11 1903								
	11									
	12	ENROLLMENT OF NOS. 1 HEREON								
	13	APPROVED BY THE SECRETARY								
	14	OF INTERIOR Sep 12 1903								
	15									
	16									
	17									

TRIBAL ENROLLMENT OF PARENTS

	Name of Father	Year	County	Name of Mother	Year	County
1	H. W. Owens	Dead	Non Citz	Sarah Owens		Non Citz
2	P. H. Littlepage	" "		Emma Littlepage	Dead	Atoka
3	No1			No2		
4	No1			No2		
5	No1			No2		
6						
7	No1 admitted by Dawes Com, Case					
8	No 248 as B. B. Owens No appeal					
9	Nos 2-3 were also admitted in same Case.					
10	No3 was admitted as Cordelia Owens.					
11	Nº5 Born Feby 6, 1902: enrolled March 18, 1902					
12						
13						
14					Date of Application for Enrollment.	
15					Aug 30/99	
16						
17	P.O. P.O. Krebs I.T.					

Krebs I.T.

Choctaw By Blood Enrollment Cards 1898-1914

Dawes' Roll No.	NAME	Relationship to Person First Named	AGE	SEX	BLOOD	TRIBAL ENROLLMENT		
						Year	County	No.
DEAD. 1	Brown, Rosealie	Named	45	F	1/4	1896	Atoka	1848
11726 2	" Milton 20	Son	17	M	1/8	1896	"	1850
11727 3	" Jay G 18	"	15	"	1/8	1896	"	1851
11728 4	" Cyrus 16	"	13	"	1/8	1896	"	1852
11729 5	" Lorenzo 14	"	11	"	1/8	1896	"	1853
11730 6	" Beulah 11	"[sic]	8	"	1/8	1896	"	1854
11731 7	" Ida A 7	Dau	4	F	1/8	1896	"	1855
8								
9								
10								
11	ENROLLMENT							
12	OF NOS. 2,3,4,5,6 and 7 HEREON APPROVED BY THE SECRETARY							
13	OF INTERIOR MAR 10 1903							
14	No 1 HEREON DISMISSED UNDER							
15	ORDER OF THE COMMISSION TO THE FIVE							
16	CIVILIZED TRIBES OF MARCH 31, 1905.							
17								

TRIBAL ENROLLMENT OF PARENTS

	Name of Father	Year	County	Name of Mother	Year	County
1	Jim Morris	Dead	Non Citz	Hannah Thomas		Atoka
2	Tom Brown		Colored man	No1		
3	" "		" "	No1		
4	" "		" "	No1		
5	" "		" "	No1		
6	" "		" "	No1		
7	" "		" "	No1		
8						
9						
10						
11	For children of No2 see NB (Apr 26-06) Card #411 & 1299					
12	No1 on 1896 roll as Rose Lee Brown					
13	No3 " 1896 " " Jay Gould "					Date of Application for Enrollment.
	No6 " 1896 " " Beulo "					
14	No1 died January 27, 1900: proof of death filed Nov 26, 1902					Aug 30/99
15						
16						
17						

Choctaw By Blood Enrollment Cards 1898-1914

RESIDENCE: Jackson   COUNTY. **Choctaw Nation**   CARD NO.

POST OFFICE: Mayhew, I.T.   Choctaw Roll   FIELD NO. **4181**

Dawes' Roll No.	NAME	Relationship to Person First Named	AGE	SEX	BLOOD	TRIBAL ENROLLMENT Year	County	No.
11732	1 Durant, Reuben 43		40	M	Full	1896	Jackson	3474
11733	2 " Sealy 53	Wife	50	F	"	1896	"	3476
	3							
	4							
	5							
	6	ENROLLMENT						
	7	OF NOS. 1 and 2 HEREON APPROVED BY THE SECRETARY						
	8	OF INTERIOR Mar. 10, 1903						
	9							
	10							
	11							
	12							
	13							
	14							
	15							
	16							
	17							

TRIBAL ENROLLMENT OF PARENTS

Name of Father	Year	County	Name of Mother	Year	County
1 Peter Durant	dead	Kiamitia	Sealy Durant	Dead	Red River
2 Ta-nubbee	"	"	Ho-te-ma	"	Kiamitia
3					
4					
5					
6 No.2 on 1896 roll as Sally Durant					
7					
8					
9					
10					
11					
12					
13					
14				Date of Application for Enrollment.	
15				Aug 30/99	
16					
17 P.O. Boswell, IT 5/17/07					

281

Choctaw By Blood Enrollment Cards 1898-1914

RESIDENCE:	Jackson		**Choctaw Nation**				**Choctaw Roll** *(Not Including Freedmen)*		CARD NO.	
POST OFFICE:	Mayhew,								FIELD NO. 4182	

Dawes' Roll No.	NAME		Relationship to Person First Named	AGE	SEX	BLOOD	TRIBAL ENROLLMENT			
							Year	County		No.
11734	1	Belvin, Robinson ³¹	First Named	28	M	Full	1896	Jackson		1508
	2									
	3									
	4									
	5	ENROLLMENT								
	6	OF NOS. 1 HEREON APPROVED BY THE SECRETARY								
	7	OF INTERIOR MAR 10 1903								
	8									
	9									
	10									
	11									
	12									
	13									
	14									
	15									
	16									
	17									

TRIBAL ENROLLMENT OF PARENTS

	Name of Father	Year	County	Name of Mother	Year	County
1	Stephen Belvin		Jackson	Isabelle Belvin	Dead	Atoka
2						
3						
4						
5						
6						
7	On 1896 roll as Roberson Belvin					
8	No1 is now the husband of Lizzie Hayes on Choctaw Card #4238				Sept 26, 1901	
9						
10						
11						
12						
13						Date of Application for Enrollment.
14						
15						Aug 30/99
16						
17	P.O. Boswell, I.T. 5/15/07					

282

Choctaw By Blood Enrollment Cards 1898-1914

RESIDENCE:	Jacks Fork	COUNTY.	**Choctaw Nation**			**Choctaw Roll**	CARD No.	
POST OFFICE:	Stringtown, I.T					(Not Including Freedmen)	FIELD No. 4183	

Dawes' Roll No.	NAME	Relationship to Person First Named	AGE	SEX	BLOOD	TRIBAL ENROLLMENT		
						Year	County	No.
11735	1 Folota, Betsy 51		48	F	Full	1896	Jacks Fork	4549
	2							
	3							
	4							
	5	ENROLLMENT						
	6	OF NOS. 1 HEREON APPROVED BY THE SECRETARY						
	7	OF INTERIOR MAR 10 1903						
	8							
	9							
	10							
	11							
	12							
	13							
	14							
	15							
	16							
	17							

TRIBAL ENROLLMENT OF PARENTS

	Name of Father	Year	County	Name of Mother	Year	County
1	Ta-nok-homa	Dead	Gaines	Ta-li-o-na	Dead	Gaines
2						
3						
4						
5						
6	No 1 is the wife of Martin Folota on					
7	Chickasaw card #1383.	transferred to Choc Card 5594 10/28/02				
8						
9						
10						
11						
12						
13						
14						Date of Application for Enrollment.
15						Aug 30/99
16						
17		P.O. Lehigh I.T.				

Choctaw By Blood Enrollment Cards 1898-1914

Card No. 4284

Dawes' Roll No.	NAME	Relationship to Person First Named	AGE	SEX	BLOOD	TRIBAL ENROLLMENT Year	County	No.
11736	1 Harrison, Ina 27		24	F	Full	1893	Jacks Fork	700
	2							
	3							
	4							
	5	ENROLLMENT OF NOS. 1 HEREON						
	6	APPROVED BY THE SECRETARY						
	7	OF INTERIOR MAR 10 1903						
	8							
	9							
	10							
	11							
	12							
	13							
	14							
	15							
	16							
	17							

TRIBAL ENROLLMENT OF PARENTS

Name of Father	Year	County	Name of Mother	Year	County
1 King Harrison	Dead	Towson	Eliz. Jacob		Towson
2					
3					
4					
5					
6 On 1893 Pay Roll, Page 79, No 700					
7 Jacks Fork Co, as Enie Tims					
8 * "Duplicate enrollment of No. 15602; not entitled to land or money under					
9 this number; see I.D.L. O.I. #916-1911					
10					
11					
12					
13					
14					
15			Date of Application for Enrollment.	Aug 30/99	
16					
17					

RESIDENCE:	Atoka		COUNTY.						

Choctaw Nation — **Choctaw Roll** *(Not Including Freedmen)*

POST OFFICE: Atoka, I.T.

CARD NO. FIELD NO. **4185**

Dawes' Roll No.	NAME		Relationship to Person First Named	AGE	SEX	BLOOD	TRIBAL ENROLLMENT		
							Year	County	No.
11737	1 Billy, Wesley	35	First Named	32	M	Full	1896	Atoka	1748
11738	2 " Elsie	37	Wife	34	F	"	1896	"	1749
11739	3 " Ida	5	Dau	2	"	"			
DEAD	4 Webster, Sarah	15	S.D.	12	"	"	1896	Atoka	13923
11740	5 Billy, McKinley	2	Son	7m	M	"			
11741	6 " Daniel	1	"	4mo	M	"			
	7								
	8								
	9								
	10	ENROLLMENT OF NOS 1,2,3,5 and 6 HEREON							
	11	APPROVED BY THE SECRETARY OF INTERIOR Mar 10 1903							
	12								
	13	No.4 hereon dismissed under order of							
	14	the Commission to the Five Civilized							
	15	Tribes of March 31, 1905.							
	16								
	17								

TRIBAL ENROLLMENT OF PARENTS

	Name of Father	Year	County	Name of Mother	Year	County
1	Witness Billy	Dead	Nashoba	Bicy Billy	Dead	Nashoba
2	Francis Webster	"	Atoka	Eliz. Webster	"	Atoka
3	No1			No2		
4	Impson Johnson	Dead	Jackson	No2		
5	No1			No2		
6	No1			No2		
7						
8	No3- Affidavit of birth to be					
9	supplied:- Recd Oct 26/99					
10	No.5 Enrolled January 29, 1901					
11	No6 Born March 17 1902: enrolled Aug 4, 1902					
12	No.2 on 1896 roll as Elsey Billy					
13	No4 died Nov. 8, 1901: proof of death filed Nov. 25, 1902					
	For child of Nos 1&2 see NB (Apr 26-06) Card #743					#1 to 4
14						
15					Date of Application for Enrollment. Aug 30/99	
16						
17						

Choctaw By Blood Enrollment Cards 1898-1914

RESIDENCE:	Atoka	COUNTY.		
POST OFFICE:	Lehigh, I.T.			

Choctaw Nation — **Choctaw Roll** *(Not Including Freedmen)* — CARD NO. FIELD NO. **4186**

Dawes' Roll No.	NAME		Relationship to Person First Named	AGE	SEX	BLOOD	TRIBAL ENROLLMENT		
							Year	County	No.
11742	1 Foster, Abel	43	First Named	40	M	Full	1896	Atoka	4473
11743	2 " Joel	16	Son	13	"	"	1896	"	4474
11744	3 " Daniel	6	"	3	"	"	1896	"	4475
	4								
	5								
	6								
	7								
	8								
	9								
	10								
	11								
	12								
	13								
	14								
	15								
	16								
	17								

ENROLLMENT
OF NOS. 1,2 and 3 HEREON
APPROVED BY THE SECRETARY
OF INTERIOR Mar 10 1903

TRIBAL ENROLLMENT OF PARENTS

	Name of Father	Year	County	Name of Mother	Year	County
1	Lewis Foster	Dead	Kiamitia	Jane Foster	Dead	Cedar
2	No 1			Becky Foster	"	Atoka
3	No 1			Julia A Foster	"	"
4						
5						
6						
7						
8						
9						
10						
11						
12						
13						
14					Date of Application for Enrollment. Aug 30/99	
15					Aug 30/99	
16						
17	P.O. Owl I.T. 6/8/03					

286

RESIDENCE:	Atoka		COUNTY.				Choctaw Roll		CARD NO.	
POST OFFICE:	Atoka, I.T.		**Choctaw Nation**				(Not Including Freedmen)		FIELD NO. **4187**	

Dawes' Roll No.	NAME		Relationship to Person First Named	AGE	SEX	BLOOD	TRIBAL ENROLLMENT		
							Year	County	No.
11745	1 Woods, Abner	47		44	M	Full	1896	Atoka	13963
11746	2 " McGee	23	Son	20	"	"	1896	"	13965
11747	3 " Willie	15	"	12	"	"	1896	"	13966
11748	4 " Louisa	11	Dau	8	F	"	1896	"	13968
11749	5 " Nancy	9	"	6	"	"	1896	"	13969
	6								
	7								
	8								
	9								
	10								
	11								
	12								
	13								
	14								
	15								
	16								
	17								

ENROLLMENT
OF NOS. 1,2,3,4 and 5 HEREON
APPROVED BY THE SECRETARY
OF INTERIOR Mar 10 1903

TRIBAL ENROLLMENT OF PARENTS

	Name of Father	Year	County	Name of Mother	Year	County
1	Tunup Noah	Dead	Kiamitia	Winnie Noah	Dead	Atoka
2	No 1			Sally A Woods	"	"
3	No 1			Mary Woods	"	Blue
4	No 1			" "	"	"
5	No 1			" "	"	"
6						
7						
8						
9						
10						
11						
12						
13						
14						
15				Date of Application for Enrollment.	Aug 30/99	
16						
17						

287

Choctaw By Blood Enrollment Cards 1898-1914

RESIDENCE:	Atoka		COUNTY.	**Choctaw Nation**				**Choctaw Roll**		CARD No.	
POST OFFICE:	Atoka, I.T.							(Not Including Freedmen)		FIELD No.	**4188**

Dawes' Roll No.	NAME		Relationship to Person First Named	AGE	SEX	BLOOD	TRIBAL ENROLLMENT			
							Year	County		No.
11750	1 Hokubbi, Peter	22	First Named	19	M	Full	1893	Atoka		296
	2									
	3									
	4									
	5		~~ENROLLMENT HEREON OF NOS. 1 APPROVED BY THE SECRETARY~~							
	6		~~OF INTERIOR Mar 10 1903~~							
	7									
	8									
	9									
	10									
	11									
	12									
	13									
	14									
	15									
	16									
	17									

TRIBAL ENROLLMENT OF PARENTS

Name of Father	Year	County	Name of Mother	Year	County
1 Davis Hokabi	Dead	Tobucksy	Betsy Frazier	Dead	Atoka
2					
3					
4					
5 On 1893 Pay Roll, Page 28, No 296 Atoka					
6 Co. as Peter Frazier. Also on 1896					
7 roll as Peter Tahokubbi, Page 325, No 12461					
8 Atoka Co					
No.1 is now the husband of Sisley Fletcher on Choctaw card #3879 Aug 2, 1902					
9 Nº1 was formerly husband of Ellen Lewis and is father of Mulbert Lewis on					
10 Chickasaw card #1483-7-5502					
For child of No1 see NB (Act Mar 3-05 Card #270					
11					
12					
13					
14				Date of Application for Enrollment.	
15				Aug 30/99	
16					
17					

Choctaw By Blood Enrollment Cards 1898-1914

RESIDENCE:	Atoka		COUNTY.							
POST OFFICE:	Atoka, I.T.									

Choctaw Nation — **Choctaw Roll** *(Not Including Freedmen)*

CARD NO. FIELD NO. **4189**

Dawes' Roll No.	NAME	Relationship to Person First Named	AGE	SEX	BLOOD	TRIBAL ENROLLMENT		
						Year	County	No.
11751	1 Thomas, Hannah 71		68	F	1/2	1896	Atoka	12475
	2							
	3							
	4							
	5 ENROLLMENT OF NOS. 1 HEREON APPROVED BY THE SECRETARY OF INTERIOR March 10 1903							
	8							
	9							
	10							
	11							
	12							
	13							
	14							
	15							
	16							
	17							

TRIBAL ENROLLMENT OF PARENTS

Name of Father	Year	County	Name of Mother	Year	County
1 Jack Thomas	Dead	Colored man	I-le-to-na	Dead	in Alabama
2					
3					
4					
5					
6					
7					
8					
9					
10					
11					
12					
13					
14				Date of Application for Enrollment	
15				Aug 30/99	
16					
17					

Choctaw By Blood Enrollment Cards 1898-1914

RESIDENCE: **Atoka**   COUNTY. **Choctaw Nation**   **Choctaw Roll** *(Not Including Freedmen)*   CARD NO. FIELD NO. **4190**

POST OFFICE: **Atoka, I.T.**

Dawes' Roll No.	NAME	Relationship to Person First Named	AGE	SEX	BLOOD	TRIBAL ENROLLMENT		
						Year	County	No.
DEAD	1 ~~Black, Joanna~~	~~Named~~	~~34~~	~~F~~	~~1/4~~	~~1893~~	~~Atoka~~	~~72~~
11752	2 " Maggie E ¹⁹	Dau	16	"	1/8	1893	"	76
11753	3 " Sylvanns ¹⁷	Son	14	M	1/8	1893	"	73
11754	4 " John ¹⁵	"	12	"	1/8	1893	"	74
11755	5 " Willie ¹³	"	10	"	1/8	1893	"	75
11756	6 " Clara ¹⁰	Dau	7	F	1/8	1893	"	77
	7							
	8							
	9							
	10 ENROLLMENT							
	OF NOS. 2,3,4,5 and 6 HEREON 11 APPROVED BY THE SECRETARY							
	12 OF INTERIOR Mar 10 1903							
	13 No.1 hereon dismissed under order of							
	14 the Commission to the Five Civilized							
	15 Tribes of March 31, 1905.							
	16							
	17							

TRIBAL ENROLLMENT OF PARENTS

Name of Father	Year	County	Name of Mother	Year	County
1 ~~Douglas Cooper~~	~~Dead~~	~~Non Citz~~	~~Mary A. Brown~~		~~Atoka~~
2 William Black		" "	No1		
3 " "		" "	No1		
4 " "		" "	No1		
5 " "		" "	No1		
6 " "		" "	No1		
7					
8					
9					
10 All on 1893 Pay roll, Page 7, Atoka Co					
11 No1 " " " " 7 " " as					
12 Jonany Black					
13 Husband of Nº1 and father of the children on this card, is on Choctaw card #D.682					
14 No1 died January 10, 1900: proof of death filed Nov 26, 1902			Date of Application for Enrollment.		
15 2 to 6 incl. now living with Mary A Brown, Choctaw card $4191 ~~For child of No.2 see NB (March 3,1905) #732~~			Aug 30/99		
16					
17					

Choctaw By Blood Enrollment Cards 1898-1914

RESIDENCE: Atoka   COUNTY. **Choctaw Nation**   **Choctaw Roll** *(Not Including Freedmen)*   CARD No.

POST OFFICE: Atoka, I.T.   FIELD No. 4191

Dawes' Roll No.	NAME	Relationship to Person First Named	AGE	SEX	BLOOD	TRIBAL ENROLLMENT Year	County	No.
11757	1 Brown, Mary A ⁶¹		58	F	1/2	1893	Atoka	62
DEAD,	2 Banks, Dorothy	Dau	21	"	1/4	1893	"	64
11758	3 Banks, Edith ¹	Gr. Dau	1mo	F	1/8			
	4							
	5							
	6							
	7	ENROLLMENT						
	8	OF NOS. 1 and 3 HEREON APPROVED BY THE SECRETARY						
	9	OF INTERIOR MAR 10 1903						
	10	No. 2 HEREON DISMISSED UNDER						
	11	ORDER OF THE COMMISSION TO THE FIVE CIVILIZED TRIBES OF MARCH 31, 1905.						
	12							
	13							
	14							
	15							
	16							
	17							

TRIBAL ENROLLMENT OF PARENTS

	Name of Father	Year	County	Name of Mother	Year	County
1	Jack Thomas	Dead	Colored man	I-le-to-na	Dead	in Alabama
2	Albert Brown		Non Citz	No1		
3	Chas L Banks		" "	Nº2		
4						
5						
6						
7						
8						
9	Both on 1893 Pay roll, Page 6, Atoka Co					
10	No1 on 1893 Pay roll as Mary Ann Brown					
11	Nº2 " 1893 " " " Dortha "					
12	Nº2 was married to Chas L Banks a non-citizen Sept. 17, 1902 marriage filed Oct 2, 1902					
13	Nº2 Died Sept. 12. 1902. See affidavit of C. L. Banks attached to application for #1 & 2					
14	enrollment of Nº3. Proof of death filed Oct. 9, 1902				Date of Application for Enrollment	
15	N³03 Born Sept. 5, 1902, enrolled Oct. 2, 1902.				Aug 30/99	
16						
17						

Choctaw By Blood Enrollment Cards 1898-1914

RESIDENCE:	Atoka	COUNTY.							
POST OFFICE:	Atoka, I.T.								

Choctaw Nation

Choctaw Roll (Not Including Freedmen)

CARD NO.

FIELD NO. **4192**

Dawes' Roll No.	NAME	Relationship to Person	AGE	SEX	BLOOD	TRIBAL ENROLLMENT		
						Year	County	No.
11759	1 Banks, Ida M. 25	First Named	22	F	1/4	1896	Atoka	1856
11760	2 Bryant, Minnie M 5	Dau	2	"	1/8			
	3							
	4							
	5							
	6 ENROLLMENT							
	7 OF NOS. 1 and 2 HEREON APPROVED BY THE SECRETARY							
	8 OF INTERIOR Mar. 10 1903							
	9							
	10							
	11							
	12							
	13							
	14							
	15							
	16							
	17							

TRIBAL ENROLLMENT OF PARENTS

	Name of Father	Year	County	Name of Mother	Year	County
1	Albert Brown	Dead	Non Citz	Mary A. Brown		Atoka
2	William Bryant	"	"	No 1		
3						
4						
5						
6						
7						
8						
9	Affidavit as to birth of No.2 to be					
10	supplied:- Filed Nov. 2/99					
11	No.2 on 1896 roll as Ida May Bryant. This notation should read No.1 instead of No2, Sept 24, 1902					
12						
13	No.1 is now the wife of Charles L Banks, non citizen					
14	Evidence of marriage filed 11/26/02					
15						Date of Application for Enrollment,
16						Aug 30/99
17						

292

RESIDENCE:	Atoka	COUNTY.	**Choctaw Nation**				**Choctaw Roll**	CARD NO.	
POST OFFICE:	Wapanucka, I.T.						*(Not Including Freedmen)*	FIELD NO. 4193	

Dawes' Roll No.	NAME		Relationship to Person First Named	AGE	SEX	BLOOD	TRIBAL ENROLLMENT		
							Year	County	No.
I.W. 401	1 Hendrix, Jasper	49		46	M	IW			
14399	2 " Belle	52	Wife	49	F	1/8	1896	Atoka	6053
14300	3 " James	19	Son	16	M	1/16	1896	"	6055
14301	4 " Brit	17	"	14	"	1/16	1896	"	6056
14302	5 " Birtie	15	Dau	12	F	1/16	1896	"	6060
14303	6 " Emmet	13	Son	10	M	1/16	1896	"	6057
14304	7 " Elmer	12	"	9	"	1/16	1896	"	6058
	8								
	9	ENROLLMENT							
	10	OF NOS. 2,3,4,5,6 and 7 HEREON APPROVED BY THE SECRETARY							
	11	OF INTERIOR APR 11 1903							
	12	Nos 2,3,4 were admitted by U.S. Indian Agent Feb 8 1896							
	13	See decision of D.M. Wisdom, U.S. Indian Agt, filed							
	14	in Choctaw #3554, Oct. 21, 1902							
	15	ENROLLMENT							
	16	OF NOS. 1 HEREON APPROVED BY THE SECRETARY		For child of No4 see NB (Apr 25-06) Card #482						
	17	OF INTERIOR SEP 12 1903	"	"	" No5	"	"	"	" #1294	

TRIBAL ENROLLMENT OF PARENTS

Name of Father	Year	County	Name of Mother	Year	County
1 Edwin Hendrix	Dead	Non Citz	Jane Hendrix	Dead	Non Citz
2 Murrill[sic] Askew	"	Chick Dist	Eliz Askew	"	" "
3	No1			No2	
4	No1			No2	
5	No1			No2	
6	No1			No2	
7	No1			No2	
8					
9	All admitted by Dawes Com Case No 1130. No appeal				
10	No5 admitted as Berta Hendricks				
11	No6 " " Emmitt "				
	No5 on 1896 roll as Birt Hendrix				
12	No6 " 1896 " " Emmitt "		No3 is past 21 years of age. See testimony		
13	No7 " 1896 " " Elma "		of July 8, 1903		
14	As to residence, see testimony of No2				
15	All admitted by Dawes Com under			Date of Application for Enrollment.	
	name of Hendricks			Aug 30/99	
16					
17					

Choctaw By Blood Enrollment Cards 1898-1914

RESIDENCE: Atoka   COUNTY. **Choctaw Nation**   Choctaw Roll   CARD NO.

POST OFFICE: Wapanucka I.T.   *(Not Including Freedmen)*   FIELD NO. **4194**

Dawes' Roll No.	NAME		Relationship to Person First Named	AGE	SEX	BLOOD	TRIBAL ENROLLMENT		
							Year	County	No.
I.W. 402	1 Daniel, Joe E.	41	First Named	36	M	I.W.			
14405	2 " Zora	27	Wife	24	F	1/16			
14406	3 " Sidney T	4	Son	1½	M	1/32			
14407	4 " Lela May	1	Dau	2mo	F	1/32			
14408	5 " Eunice B	3	Dau	3wks	F	1/32			
	6								
	7								
	8	ENROLLMENT OF NOS. 2,3,4 and 5 HEREON							
	9	APPROVED BY THE SECRETARY							
	10	OF INTERIOR Apr 11 1903							
	11	ENROLLMENT							
	12	OF NOS. 1 HEREON APPROVED BY THE SECRETARY							
	13	OF INTERIOR Sep 12 1903							
	14								
	15								
	16								
	17								

TRIBAL ENROLLMENT OF PARENTS

	Name of Father	Year	County	Name of Mother	Year	County
1	R. P. Daniel	Dead	Non Citz	Eliz. Daniel	Dead	Non Citz
2	Jasper Hendrix		Intermarried	Belle Hendrix		Atoka
3	No1			No2		
4	No1			No2		
5	No1			No2		
6	No2 was admitted by U.S. Indian Agent Feb 8, 1896 as Zora H					
7	Nos 1-2 were admitted by Dawes Com					
8	Case No 1130 under name of Daniels. No appeal					
	As to residence see testimony of No1					
9	No3- Affidavit of birth to be					
10	supplied:- Recd Oct 26/99					
11						
12	Eunice B Daniel, born Dec 24/99 on					
13	Card No D-550					
14	No.4 born Dec 29, 1901: Enrolled Feby 24, 1902					
15	No5 born December 24 1899: transferred to this card May 24, 1902					#1 to 3 inc
	For child of Nos 1&2 see NB (Apr 26-06) #1287					
16	P.O. Hart, Okla 12-1908				Date of Application for Enrollment.	Aug 30/99
17	P.O. Sulphur I.T. 3/6/03					

Choctaw By Blood Enrollment Cards 1898-1914

RESIDENCE:	Jackson	COUNTY.							
POST OFFICE:	Mayhew, I.T.		**Choctaw Nation**				**Choctaw Roll** (Not Including Freedmen)	CARD No.	FIELD No. 4195

Dawes' Roll No.	NAME		Relationship to Person First Named	AGE	SEX	BLOOD	TRIBAL ENROLLMENT		
							Year	County	No.
11761	1 Durant, Sammie	23		20	M	Full	1896	Jackson	3475
	2								
	3								
	4								
	5	ENROLLMENT							
	6	OF NOS. 1 HEREON APPROVED BY THE SECRETARY							
	7	OF INTERIOR MAR 10 1903							
	8								
	9								
	10								
	11								
	12								
	13								
	14								
	15								
	16								
	17								

TRIBAL ENROLLMENT OF PARENTS

	Name of Father	Year	County	Name of Mother	Year	County
1	Wilson Durant		Jackson	Wicey Durant	Dead	Jackson
2						
3						
4						
5						
6						
7						
8	No 1 is now the husband of No 2 on Choctaw card #4142					
9				12/1/02		
10						
11						
12						
13						
14						
15				Date of Application for Enrollment.	Aug 30/99	
16						
17						

Choctaw By Blood Enrollment Cards 1898-1914

RESIDENCE:	Atoka	COUNTY.				CARD NO.
POST OFFICE:	Lehigh, I.T.		Choctaw Nation	Choctaw Roll (Not Including Freedmen)		FIELD NO. 4196

Dawes' Roll No.	NAME		Relationship to Person First Named	AGE	SEX	BLOOD	TRIBAL ENROLLMENT		
							Year	County	No.
I.W. 403	1 Danenhour, Thomas	43	First Named	41	M	IW			
11762	2 " Fannie	13	Dau	10	F	3/8	1896	Atoka	3582
11763	3 " Hittie[sic]	11	"	8	"	3/8	1896	"	3583
11764	4 " George	9	Son	6	M	3/8	1896	"	3585
11765	5 " Annie	7	Dau	4	F	3/8	1896	"	3586
11766	6 " Frank	5	Son	2	M	3/8			
	7								
	8								
	9								
	10	ENROLLMENT							
	11	OF NOS. 2,3,4,5 and 6 HEREON APPROVED BY THE SECRETARY							
	12	OF INTERIOR MAR 10 1903							
	13	ENROLLMENT							
	14	OF NOS. 1 HEREON APPROVED BY THE SECRETARY							
	15	OF INTERIOR SEP 12 1903							
	16								
	17								

TRIBAL ENROLLMENT OF PARENTS

	Name of Father	Year	County	Name of Mother	Year	County
1	Geo Danenhour		Non Citz	Rebecca Danenhour		Non Citz
2	No 1			Mary "	Dead	Atoka
3	No 1			" "	" "	
4	No 1			" "	" "	
5	No 1			" "	" "	
6	No 1			" "	" "	
7						
8	No 1 admitted by Dawes Com, Case No 304					
9	as Thos. Danenhour					
10	Surnames on 1896 roll as Danenhower No 3 on 1896 roll as Allie "					
11						
12						
13						
14					Date of Application for Enrollment.	
15					Aug 30/99	
16						
17						

Choctaw By Blood Enrollment Cards 1898-1914

RESIDENCE: Atoka COUNTY.

Choctaw Nation

POST OFFICE: Atoka, I.T.

Choctaw Roll
(Not Including Freedmen)

CARD NO.

FIELD NO. 4197

Dawes' Roll No.	NAME	Relationship to Person First Named	AGE	SEX	BLOOD	TRIBAL ENROLLMENT		
						Year	County	No.
11767	1 Folsom, Simon 63		60	M	3/4	1896	Atoka	4431
11768	2 " Robert 19	Ward	16	"	Full	1896	"	4480
	3							
	4							
	5							
	6	ENROLLMENT						
	7	OF NOS. 1 and 2 HEREON APPROVED BY THE SECRETARY						
	8	OF INTERIOR MAR 10 1903						
	9							
	10							
	11							
	12							
	13							
	14							
	15							
	16							
	17							

TRIBAL ENROLLMENT OF PARENTS

	Name of Father	Year	County	Name of Mother	Year	County
1	Adam Folsom	Dead	Atoka		Dead	Gaines
2	Daniel Folsom	"	"	Dixie Folsom	"	Atoka
3						
4						
5						
6						
7						
8						
9						
10						
11						
12						
13						
14						
15				Date of Application for Enrollment.	Aug 30/99	
16						
17						

Choctaw By Blood Enrollment Cards 1898-1914

RESIDENCE:	Atoka	COUNTY.	**Choctaw Nation**			**Choctaw Roll** *(Not Including Freedmen)*	CARD NO.
POST OFFICE:	Lehigh, I.T.						FIELD NO.

Dawes' Roll No.	NAME		Relationship to Person First Named	AGE	SEX	BLOOD	TRIBAL ENROLLMENT		
							Year	County	No.
11769	1 Wilson, Henry C	41	First Named	38	M	Full	1896	Atoka	13954
11770	2 " Lizzie	38	Wife	25	F	"	1896	"	13955
11771	3 " Robinson	14	Son	11	M	"	1896	"	13956
11772	4 " Addie	12	Dau	9	F	"	1896	"	13959
11773	5 " Hugo	9	Son	6	M	"	1896	"	13957
11774	6 " William	7	"	4	"	"	1896	"	13958
11775	7 " Leighton	3	"	3mo	"	"			
11776	8 " Theodore R	1	Son	4mo	M	"			
	9								
	10								
	11								
	12	ENROLLMENT OF NOS. 1,2,3,4,5,6,7 and 8 HEREON APPROVED BY THE SECRETARY							
	13								
	14	OF INTERIOR MAR 10 1903							
	15								
	16								
	17								

TRIBAL ENROLLMENT OF PARENTS

	Name of Father	Year	County	Name of Mother	Year	County
1	Henry Wilson	Dead	Atoka	Lucy Wilson		Atoka
2	Alfred Battiest	"	Kiamitia	Susan Bond		"
3	No1			No2		
4	No1			No2		
5	No1			No2		
6	No1			No2		
7	No1			No2		
8	No.1			No.2		
9						
10			No1 on 1896 roll as Henry Wilson Jr			
11			No2 " 1896 " " Liza "			
12			No4 " 1896 " " Ada "			
			No6 " 1896 " " Willie "			
13			No7- Affidavit of birth to be		#1 to 7 inc	
14			supplied:- Filed Oct 26/99		Date of Application for Enrollment.	
15			No.8 born Oct. 14, 1901: Enrolled Feby 13, 1902		Aug 30/99	
16						
17			P.O. Wapanucka, I.T.			

12/31/02

Choctaw By Blood Enrollment Cards 1898-1914

RESIDENCE: Jackson COUNTY. **Choctaw Nation** **Choctaw Roll** CARD NO.
POST OFFICE: Mayhew, I.T. (Not Including Freedmen) FIELD NO. **4199**

Dawes' Roll No.	NAME	Relationship to Person First Named	AGE	SEX	BLOOD	TRIBAL ENROLLMENT		
						Year	County	No.
11777	1 Wade, Molsey ⁵⁰	First Named	47	F	Full	1893	Jackson	672
11778	2 Williams, Eastman ²¹	Son	18	M	"	1893	"	673
11779	3 Wade, Manassas S. G. ¹⁵	"	12	"	"	1893	"	674
11780	4 Folsom, Solomon ⁵	"	1½	"	"			
	5							
	6							
	7							
	8							
	9							
	10							
	11							
	12							
	13							
	14							
	15							
	16							
	17							

ENROLLMENT
OF NOS. 1,2,3 and 4 HEREON
APPROVED BY THE SECRETARY
OF INTERIOR Mar 10 1903

TRIBAL ENROLLMENT OF PARENTS

	Name of Father	Year	County	Name of Mother	Year	County
1	William Chukunnubby	Dead	Kiamitia		Dead	Kiamitia
2	Esias Williams	"	Jackson	No1		
3	Moses Wade	"	"	No1		
4	Sim Folsom		Kiamitia	No1		
5						
6	No1 on 1893 Pay Roll, Page 78, No 672, Jackson Co as Molcey Wade					
7	No2 " 1893 " " " 78 " 673 " " as Eastman Wade					
8	No3 " 1893 " " " 78 " 674 " " " M.S.G. "					
9						
10	No4 Affidavit of birth filed [blank]					
11	No.1 on 1896 Choctaw roll as Millie Wade page 368 #14040					
12	No.3 " " " " " Maria Wade " " #14041					
13	Nº1 is now the wife of Anderson Cole, Choctaw card #1825					
14						Date of Application for Enrollment.
15						Aug 30/99
16						
17						

Choctaw By Blood Enrollment Cards 1898-1914

Choctaw Nation

POST OFFICE: Mayhew, I.T. Lehigh

Choctaw Roll (Not Including Freedmen)

CARD NO.
FIELD NO. 4200

Dawes' Roll No.		NAME		Relationship to Person First Named	AGE	SEX	BLOOD	TRIBAL ENROLLMENT		
								Year	County	No.
DEAD.	1	Wesley, Joseph			23	M	Full	1896	Jackson	13841
11781	2	" Melvina	26	Wife	23	F	"	1896	Atoka	2934
11782	3	" Sealey	3	Dau	3 wks	"	"			
	4									
	5									
	6	ENROLLMENT								
	7	OF NOS. 2 and 3 HEREON APPROVED BY THE SECRETARY								
	8	OF INTERIOR MAR 10 1903								
	9	No.___1___ HEREON DISMISSED UNDER								
	10	ORDER OF THE COMMISSION TO THE FIVE CIVILIZED TRIBES OF MARCH 31, 1905.								
	11									
	12									
	13									
	14									
	15									
	16									
	17									

TRIBAL ENROLLMENT OF PARENTS

	Name of Father	Year	County	Name of Mother	Year	County
1	Stephen Lewis	Dead	Atoka	Edna Lewis	Dead	Atoka
2	James Collins	"	"	Eliz. Collins	"	"
3	No1			No2		
4						
5						
6						
7			No2 on 1896 roll as Melvina Collins			
8						
9			No3 Affidavit of birth to be			
10			supplied:-	Filed Oct 26/99		
11						
12			Nº1 died Nov – 1901 proof of death filed Nov 22. 1902			
13						
14					Date of Application for Enrollment.	
15					Aug 30/99	
16						
17			P.O. Lehigh, Ind Ter.			

Index

MORRIS
Allington 256
Easter 228
Eliz 256
Emma 256
Forbis 256
Hannah 280
Jim 256,280
Malinda 256
Peter 256
Solomon 228
Temelius 256
William 256
MORRISON
Allington 256
Dammeris 256
Emma 256
Forbis 256
Malinda 256
Melinda 256
Peter 256
Selina 257
Temelius 256
William 256
MOSELY, William 114
MOSLY, William 114
MULLEN
Ada 87
Eliz C 87
Jos P 87
Joseph S 87
Joseph S, Jr 87
Sallie 218
Silas 218
MULLIN, Sallie 267
MURPHEY
A M 17
Mary 17
MURPHY, Annie 275
MYER, James 202
NAIL
Emma F 59
Louvina 34
Melissa 156
NALE, Ransom 102
NA-NE-MA 274
NELSON

Morris 267
Rachel 177
Rhoda 177
NE-TAK-EN-LUBBEE 242
NICHOLAS, Emily 201
NICHOLSON, Omer R 39,195
NINAS
Alice 60
Flora B 60
H C 60
Josephine 60
Mary 60
Simeon 60
Tennessee 60
William 60
NOAH
Alfred 190
Aurora 216
Cha-fa-tubbee 191
Chafatubbee 216
Elisha 130
Elizabeth 130
Esias 190
Irvin 216
Isabinda 190
Jackson 190
Libbey 216
Lottie 191
Mary 190,191,216
Mulsey 216
Salena 191
Sarah 130
Tunup 287
Winnie 287
NONAH-HACHALE 18
NORMAN, Thos 68
NOWA
Alfred 190
Ervin 216
Mary 191
Salaskey 191
Sarah 130
Sebindee 190
Selina 191
NOWABBEE, Charlie 124
NO-WABBI 254
NOWABBI

320

325